6th Workshop on Technologies for Machine Translation of Low Resource Languages (LoResMT 2023)

Dubrovnik, Croatia
6 May 2023

ISBN: 978-1-7138-7385-3

Printed from e-media with permission by:

Curran Associates, Inc.
57 Morehouse Lane
Red Hook, NY 12571

Some format issues inherent in the e-media version may also appear in this print version.

Association for Computational Linguistics
209 N. Eighth Street
Stroudsburg, Pennsylvania 18360

Phone: 1-570-476-8006
Fax: 1-570-476-0860

acl@aclweb.org

Additional copies of this publication are available from:

Curran Associates, Inc.
57 Morehouse Lane
Red Hook, NY 12571 USA
Phone: 845-758-0400
Fax: 845-758-2633
Email: curran@proceedings.com
Web: www.proceedings.com

LoResMT 2023

The Sixth Workshop on Technologies for Machine Translation of Low-Resource Languages (LoResMT 2023)

Proceedings of the Workshop

May 6, 2023

The LoResMT organizers gratefully acknowledge the support from the following sponsors.

In cooperation with

Preface

Based on the success of past low-resource machine translation (MT) workshops at AMTA 2018, MT Summit 2019, AACL-IJCNLP 2020, AMTA 2021, and COLING 2022, we introduce LoResMT 2023 workshop at EACL 2023 (https://2023.eacl.org/). In the past few years, machine translation (MT) performance has improved significantly. With the development of new techniques such as multilingual translation and transfer learning, the use of MT is no longer a privilege for users of popular languages. However, the goal of expanding MT coverage to more diverse languages is hindered by the fact that MT methods require large amounts of data to train quality systems. This has made developing MT systems for low-resource languages challenging. Therefore, the need for developing comparable MT systems with relatively small datasets remains highly desirable.

Despite the advancements in MT technologies, creating an MT system for a new language or enhancing an existing one still requires a significant amount of effort to gather the necessary resources. The data-intensive nature of neural machine translation (NMT) approaches necessitates parallel and monolingual corpora in various domains, which are always in high demand. Developing MT systems also require dependable evaluation benchmarks and test sets. Furthermore, MT systems rely on numerous natural language processing (NLP) tools to pre-process human-generated texts into the required input format and post-process MT output into the appropriate textual forms in the target language. These tools include word tokenizers/de-tokenizers, word segmenters, and morphological analyzers, among others. The quality of these tools significantly impacts the translation output, yet there is a limited discourse on their methods, their role in training different MT systems, and their support coverage in different languages.

LoResMT is a platform that aims to facilitate discussions among researchers who are working on machine translation (MT) systems and methods for low-resource, under-represented, ethnic, and endangered languages. The goal of the platform is to address the challenges associated with the development of MT systems for languages that have limited resources or are at risk of being lost.

This year, LoResMT received research papers covering a wide range of languages spoken around the world. In addition to research papers, the workshop also accepts relevant findings papers at EACL 2023 to be presented at LoResMT. Aside from the research papers, LoResMT also featured two invited talks. These talks allowed participants to hear from experts in the field of MT and learn about the latest developments and challenges in MT for low-resource languages.

The program committee members play a crucial role in ensuring the success of the workshop. They review the submissions and provide constructive feedback to help the authors refine their papers and ensure they meet the set standards. Without their dedication, expertise, and hard work, the workshop would not be possible. The authors who submitted their work to LoResMT are also an integral part of the workshop's success. Their research and contributions offer new insights into the field of machine translation for low-resource languages, and their participation enriches the discussions and fosters collaboration. We are sincerely grateful to both the program committee members and the authors for their invaluable contributions and for making LoResMT a success.

Kat, Valentin, Nathaniel, Atul, Chao
(On behalf of the LoResMT chairs)

Program Committee

Workshop Chairs

Atul Kr. Ojha, Atul Kr. Ojha, Data Science Institute, Insight Centre for Data Analytics, University of Galway & Panlingua Language Processing LLP
Chao-hong Liu, Potamu Research Ltd
Ekaterina Vylomova, University of Melbourne, Australia
Flammie Pirinen, UiT Norgga árktalaš universitehta
Jade Abbott, Retro Rabbit
Jonathan Washington, Swarthmore College
Nathaniel Oco, De La Salle University
Valentin Malykh, Huawei Noah's Ark lab and Kazan Federal University
Varvara Logacheva Skolkovo, Institute of Science and Technology
Xiaobing Zhao, Minzu University of China

Program Committee

Abigail Walsh, ADAPT Centre, Dublin City University, Ireland
Alberto Poncelas, Rakuten, Singapore
Alina Karakanta, Fondazione Bruno Kessler (FBK), University of Trento
Amirhossein Tebbifakhr, Fondazione Bruno Kessler
Anna Currey, AWS AI Labs
Aswarth Abhilash Dara, Amazon
Atul Kr. Ojha, University of Galway & Panlingua Language Processing LLP
Bharathi Raja Chakravarthi, University of Galway
Bogdan Babych, Heidelberg University
Chao-hong Liu, Potamu Research Ltd
Constantine Lignos, Brandeis University, USA
Daan van Esch, Google
Diptesh Kanojia, University of Surrey, UK
Duygu Ataman, University of Zurich
Ekaterina Vylomova, University of Melbourne, Australia
Eleni Metheniti, CLLE-CNRS and IRIT-CNRS
Flammie Pirinen, UiT Norgga árktalaš universitehta
Jade Abbott, Retro Rabbit
Jasper Kyle Catapang, University of the Philippines
Jindřich Libovický, Charles Univeristy
Jonathan Washington, Swarthmore College
Majid Latifi, UPC University
Maria Art Antonette Clariño, University of the Philippines Los Baños
Mathias Müller, University of Zurich
Nathaniel Oco, De La Salle University
Rajdeep Sarkar, University of Galway
Rico Sennrich, University of Zurich
Saliha Muradoglu, The Australian National University
Sangjee Dondrub, Qinghai Normal University
Sardana Ivanova, University of Helsinki
Shantipriya Parida, Silo AI
Sunit Bhattacharya, Charles University

Surafel M. Lakew, Amazon.com, Inc
Wen Lai, LMU Munich
Valentin Malykh, Huawei Noah's Ark lab and Kazan Federal University
Varvara Logacheva Skolkovo, Institute of Science and Technology

Secondary Reviewers

Gaurav Negi, University of Galway

Table of Contents

Program

Saturday, May 6, 2023

09:00 - 09:15 *Opening Remarks*

09:15 - 10:05 *Invited Talk 1*

10:05 - 10:30 *Session 1: Finding Papers*

10:30 - 11:15 *COFFEE/TEA BREAK*

11:15 - 12:45 *Session 2: Scientific Research Papers*

Train Global, Tailor Local: Minimalist Multilingual Translation into Endangered Languages
Zhong Zhou, Jan Niehues and Alexander Waibel

Measuring the Impact of Data Augmentation Methods for Extremely Low-Resource NMT
Annie Lamar and Zeyneb Kaya

Language-Family Adapters for Low-Resource Multilingual Neural Machine Translation
Alexandra Chronopoulou, Dario Stojanovski and Alexander Fraser

Multilingual Bidirectional Unsupervised Translation through Multilingual Fine-tuning and Back-Translation
Bryan Li, Mohammad Sadegh Rasooli, Ajay Patel and Chris Callison-burch

12:45 - 14:15 *Lunch*

14:15 - 15:00 *Invited Talk 2*

15:00 - 15:30 *Session 3: Finding Papers*

A Simplified Training Pipeline for Low-Resource and Unsupervised Machine Translation
Àlex R. Atrio, Alexis Allemann, Ljiljana Dolamic and Andrei Popescu-belis

15:45 - 16:30 *COFFEE/TEA BREAK*

Saturday, May 6, 2023 (continued)

16:30 - 18:05 *Session 4: Scientific Research Papers*

Improving Neural Machine Translation of Indigenous Languages with Multilingual Transfer Learning
Wei-rui Chen and Muhammad Abdul-mageed

PEACH: Pre-Training Sequence-to-Sequence Multilingual Models for Translation with Semi-Supervised Pseudo-Parallel Document Generation
Alireza Salemi, Amirhossein Abaskohi, Sara Tavakoli, Azadeh Shakery and Yadollah Yaghoobzadeh

Investigating Lexical Replacements for Arabic-English Code-Switched Data Augmentation
Injy Hamed, Nizar Habash, Slim Abdennadher and Ngoc Thang Vu

Evaluating Sentence Alignment Methods in a Low-Resource Setting: An English-YorùBá Study Case
Edoardo Signoroni and Pavel Rychlý

Findings from the Bambara - French Machine Translation Competition (BFMT 2023)
Ninoh Agostinho Da Silva, Tunde Ajayi, Alex Antonov, Panga Azazia Kamate, Moussa Coulibaly, Mason Del Rio, Yacouba Diarra, Sebastian Diarra, Chris Emezue and Joel Hamilcaro

18:05 - 18:15 *Closing remarks*

Train Global, Tailor Local: Minimalist Multilingual Translation into Endangered Languages

Zhong Zhou
Carnegie Mellon University
zhongzhou@cmu.edu

Jan Niehues
Karlsruhe Institute of Technology
jan.niehues@kit.edu

Alex Waibel
Carnegie Mellon University
Karlsruhe Institute of Technology
alex@waibel.com

Abstract

In many humanitarian scenarios, translation into severely low resource languages often does not require a universal translation engine, but a dedicated *text-specific* translation engine. For example, healthcare records, hygienic procedures, government communication, emergency procedures and religious texts are all limited texts. While generic translation engines for all languages do not exist, translation of multilingually known limited texts into new, endangered languages may be possible and reduce human translation effort. We attempt to leverage translation resources from many rich resource languages to efficiently produce best possible translation quality for a well *known text*, which is available in multiple languages, in a new, severely low resource language. We examine two approaches: 1.) best selection of seed sentences to jump start translations in a new language in view of best generalization to the remainder of a larger targeted text(s), and 2.) we adapt large general multilingual translation engines from many other languages to focus on a specific text in a new, unknown language. We find that adapting large pretrained multilingual models to the domain/text first and then to the severely low resource language works best. If we also select a best set of seed sentences, we can improve average chrF performance on new test languages from a baseline of 21.9 to 50.7, while reducing the number of seed sentences to only ∼1,000 in the new, unknown language.

1 Introduction

A language dies when no one speaks it. An endangered language is a language that is spoken by enough people that it could survive under favorable conditions but few or no children are learning it (Crystal, 2002; Kincade, 1991; Wurm, 2001). More than half of the 7,139 languages will die in the next 80 years (Austin and Sallabank, 2011; Eberhard et al., 2021). Endangered languages may survive and thrive if they gain prestige, power and visibility

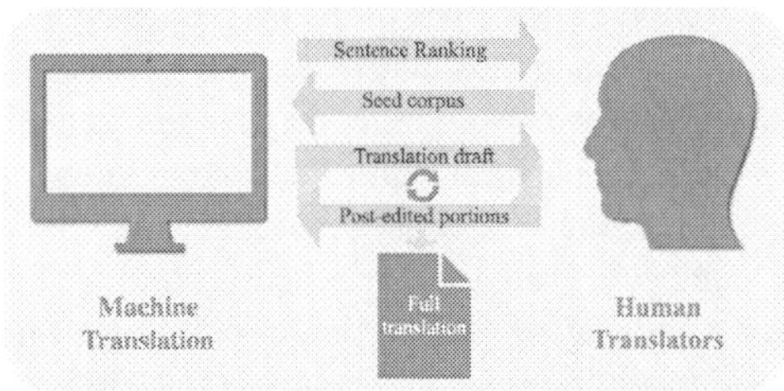

Figure 1: Translation workflow for endangered languages.

(Crystal, 2002). Frisian, for example, struggles to gain prestige in Germany, and is endangered even though it has a large number of speakers. Hebrew, conversely, has been revived as a spoken language because it is critical to the development and identity of the Jewish community. We empower endangered language communities by exercising a language. This can be achieved by translating important texts to their language so that these communities can gain information, knowledge, power and visibility in their own language. One life-saving example of this knowledge-transfer is translating water, sanitation and hygiene (WASH) text into their languages, a process that has long started before the COVID-19 pandemic but has gained much attention since then (Thampi et al., 2020; Reddy et al., 2017).

The problem in these scenarios, therefore, is not to build a high accuracy translation engine for *any texts* using huge data corpora, but rather to build a good translation for a *known* text (for which translations in many other languages exist), but in a new language with only extremely little seed data (a few hundred sentences). We assume there is little to no endangered language data and few human translators. To produce high quality translation, existing methods rely on a seed corpus produced by human translators. Previous work has shown progress in using extremely small seed corpora with as small as ∼1,000 lines of data and has found that random sampling performs better than choosing a fixed por-

Proceedings of the The Sixth Workshop on Technologies for Machine Translation of Low-Resource Languages (LoResMT 2023), pages 1–15
May 6, 2023

tion of the text to build a seed corpus (Zhou and Waibel, 2021b; Lin et al., 2020; Qi et al., 2018). But researchers have yet to 1.) examine various Active Learning (AL) methods to improve accuracy and effectiveness in building better optimized seed corpora so as to minimize the initial human effort and 2.) completely solve the problem of using large multilingual models for representational learning so that we can train (or adapt) them to a new language using an extremely small seed corpus.

To solve these two problems, we propose explainable and robust active learning methods that perform as well as or better than random sampling; we transfer methods learned on data of known languages to the new, endangered language. We also examine different training schedules and we find a strategic way of growing large multilingual models in a multilingual and multi-stage fashion with extremely small endangered seed corpora.

In our translation workflow, human translators are informed by machine sentence ranking to produce a seed corpus. Machine systems then use this seed corpus to produce a full translation draft. Human translators post-edit the draft, and feed new data to machines each time they finish post-editing a portion of the text. In each iteration, machines produce better and better drafts with new data, and human translators find it easier and faster to post-edit. Together they complete the translation of the whole text into an endangered language (Figure 1).

To produce sentence ranking, traditional active learning approaches assume abundant data, but we have little to no data in the target endangered language. We question this assumption and build seed corpora by ranking all sentences in existing translations from other languages to generalize to a new, endangered language. This ranking is target-independent as we do not require any endangered language data. To produce such a ranking, we explore active learning methods (Table 1). For each reference language, we build unigram, n-gram and entropy models (Figure 2). To prevent any language from overpowering the ranking, we aggregate sentence scores across multiple languages and rank the final aggregation. To select the pool of languages for aggregation, we build methods on different voting mechanisms.

To curate a seed corpus in the new, endangered language where we have no data initially, we pass the sentence ranking learned from known languages to human translators. Human translators take this ranking, and translate the top few ($\sim$1,000 or less) sentences, curating the seed corpus.

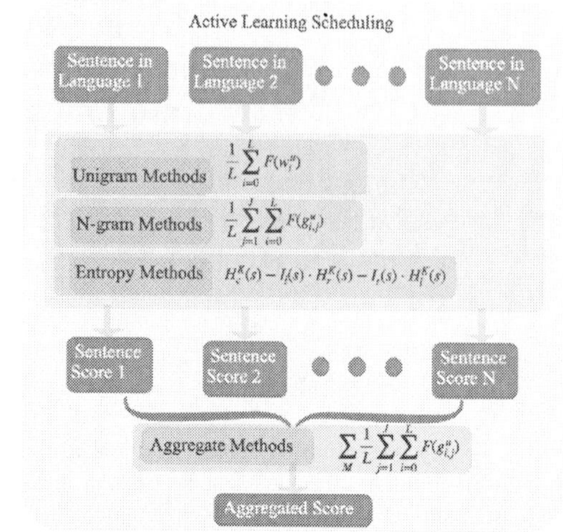

Figure 2: Visualizing different active learning methods. We score and rank each sentence in a text corpus.

To train on such small seed corpus, we find pretraining to be key. For the pretrained model, we either create our own pretrained model by training on known languages, or use an existing pretrained model. We explore both paths in our work, with and without activating the knowledge in existing large pretrained models. We observe an average increase of 28.8 in chrF score over the baselines.

Our contribution is three-fold: 1. We develop 14 active learning methods on known languages and transfer ranking to the new, endangered language; 2. We activate the knowledge of large multilingual models by proposing multilingual and multi-stage adaptations through 24 different training schedules; we find that adapting pretrained models to the domain and then to the endangered language works best; 3. We aggregate scores from 115 languages to provide a universal ranking and increase robustness by *relaxed memoization* method.

2 Related Works

2.1 Translation into Endangered Languages

Recent advances have succeeded in building multilingual methods to translate from multiple rich resource languages to a new, endangered language (Johnson et al., 2017; Ha et al., 2016; Firat et al., 2016; Zhou et al., 2018a,b). Many have demonstrated good transfer learning to low resource languages (Zhou and Waibel, 2021b; Lin et al., 2020; Qi et al., 2018), while some work on zero-shot learning (Neubig and Hu, 2018; Pham et al., 2019; Philip et al., 2020; Karakanta et al., 2018; Zhang et al., 2020; Chen et al., 2022, 2021). However, zero-shot learning is volatile and unstable, so we choose to use extremely small data instead.

2.2 Active Learning in Machine Translation

Active learning has a long history in machine translation (Settles, 2012; Eck et al., 2005; González-Rubio et al., 2012). Random sampling is often surprisingly powerful (Kendall and Smith, 1938; Knuth, 1991; Sennrich et al., 2016a). There is extensive research to beat random sampling by methods based on entropy (Koneru et al., 2022), coverage and uncertainty (Peris and Casacuberta, 2018; Zhao et al., 2020), clustering (Haffari et al., 2009; Gangadharaiah et al., 2009), consensus (Haffari and Sarkar, 2009), syntactic parsing (Miura et al., 2016), density and diversity (Koneru et al., 2022; Ambati et al., 2011), and learning to learn active learning strategies (Liu et al., 2018).

2.3 Large Pretrained Multilingual Model

The state-of-the-art multilingual machine translation systems translate from many source languages to many target languages (Johnson et al., 2017; Ha et al., 2016; Zoph and Knight, 2016). The bottleneck in building such systems is in computation limits, as the training data increases quadratically with the number of languages. Some companies have built and released large pretrained multilingual models (Liu et al., 2020; Tang et al., 2020). M2M100 is trained in 100 languages (Fan et al., 2021; Schwenk et al., 2021; El-Kishky et al., 2020) and covers a few endangered languages.

3 Methods

We translate a fixed text that is available in many languages to a new, endangered language. In our translation workflow, we first develop active learning methods to transfer sentence ranking from known languages to a new, endangered language. We then pass this ranking to human translators for them to translate the top few ($\sim$1,000 or less) sentences into the endangered language, curating the seed corpus. We finally train on the seed corpus, either from scratch or from a pretrained model.

We build training schedules on an extremely small seed corpus, we also build active learning strategies of creating and transferring the sentence ranking to the new, endangered language. We propose and compare 24 training schedules and 14 active learning methods for machine translation into a new, endangered language. To compare all active learning algorithms fairly, we use the same translation system unit as a control for all experiments, varying only the seed corpora built by different methods. We select the same number of words in all seed corpora as most translators are paid by the number of words (Bloodgood and Callison-Burch, 2010; Eck, 2008; Tomanek and Hahn, 2009).

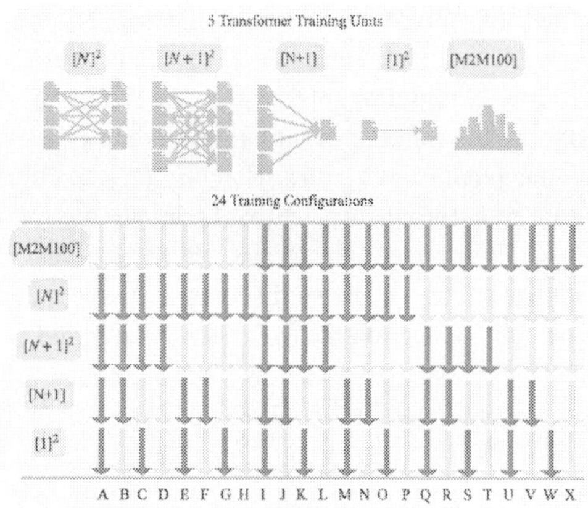

Figure 3: 24 different training schedules.
[N]: multilingual model on N neighboring languages
$[N+1]^2$: multi-target model with endangered language
[N+1]: single-target model with endangered language
$[1]^2$: autoencoder in endangered language.

3.1 Training Schedules

In our setup we have the new, endangered language as the target language, and we have a few neighboring languages as the source languages that are either in the same linguistic language family or geographically close to facilitate linguistic transfer. In effect, we have N source languages with full translations of the text and a new and endangered language that has an extremely small seed corpus.

We use the state-of-the-art multilingual transformer prepending both source and target language labels to each source sentence (Johnson et al., 2017; Ha et al., 2016). For precise translation for all named entities, we use an existing method of *order-preserving named entity translation* by masking each named entity with ordered __NEs using a parallel multilingual lexicon table in 125 languages (Zhou and Waibel, 2021b; Wu et al., 2018).

Using this multilingual transformer architecture as a base, we build 5 training units on the small seed corpus of the new, endangered language and the existing translations of known languages. We let $[N]^2$ denote the training of all source languages in a N-by-N multilingual transformer. We let $[N+1]^2$ denote the training of all languages including the endangered language in a (N+1)-by-(N+1) multilingual transformer. We let [N+1] denote the (N+1)-by-1 multilingual transformer that focuses on translating into the endangered language. We let $[1]^2$ be the autoencoder on the endangered language.

Our translation system is built on these 5 training units: an optional [M2M100] (Fan et al., 2021), $[N]^2$, $[N+1]^2$, [N+1] and $[1]^2$. These 5 stages increase in specificity while they decrease in data size. Building on them, we show 24 different training schedules, among which 8 are pretrained with in-domain data and 16 are pretrained with out-of-domain large multilingual models (Figure 3). We only consider models with pretraining and therefore do not exhaust all 32 training schedules.

3.2 Active Learning Strategies

We have two baselines: the linguistic baseline of the excerpt-based approach, *Luke*, and the statistical baseline of random sampling, *Rand*. The excerpt-based approach, which selects a portion of the text with consecutive sentences, preserves the text's formality, cohesion and context but lacks global coverage. Random sampling increases global coverage but sacrifices local coherence.

3.2.1 N-gram Approach

Many researchers count the number of unknown n-grams as score functions to solve the knapsack problem, covering all vocabulary (Eck, 2008; Eck et al., 2005; Haffari et al., 2009). Instead of solving the knapsack problem, we choose sentences to partially cover the vocabulary and build an extremely small seed corpus. To cover the vocabulary strategically, we sum the frequency counts of the unknown n-grams to increase density. These frequency counts promote frequent words for learning to be meaningful in the extremely low resource scenario. In Table 1 we denote frequency function by $F(\cdot)$, denote sequence length by L and denote the highest n-gram order by J.

3.2.2 Entropy Approach

Many have worked on entropy methods in modelling density and diversity (Ambati et al., 2011; Eck, 2008; Zeng et al., 2019; Haffari et al., 2009). We use traditional Language Models (LMs) instead of neural language models, as our data size is extremely small. For implementations of LMs, we use KenLM and NLTK's LM because of their simplicity and speed, especially KenLM (Heafield, 2011; Bird and Loper, 2004). In Table 1 we let $H(\cdot)$ be the cross entropy function, with the choice of KenLM (K) or NLTK (N). To separate training from testing in using language models, we divide the data into three portions, the sentences that we have chosen (*c*), and the remaining that are split equally into two parts, left (*l*) and right (*r*). Let $I_l(\cdot)$ and $I_r(\cdot)$ be indicator functions to show whether a sentence belongs to the left or the right. We aim to maximize the diversity H_c and optimize density by adjusting H_l and H_r (Koneru et al., 2022).

Name	Description	Score Function
S	Frequency sum of unknown words	$\sum_{i=0}^{L} F(w_i^u)$
SN	Normalized S by L	$\frac{1}{L}\sum_{i=0}^{L} F(w_i^u)$
SNG_J	Normalized Frequency sum of n-grams up to J	$\frac{1}{L}\sum_{j=1}^{J}\sum_{i=0}^{L} F(g_{i,j}^u)$
AGG_J^M	Aggregation of n-gram scores up to J with set M	$\sum_{M}\frac{1}{L}\sum_{j=1}^{J}\sum_{i=0}^{L} F(g_{i,j}^u)$
ENT^K	Entropy methods, K is KenLM or not	$H_c^K(s) - I_l(s)\cdot H_r^K(s) - I_r(s)\cdot H_l^K(s)$

Table 1: Summary of score functions.

3.2.3 Aggregation Approach

To prevent any language from overpowering the ranking, we aggregate sentence scores across different languages (Figure 2). We investigate the use of a customized set of languages for each endangered language, versus the use of a universal set of languages representing world languages. The former requires some understanding of the neighboring languages, the latter requires careful choices of the representative set (Blasi et al., 2022).

We have 4 aggregation methods: *one-vote-per-language* (L), where we aggregate over all languages, *one-vote-per-family* (F), where we aggregate over languages representing the top few families, *one-vote-per-person* (P), where we aggregate over the top few most spoken languages, and *one-vote-per-neighbor* (N), where we aggregate over a customized set of neighboring languages. For the world language distribution, L covers all, F samples across it, P covers the head, while N creates a niche area around the endangered language.

Target	L	Family	Source Languages
Frisian	0	Germanic	English*, German, Dutch, Norwegian, Afrikaans, Swedish, French, Italian, Portuguese, Romanian
Hmong	0	Hmong–Mien	Komrem*, Vietnamese, Thai, Chinese, Myanmar, Haka, Tangsa, Zokam, Siyin, Falam
Pokomchi	0	Mayan	Chuj*, Cakchiquel, Mam, Kanjobal, Cuzco, Ayacucho, Bolivian, Huallaga, Aymara, Guajajara
Turkmen	1	Turkic	Kyrgyz*, Tuvan, Uzbek, Karakalpak, Kazakh, Azerbaijani, Japanese, Korean, Finnish, Hungarian
Sesotho	1	Niger–Congo	Yoruba*, Gikuyu, Xhosa, Kuanyama, Kpelle, Fon, Bulu, Swati, Venda, Lenje
Welsh	1	Celtic	English*, German, Danish, Dutch, Norwegian, Swedish, French, Italian, Portuguese, Romanian
Xhosa	2	Nguni	Swati*, Gikuyu, Sesotho, Yoruba, Lenje, Gbaya, Afrikaans, Wolaitta, Kuanyama, Bulu
Indonesian	3	Austronesian	Javanese*, Malagsy, Tagalog, Ilokano, Cebuano, Fijian, Sunda, Zokam, Wa, Maori
Hungarian	4	Uralic	Finnish*, French, English, German, Latin, Romanian, Swedish, Spanish, Italian, Portuguese
Spanish	5	Romance	English*, German, Danish, Dutch, Norwegian, Swedish, French, Italian, Portuguese, Romanian

Table 2: Summary of different target languages used (Campbell and Belew, 2018; Collin, 2010). L, resource level, is from a scale of 0 to 5 (Joshi et al., 2020). Reference languages used for active learning methods except aggregate methods are starred.

Aggregation decreases variance and increases accuracy. Typical aggregation involve taking the sum or the average. Since they have the same effect on sentence ranking, we take the sum for simplicity.

To save space and time, we devise *relaxed memoization*. At every step, we compute sentence score for each language, producing a score matrix of languages versus sentences. We update entries that are affected by the selected sentence, cache and reuse other entries. Further parallelism results in >360 times speedup, from ∼6.5 months to ∼13 hours.

3.3 Evaluation Method and Metrics

Existing multilingual systems produce multiple outputs from all source languages, rendering comparison messy. To simplify, we combine translations from all source languages into one by an existing *centeredness method* (Zhou and Waibel, 2021b). Using this method, we score each translated sentence by the sum of its similarity scores to all others. We rank these scores and take the highest score as our combined score. The expected value of the combined score is higher than that of each source.

To compare effectively, we control all test sets to be the same. Since different active learning strategies produce different seed corpora to be used as training and validation sets, the training and validation sets vary. Their complement, the test sets therefore also vary, rendering comparison difficult. To build the same test set, we devise an *intersection method*. We take the whole text and carve out all seed corpora, that is, all training and validation sets from all experiments. The remaining is the final test set, which is the intersection of all test sets.

Our metrics are: chrF, characTER, BLEU, COMET score, and BERTscore (Popović, 2015; Wang et al., 2016; Post, 2018; Zhang et al., 2019; Stewart et al., 2020; Rei et al., 2021). We prioritize chrF over BLEU for better accuracy, fluency and expressive power in morphologically-rich languages (Papineni et al., 2002).

4 Data

Existing research classifies world languages into Resource 0 to 5, with 0 having the lowest resource and 5 having the highest (Joshi et al., 2020). We choose 10 target languages ranging from Resource 0 to 5 (Table 2). For each target language we choose ten neighboring languages as source languages (Table 2). We prioritize Resource 0 to 2 languages as real endangered languages, and we use Resource 3 to 5 languages as hypothetical ones.

To translate into these languages, our text is the Bible in 125 languages (Mayer and Cysouw, 2014). Each endangered seed corpus contains ∼3% of the text, while all other languages have full text. Our goal is to translate the rest of the text into the endangered language. In pretraining, we use a 80/10/10 split for training, validation and testing, respectively. In training, we use approximately a 3.0/0.2/96.8 split for training, validation and testing, respectively. Our training data for each experiment is ∼1,000 lines. We use BPE with size of ∼3,000 for the endangered language and ∼9,000 for the combined (Sennrich et al., 2016b).

Training on ∼100 million parameters with Geforce RTX 2080 Ti and RTX 3090, we use a 6-layer encoder and a 6-layer decoder with 512 hidden states, 8 attention heads, 512 word vector size, 2,048 hidden units, 6,000 batch size, 0.1 label smoothing, 2.5 learning learning rate and 1.0 finetuning learning rate, 0.1 dropout and attention dropout, a patience of 5 after 190,000 steps in $[N]^2$ with an update interval of 1000, a patience of 5 for $[N+1]^2$ with an update interval of 200, and a patience of 25 for [N+1] and $[1]^2$ with an update interval of 50, "adam" optimizer and "noam" decay method (Klein et al., 2017; Papineni et al., 2002).

↑chrF	Frisian	Hmong	Pokomchi	Turkmen	Sesotho	Welsh	Xhosa	Indonesian	Hungarian	Spanish	Average
Baselines:											
+ Bilingual	23.1	25.0	28.7	18.9	25.2	22.2	21.4	27.2	20.1	22.1	23.4
+ Multilingual	28.0	28.1	31.9	22.6	28.3	26.5	23.9	29.7	22.3	26.8	26.8
Our Models:											
+ Schedule B	50.5	43.9	42.8	38.9	43.2	46.0	34.9	47.2	37.4	50.1	43.5
+ Active (AL)	53.6	45.7	44.4	40.3	44.9	47.7	36.8	49.1	39.0	52.7	45.4

Table 3: Results for translation into 10 languages that are new and severely low resourced to the system, independent of M2M100.

↑chrF	Frisian	Welsh	Hungarian	Spanish	Average
Baselines:					
+ Bilingual	23.1	22.2	20.1	22.1	21.9
+ Multilingual	28.0	26.5	22.3	26.8	25.9
+ M2M100	26.0	9.9	38.8	47.5	24.9
Our Models:					
+ Schedule I	53.5	49.5	42.2	53.2	49.6
+ Active (AL)	54.9	49.8	43.2	54.9	50.7

Table 4: Results for translation into 4 languages that are new and severely low resourced to the system, activating knowledge in M2M100 and leveraging active learning.

5 Results

For simplicity, we use the centeredness method to combine translations from all source languages and have one score per metric. To compare across different methods, all experiments have the same test set (3,461 lines), the intersection of all test sets.

Our models improve over the baselines: With Schedule *I*, we observe an average improvement of 24.7 in chrF score over the M2M100 baseline (Table 4). By active learning with 4-gram model, we observe an increase of 28.8 in chrF score over the bilingual baseline.

Our strategic training schedule improves the translation further by activating the knowledge of M2M100 : With Schedule *B* and the 4-gram model, we observe an average improvement of 18.6 in chrF score over the multilingual baseline (Table 3). For Schedule *I*, the increase is 24.8 over the multilingual baseline (Table 4). Indeed, the increase with the activation of M2M100 is greater.

5.1 Training Schedules

We compare 24 training schedules using a randomly sampled seed corpus (∼1,000 lines) to translate into Frisian (Table 5 and 6).

Pretraining with [N]^2 works well without M2M100: We compare 8 training schedules without M2M100 (Table 6). We find that Schedule *B* (pretraining on [N]^2 and training on [N+1]^2 and [N+1]) and Schedule *F* (pretraining on [N]^2 and training on [N+1]) work well without M2M100. Schedule *B* gives a chrF score of 51.1 and Schedule *F* gives a chrF score of 51.2.

M2M100 is useful when a target language and its corresponding source languages are in the M2M100 list and the test set does not overlap with the M2M100 training set. However, we strongly advise discretion, as training data for large pretrained models is usually not clearly specified and most are not trained with endangered languages in mind. M2M100 training data may very likely contain the Bible data, so it only serves as a comparison and provides an alternative view to show that our model is robust with large models. When M2M100 does not apply, our models pretrained with [N]^2 suffice.

Full stage training increases robustness: For models without M2M100 we can use Schedule *B* (Table 7) or F (Table 10). Though the results for Frisian are similar, B is much better than F for morphologically rich languages like Pokomchi, Turkmen and Xhosa. Indeed, B with full training is more robust than F, which skips [N+1]^2. Similarly, for models with M2M100, we can use Schedule *I* (Table 8) or *L* (Table 9). Again, Schedule *I* with full training stages perform better than Schedule *L*.

Applying M2M100 alone gives poor results: Schedule *X* produces poor results (Table 5). Problems include catastrophic forgetting, bias towards rich resource languages, and unclean data. Existing research shows some released models mislabel their English data as Welsh (Radford et al.).

Mixed models with M2M100 perform well: A few training schedules beat those pretrained with [N]^2 (Table 6). Schedule *I* (training on 5 stages) gives a chrF score of 52.9, L (training 3 stages skipping [N+1] and [1]^2) gives 52.8, M (training 4 stages skipping [N+1]^2) gives 52.7, J (training 4 stages skipping [1]^2) gives 51.8, and N (training 3 stages skipping [N+1]^2 and [1]^2) gives 51.9. All are higher than those without M2M100.

Adapting M2M100 to the domain and then to the endangered language works best: Schedule *I*

Network	I	J	K	L	M	N	O	P	Q	R	S	T	U	V	W	X
[M2M100]	⇓	⇓	⇓	⇓	⇓	⇓	⇓	⇓	⇓	⇓	⇓	⇓	⇓	⇓	⇓	⇓
$[N]^2$	⇓	⇓	⇓	⇓	⇓	⇓	⇓	⇓								
$[N+1]^2$	⇓	⇓	⇓	⇓					⇓	⇓	⇓	⇓				
[N+1]	⇓	⇓			⇓	⇓			⇓	⇓			⇓	⇓		
$[1]^2$	⇓		⇓		⇓		⇓		⇓		⇓		⇓		⇓	
↑chrF	**52.9**	**51.8**	49.5	**52.8**	**52.7**	**51.9**	27.4	16.9	49.6	48.5	39.6	48.7	48.5	45.7	27.8	26.3
↓cTER	0.492	0.508	0.482	0.488	0.493	0.502	0.654	0.800	0.530	0.546	0.553	0.539	0.538	0.579	0.650	0.667
↑BLEU	28.8	27.9	24.2	28.9	28.8	28.2	3.0	0.6	24.8	24.2	13.9	24.3	24.5	22.0	3.4	3.3
↑COMET	-0.56	-0.59	-0.63	-0.53	-0.56	-0.57	-1.28	-1.75	-0.67	-0.70	-0.89	-0.68	-0.69	-0.80	-1.21	-1.30
↑BERTS	0.891	0.889	0.886	0.892	0.891	0.890	0.813	0.775	0.883	0.881	0.861	0.882	0.880	0.873	0.823	0.819

Table 5: Comparing 16 training schedules with M2M100. BERTS is BERTScore, cTER is characTER and LRatio is length ratio.

Network	A	B	C	D	E	F	G	H
$[N]^2$	⇓	⇓	⇓	⇓	⇓	⇓	⇓	⇓
$[N+1]^2$	⇓	⇓	⇓	⇓				
[N+1]	⇓	⇓			⇓	⇓		
$[1]^2$	⇓		⇓		⇓		⇓	
↑chrF	38.7	**51.1**	35.6	50.8	43.4	**51.2**	25.6	24.1
↓cTER	0.555	0.517	0.572	0.515	0.523	0.507	0.650	0.682
↑BLEU	12.5	24.9	9.2	24.5	17.5	26.2	2.5	2.1
↑COMET	-0.87	-0.66	-0.91	-0.65	-0.81	-0.63	-0.99	-1.02
↑BERTS	0.850	0.882	0.839	0.884	0.865	0.885	0.801	0.794

Table 6: Comparing 8 training schedules without M2M100.
$[N]^2$: multilingual model on N neighboring languages
$[N+1]^2$: multi-target model with endangered language
[N+1]: single-target model with endangered language
$[1]^2$: autoencoder in endangered language.

(training on 5 stages) with score 52.9 performs best. These models first adapt M2M100 to the domain by doing another pretraining on N^2. After adapting M2M100 to the domain, we adapt the model to the endangered language by training on $[N+1]^2$. The final two stages [N+1] and $[1]^2$ are optional.

5.2 Active Learning Methods

Using Schedule *B* without M2M100, and *L* with M2M100, we compare 14 active learning methods across languages (Table 7 and 8).

Normalizing by sequence length improves density: Without normalization, the model chooses longer sentences with many rare words. Normalization improves density. For Sesotho, the chrF score is 39.0 without normalization and 41.6 with it.

Marginal benefit of increasing n-gram order wanes: Existing research shows bigrams suffice (Eck, 2008). As the n-gram order increases, the data gets sparser and the marginal benefit subsides. Hmong has the best score (46.1) using bigrams.

Tipping points vary with language: The optimal highest n-gram order may differ from language to language. 4-grams work best for Frisian while bigrams work best for Hmong. Hmong is an isolating language while Frisian is a fusional language. A possible explanation is that higher n-grams may have more impact on fusional languages.

Entropy and n-gram methods both beat baselines and higher n-gram models perform best: KenLM is much faster and performs better than NLTK. The entropy method using KenLM beats both baselines. Frisian has a chrF score of 52.7 with the entropy method using KenLM. This is much higher than the baselines: *Luke* (47.5) and *Rand* (50.5). The 4-gram model (53.6) is higher because building LMs from a few lines of data may not be accurate. Simpler n-gram models work better than more evolved entropy models with small data.

Aggregation over all languages serves as a universal ranking: The first 10 active learning methods are based on learning from one reference language and generalizing to the endangered language, while the last 4 focus on aggregation over multiple languages (Table 7 and 8). For Welsh, aggregation over multiple languages (48.2 with most spoken languages) performs better than those that rely on one reference language; but for other languages aggregation performs worse. Aggregation over all languages performs better than other aggregation methods for all languages except Welsh. This hinges on the reference language. For Frisian, choosing English (a Germanic language) as a reference language, performs better than aggregation. For Welsh (a Celtic language), choosing a reference language that is not as close, performs worse. But we often do not have such information for endangered languages. In such cases, universal ranking by aggregating over all languages is useful.

Our active learning methods mimic curriculum learning: Our models pick short and simple sentences first, emulating curriculum learning and helping human translators (Bengio et al., 2009;

↑chrF	Frisian	Hmong	Pokomchi	Turkmen	Sesotho	Welsh	Xhosa	Indonesian	Hungarian	Spanish	Average
Baselines:											
+ *Luke*	47.5	41.6	39.4	34.9	41.2	41.2	32.0	43.3	34.4	46.7	40.2
+ *Rand*	50.5	43.9	42.8	38.9	43.2	46.0	34.9	47.2	37.4	50.1	43.5
Our Models:											
+ *S*	49.2	38.5	40.4	35.2	39.0	41.9	32.5	43.5	35.1	48.0	40.3
+ *SN*	50.9	43.9	43.2	38.3	41.6	43.2	36.1	46.9	36.7	50.3	43.1
+ SNG_2	53.2	**46.1**	43.3	39.5	44.4	45.8	36.6	48.4	37.8	51.8	44.7
+ SNG_3	52.7	46.0	**44.5**	39.6	**45.5**	47.5	**36.8**	48.9	**39.2**	52.3	45.3
+ SNG_4	**53.6**	45.7	44.4	**40.3**	44.9	47.7	36.8	**49.1**	39.0	**52.7**	**45.4**
+ SNG_5	53.0	45.6	43.9	39.7	45.4	46.7	36.8	49.1	38.4	52.5	45.1
+ ENT^N	50.9	43.7	38.1	37.2	42.5	44.5	34.7	46.7	36.0	49.9	42.4
+ ENT^K	52.7	45.7	43.5	40.2	44.6	45.2	36.4	49.0	39.1	51.8	44.8
+ AGG_5^L	47.1	41.5	39.8	34.0	39.9	42.1	31.4	43.5	33.7	45.2	39.8
+ AGG_5^F	45.0	38.4	38.5	32.4	38.8	47.1	30.4	41.2	33.3	44.2	38.9
+ AGG_5^P	45.5	38.8	38.0	32.0	38.8	**48.2**	30.5	41.0	33.2	44.0	39.0
+ AGG_5^N	45.4	39.1	38.3	32.4	38.8	48.0	30.7	41.2	33.2	44.3	39.1

Table 7: 140 experiments comparing 14 active learning methods translating into 10 different languages with Schedule *B*.

↑chrF	Frisian	Welsh	Hungarian	Spanish	Average
Baselines:					
+ *Luke*	49.3	44.3	38.8	48.4	45.2
+ *Rand*	53.5	49.5	42.2	53.2	49.6
Our Models:					
+ *S*	51.9	45.9	40.4	51.1	47.3
+ *SN*	54.8	47.4	42.3	53.2	49.4
+ SNG_2	54.5	49.5	43.5	54.2	50.4
+ SNG_3	54.4	50.4	**43.9**	54.5	**50.8**
+ SNG_4	**54.9**	49.8	43.2	**54.9**	50.7
+ SNG_5	54.5	50.1	43.5	54.1	50.6
+ ENT^N	52.7	47.2	40.9	52.9	48.4
+ ENT^K	54.6	49.4	43.5	53.8	50.3
+ AGG_5^A	49.4	44.2	37.3	48.2	44.8
+ AGG_5^S	46.5	49.8	36.4	46.4	44.8
+ AGG_5^M	48.6	50.4	36.5	46.9	45.6
+ AGG_5^T	48.8	**50.8**	36.4	46.9	45.7

Table 8: 56 experiments activating the knowledge in M2M100 with Schedule *I*.

Graves et al., 2017; Jiang et al., 2015).

All active learning methods cover different genres: Our methods pick a mix of sentences from different genres, sentence lengths and complexity levels. Moreover, our methods pick narrative sentences first, which is helpful for human translators.

Our model captures some language subtleties: Apart from the metrics, we showed our translation to native speakers (Table 12). We translate "He sees that it is good" to "lug ca rua huv nwg lu sab" ("He puts it in the liver") in Hmong, which uses liver to express joy. This increases lexical choice.

Our models and mixed models perform better than M2M100 alone: M2M100 often produces extremely short sentences or repetition. Our models do not have those issues.

6 Future Work

We propose 24 training schedules for translation into endangered languages. We also propose and compare 14 active learning methods to build seed corpus without any endangered language data. Our model is robust with large multilingual models.

While the industry trend is to move towards bigger models with bigger data, our minimalist approach not only uses fewer languages, but we also aggregate over fewer languages. This saves computation power and resources, and therefore time and money, while improving translation performance.

However, we still face challenges with the lack of local coherence and context. The excerpt-based approach enjoys advantage with formality, cohesion and contextual relevance. Active learning methods, on the contrary, do not have consecutive sentences and therefore lose local coherence and pose challenges to human translators (Muntés Mulero et al., 2012; Denkowski, 2015; Sperber et al., 2017; Maruf et al., 2019; Webster et al., 2020; Zhou and Waibel, 2021a; Salunkhe et al., 2016). This is an active research area.

Evaluation is still a challenge. It is difficult to find native speakers and establish long-term collaborations. There is also much variety among endangered languages. Some are more accessible than others and these might provide earlier, realistic evaluation of our method. Empowering endangered languages is not just a technology problem. It requires much efforts in communication with local communities. Through our technologies, we would like to work with local communities to revive endangered languages and bring them to flourish.

Acknowledgements

Thanks to Alan Black, Alon Lavie, Graham Neubig, Uri Alon, David Mortensen, Kevin Haworth, Christian Hallstein for the great discussions and suggestions.

References

Vamshi Ambati, Stephan Vogel, and Jaime G Carbonell. 2011. Multi-strategy approaches to active learning for statistical machine translation. In *Proceedings of the 13th Biennial Machine Translation Summit.*

Peter K Austin and Julia Sallabank. 2011. *The Cambridge handbook of endangered languages*. Cambridge University Press.

Yoshua Bengio, Jérôme Louradour, Ronan Collobert, and Jason Weston. 2009. Curriculum learning. In *Proceedings of the 26th annual international conference on machine learning*, pages 41–48.

Steven Bird and Edward Loper. 2004. NLTK: The natural language toolkit. In *Proceedings of the 48th Annual Meeting of the Association for Computational Linguistics*, pages 214–217, Barcelona, Spain. Association for Computational Linguistics.

Damián Blasi, Antonios Anastasopoulos, and Graham Neubig. 2022. Systematic inequalities in language technology performance across the world's languages. In *Proceedings of the 60th Annual Meeting of the Association for Computational Linguistics.*

Michael Bloodgood and Chris Callison-Burch. 2010. Bucking the trend: Large-scale cost-focused active learning for statistical machine translation. *Proceedings of the 48th Annual Meeting of the Association for Computational Linguistics.*

Lyle Campbell and Anna Belew. 2018. *Cataloguing the world's endangered languages*, volume 711. Routledge New York, USA.

Guanhua Chen, Shuming Ma, Yun Chen, Li Dong, Dongdong Zhang, Jia Pan, Wenping Wang, and Furu Wei. 2021. Zero-shot cross-lingual transfer of neural machine translation with multilingual pretrained encoders. *Proceedings of the 26th Conference on Empirical Methods in Natural Language Processing.*

Guanhua Chen, Shuming Ma, Yun Chen, Dongdong Zhang, Jia Pan, Wenping Wang, and Furu Wei. 2022. Towards making the most of cross-lingual transfer for zero-shot neural machine translation. In *Proceedings of the 60th Annual Meeting of the Association for Computational Linguistics (Volume 1: Long Papers)*, pages 142–157.

Richard Oliver Collin. 2010. Ethnologue. *Ethnopolitics*, 9(3-4):425–432.

David Crystal. 2002. *Language death.* Cambridge University Press.

Michael Denkowski. 2015. Machine translation for human translators. *Unpublished doctoral dissertation, Carnegie Mellon University, Pittsburgh, Pennsylvania.*

David M Eberhard, Gary F Simons, and Charles D Fennig. 2021. *Ethnologue.* SIL International, Global Publishing.

Matthias Eck. 2008. *Developing deployable spoken language translation systems given limited resources.* Ph.D. thesis, Karlsruhe Institute of Techonology.

Matthias Eck, Stephan Vogel, and Alex Waibel. 2005. Low cost portability for statistical machine translation based on n-gram frequency and tf-idf. In *International Workshop on Spoken Language Translation.*

Ahmed El-Kishky, Vishrav Chaudhary, Francisco Guzmán, and Philipp Koehn. 2020. CCAligned: A massive collection of cross-lingual web-document pairs. In *Proceedings of the 25th Conference on Empirical Methods in Natural Language Processing*, pages 5960–5969, Online. Association for Computational Linguistics.

Angela Fan, Shruti Bhosale, Holger Schwenk, Zhiyi Ma, Ahmed El-Kishky, Siddharth Goyal, Mandeep Baines, Onur Celebi, Guillaume Wenzek, Vishrav Chaudhary, et al. 2021. Beyond english-centric multilingual machine translation. *J. Mach. Learn. Res.*, 22(107):1–48.

Orhan Firat, Kyunghyun Cho, and Yoshua Bengio. 2016. Multi-way, multilingual neural machine translation with a shared attention mechanism. In *Proceedings of the 15th Conference of the North American Chapter of the Association for Computational Linguistics on Human Language Technologies*, pages 866–875.

Rashmi Gangadharaiah, Ralf D Brown, and Jaime G Carbonell. 2009. Active learning in example-based machine translation. In *Proceedings of the 17th Nordic Conference of Computational Linguistics*, pages 227–230.

Jesús González-Rubio, Daniel Ortiz-Martínez, and Francisco Casacuberta. 2012. Active learning for interactive machine translation. In *Proceedings of the 13th Conference of the European Chapter of the Association for Computational Linguistics*, pages 245–254. Association for Computational Linguistics.

Alex Graves, Marc G Bellemare, Jacob Menick, Remi Munos, and Koray Kavukcuoglu. 2017. Automated curriculum learning for neural networks. In *Proceedings of the 34th International Conference on Machine Learning*, pages 1311–1320. PMLR.

Thanh-Le Ha, Jan Niehues, and Alexander Waibel. 2016. Toward multilingual neural machine translation with universal encoder and decoder. *International Workshop on Spoken Language Translation.*

Gholamreza Haffari, Maxim Roy, and Anoop Sarkar. 2009. Active learning for statistical phrase-based machine translation. In *Proceedings of the 8th Conference of the North American Chapter of the Association for Computational Linguistics on Human Language Technologies*, pages 415–423.

Gholamreza Haffari and Anoop Sarkar. 2009. Active learning for multilingual statistical machine translation. In *Proceedings of the Joint Conference of the 47th Annual Meeting of the ACL and the 4th International Joint Conference on Natural Language Processing of the AFNLP*, pages 181–189.

Kenneth Heafield. 2011. Kenlm: Faster and smaller language model queries. In *Proceedings of the 6th workshop on Statistical Machine Translation*, pages 187–197.

Lu Jiang, Deyu Meng, Qian Zhao, Shiguang Shan, and Alexander G Hauptmann. 2015. Self-paced curriculum learning. In *Proceedings of the 29th AAAI Conference on Artificial Intelligence*.

Melvin Johnson, Mike Schuster, Quoc V Le, Maxim Krikun, Yonghui Wu, Zhifeng Chen, Nikhil Thorat, Fernanda Viégas, Martin Wattenberg, Greg Corrado, et al. 2017. Google's multilingual neural machine translation system: Enabling zero-shot translation. *Transactions of the Association for Computational Linguistics*, 5:339–351.

Pratik Joshi, Sebastin Santy, Amar Budhiraja, Kalika Bali, and Monojit Choudhury. 2020. The state and fate of linguistic diversity and inclusion in the nlp world. *Proceedings of the 58th Annual Meeting of the Association for Computational Linguistics*.

Alina Karakanta, Jon Dehdari, and Josef van Genabith. 2018. Neural machine translation for low-resource languages without parallel corpora. *Machine Translation*, 32(1):167–189.

Maurice G Kendall and B Babington Smith. 1938. Randomness and random sampling numbers. *Journal of the royal Statistical Society*, 101(1):147–166.

D. M. Kincade. 1991. *The decline of Native Language in Canada.* Stanford University Press.

Guillaume Klein, Yoon Kim, Yuntian Deng, Jean Senellart, and Alexander Rush. 2017. Opennmt: Open-source toolkit for neural machine translation. *Proceedings of the 55th annual meeting of the Association for Computational Linguistics, System Demonstrations*, pages 67–72.

Donald E Knuth. 1991. *3: 16 Bible texts illuminated.* AR Editions, Inc.

Sai Koneru, Danni Liu, and Jan Niehues. 2022. Cost-effective training in low-resource neural machine translation. *arXiv preprint arXiv:2201.05700*.

Zehui Lin, Xiao Pan, Mingxuan Wang, Xipeng Qiu, Jiangtao Feng, Hao Zhou, and Lei Li. 2020. Pre-training multilingual neural machine translation by leveraging alignment information. *Proceedings of the 25th Conference on Empirical Methods in Natural Language Processing*.

Ming Liu, Wray Buntine, and Gholamreza Haffari. 2018. Learning to actively learn neural machine translation. In *Proceedings of the 22nd Conference on Computational Natural Language Learning*, pages 334–344.

Yinhan Liu, Jiatao Gu, Naman Goyal, Xian Li, Sergey Edunov, Marjan Ghazvininejad, Mike Lewis, and Luke Zettlemoyer. 2020. Multilingual denoising pre-training for neural machine translation. *Transactions of the Association for Computational Linguistics*, 8:726–742.

Sameen Maruf, Fahimeh Saleh, and Gholamreza Haffari. 2019. A survey on document-level machine translation: Methods and evaluation. *ACM Computing Surveys*.

Thomas Mayer and Michael Cysouw. 2014. Creating a massively parallel bible corpus. *Oceania*, 135(273):40.

Akiva Miura, Graham Neubig, Michael Paul, and Satoshi Nakamura. 2016. Selecting syntactic, non-redundant segments in active learning for machine translation. In *Proceedings of the the 15th Conference of the North American Chapter of the Association for Computational Linguistics on Human Language Technologies*, pages 20–29.

Víctor Muntés Mulero, Patricia Paladini Adell, Cristina España Bonet, and Lluís Màrquez Villodre. 2012. Context-aware machine translation for software localization. In *Proceedings of the 16th Annual Conference of the European Association for Machine Translation: EAMT 2012: Trento, Italy, May 28th-30th 2012*, pages 77–80.

Graham Neubig and Junjie Hu. 2018. Rapid adaptation of neural machine translation to new languages. *Proceedings of the 23rd Conference on Empirical Methods in Natural Language Processing*.

Kishore Papineni, Salim Roukos, Todd Ward, and Wei-Jing Zhu. 2002. Bleu: a method for automatic evaluation of machine translation. In *Proceedings of the 40th annual meeting on association for computational linguistics*, pages 311–318. Association for Computational Linguistics.

Alvaro Peris and Francisco Casacuberta. 2018. Active learning for interactive neural machine translation of data streams. *Proceedings of the 23rd Conference on Computational Natural Language Learning*.

Ngoc-Quan Pham, Jan Niehues, Thanh-Le Ha, and Alex Waibel. 2019. Improving zero-shot translation with language-independent constraints. *Proceedings of the 4th conference on Machine Translation*.

Jerin Philip, Alexandre Berard, Matthias Gallé, and Laurent Besacier. 2020. Monolingual adapters for zero-shot neural machine translation. In *Proceedings of the 25th Conference on Empirical Methods in Natural Language Processing*, pages 4465–4470.

Maja Popović. 2015. chrf: character n-gram f-score for automatic mt evaluation. In *Proceedings of the Tenth Workshop on Statistical Machine Translation*, pages 392–395.

Matt Post. 2018. A call for clarity in reporting BLEU scores. In *Proceedings of the Third Conference on Machine Translation: Research Papers*, pages 186–191, Brussels, Belgium. Association for Computational Linguistics.

Ye Qi, Devendra Singh Sachan, Matthieu Felix, Sarguna Janani Padmanabhan, and Graham Neubig. 2018. When and why are pre-trained word embeddings useful for neural machine translation? *Proceedings of the 17th Conference of the North American Chapter of the Association for Computational Linguistics on Human Language Technologies.*

Alec Radford, Jong Wook Kim, Tao Xu, Greg Brockman, Christine McLeavey, and Ilya Sutskever. Robust speech recognition via large-scale weak supervision.

B Reddy, Yadlapalli S Kusuma, Chandrakant S Pandav, Anil Kumar Goswami, Anand Krishnan, et al. 2017. Water and sanitation hygiene practices for under-five children among households of sugali tribe of chittoor district, andhra pradesh, india. *Journal of environmental and public health.*

Ricardo Rei, Ana C Farinha, Craig Stewart, Luisa Coheur, and Alon Lavie. 2021. Mt-telescope: An interactive platform for contrastive evaluation of mt systems. In *Proceedings of the 59th Annual Meeting of the Association for Computational Linguistics and the 11th International Joint Conference on Natural Language Processing: System Demonstrations*, pages 73–80.

Pramod Salunkhe, Aniket D Kadam, Shashank Joshi, Shuhas Patil, Devendrasingh Thakore, and Shrikant Jadhav. 2016. Hybrid machine translation for english to marathi: A research evaluation in machine translation:(hybrid translator). In *2016 International Conference on Electrical, Electronics, and Optimization Techniques (ICEEOT)*, pages 924–931. IEEE.

Holger Schwenk, Guillaume Wenzek, Sergey Edunov, Edouard Grave, Armand Joulin, and Angela Fan. 2021. CCMatrix: Mining billions of high-quality parallel sentences on the web. In *Proceedings of the 59th Annual Meeting of the Association for Computational Linguistics and the 11th International Joint Conference on Natural Language Processing (Volume 1: Long Papers)*, pages 6490–6500, Online. Association for Computational Linguistics.

Rico Sennrich, Barry Haddow, and Alexandra Birch. 2016a. Improving neural machine translation models with monolingual data. In *Proceedings of the 54th Annual Meeting of the Association for Computational Linguistics*, pages 86–96, Berlin, Germany. Association for Computational Linguistics.

Rico Sennrich, Barry Haddow, and Alexandra Birch. 2016b. Neural machine translation of rare words with subword units. In *Proceedings of the 54th Annual Meeting of the Association for Computational Linguistics*, pages 1715–1725.

Burr Settles. 2012. Active learning. *Synthesis lectures on artificial intelligence and machine learning*, 6(1):1–114.

Matthias Sperber, Graham Neubig, Jan Niehues, Satoshi Nakamura, and Alex Waibel. 2017. Transcribing against time. *Speech communication*, 93:20–30.

Craig Stewart, Ricardo Rei, Catarina Farinha, and Alon Lavie. 2020. COMET - deploying a new state-of-the-art MT evaluation metric in production. In *Proceedings of the 14th Conference of the Association for Machine Translation in the Americas (Volume 2: User Track)*, pages 78–109, Virtual. Association for Machine Translation in the Americas.

Yuqing Tang, Chau Tran, Xian Li, Peng-Jen Chen, Naman Goyal, Vishrav Chaudhary, Jiatao Gu, and Angela Fan. 2020. Multilingual translation with extensible multilingual pretraining and finetuning. *arXiv preprint arXiv:2008.00401.*

Nisha Thampi, Yves Longtin, Alexandra Peters, Didier Pittet, and Katie Overy. 2020. It's in our hands: a rapid, international initiative to translate a hand hygiene song during the covid-19 pandemic. *Journal of Hospital Infection*, 105(3):574–576.

Katrin Tomanek and Udo Hahn. 2009. Semi-supervised active learning for sequence labeling. In *Proceedings of the Joint Conference of the 47th Annual Meeting of the ACL and the 4th International Joint Conference on Natural Language Processing of the AFNLP*, pages 1039–1047.

Weiyue Wang, Jan-Thorsten Peter, Hendrik Rosendahl, and Hermann Ney. 2016. Character: Translation edit rate on character level. In *Proceedings of the 1st Conference on Machine Translation*, pages 505–510.

Rebecca Webster, Margot Fonteyne, Arda Tezcan, Lieve Macken, and Joke Daems. 2020. Gutenberg goes neural: Comparing features of dutch human translations with raw neural machine translation outputs in a corpus of english literary classics. In *Informatics*, volume 7, page 32. MDPI.

Winston Wu, Nidhi Vyas, and David Yarowsky. 2018. Creating a translation matrix of the bible's names across 591 languages. In *Proceedings of the 11th International Conference on Language Resources and Evaluation.*

Stephen A Wurm. 2001. *Atlas of the World's Languages in Danger of Disappearing*. Unesco.

Xiangkai Zeng, Sarthak Garg, Rajen Chatterjee, Udhyakumar Nallasamy, and Matthias Paulik. 2019. Empirical evaluation of active learning techniques for neural mt. In *Proceedings of the 2nd Workshop on Deep Learning Approaches for Low-Resource NLP (DeepLo 2019)*, pages 84–93.

Biao Zhang, Philip Williams, Ivan Titov, and Rico Sennrich. 2020. Improving massively multilingual neural machine translation and zero-shot translation. *Proceedings of the 58th Annual Meeting of the Association for Computational Linguistics*.

Tianyi Zhang, Varsha Kishore, Felix Wu, Kilian Q Weinberger, and Yoav Artzi. 2019. Bertscore: Evaluating text generation with bert. *Proceedings of the 9th International Conference on Learning Representations*.

Yuekai Zhao, Haoran Zhang, Shuchang Zhou, and Zhihua Zhang. 2020. Active learning approaches to enhancing neural machine translation. In *Proceedings of the 25th Conference on Empirical Methods in Natural Language Processing*, pages 1796–1806.

Zhong Zhou, Matthias Sperber, and Alex Waibel. 2018a. Massively parallel cross-lingual learning in low-resource target language translation. In *Proceedings of the 3rd conference on Machine Translation*. Association for Computational Linguistics.

Zhong Zhou, Matthias Sperber, and Alex Waibel. 2018b. Paraphrases as foreign languages in multilingual neural machine translation. *Proceedings of the Student Research Workshop at the 56th Annual Meeting of the Association for Computational Linguistics*.

Zhong Zhou and Alex Waibel. 2021a. Active learning for massively parallel translation of constrained text into low resource languages. *Proceedings of the 4th Workshop on Technologies for Machine Translation of Low Resource Languages in the 18th Biennial Machine Translation Summit*.

Zhong Zhou and Alex Waibel. 2021b. Family of origin and family of choice: Massively parallel lexiconized iterative pretraining for severely low resource text-based translation. *Proceedings of the 3rd Workshop on Research in Computational Typology and Multilingual NLP in the 20th Conference of the North American Chapter of the Association for Computational Linguistics on Human Language Technologies*.

Barret Zoph and Kevin Knight. 2016. Multi-source neural translation. In *Proceedings of the 15th Conference of the North American Chapter of the Association for Computational Linguistics on Human Language Technologies*, pages 30–34.

A Appendices

For simplicity, in Table 2 Pokomchi is Eastern Pokomchi, Hmong is Hmong Hoa, Kanjobal is Eastern Kanjobal, Mam is Northern Mam, Cuzco is Cuzco Quechua, Ayacucho is Ayacucho Quechua, Bolivian is South Bolivian Quechua, and Huallaga is Huallaga Quechua, Chinese is Traditional Chinese, Haka is Haka Chin, Siyin is Siyin Chin, Falam is Falam Chin, Kpelle is Kpelle Guinea.

In Table 3, our model with training scheduling uses Schedule *B*, our model with active learning uses SNG_4. In Table 4, our model with training scheduling uses Schedule *I*, our model with active learning uses SNG_4.

In the entropy score function in Table 1, we use highest n-gram order of 2 for NLTK's LM, we use highest n-gram order of 2 for the two halves (H_l^K and H_r^K) and order of 5 for the sampled data (H_c^K) for KenLM. Since KenLM needs at least a few words to start with, we use MLE as a warm start to select up to 5 sentences before launching KenLM.

For finetuning from a M2M100 Model, training on ~418 million parameters with Geforce RTX 3090, we use a 12-layer encoder and a 12-layer decoder with 1024 hidden states, 16 attention heads, 1024 word vector size, 4,096 hidden units, 0.2 label smoothing, 0.0002 training learning rate and finetuning 0.00005 learning rate, 0.1 dropout and attention dropout, "adam" optimizer and "noam" decay method (Fan et al., 2021; Schwenk et al., 2021; El-Kishky et al., 2020).

↑chrF	Frisian	Welsh	Hungarian	Spanish	Average
Baselines:					
Luke	49.1	41.7	38.3	48.7	44.5
Rand	52.8	46.8	41.9	52.9	48.6
Our Models:					
S	51.6	44.8	40.7	52.0	47.3
SN	53.2	45.8	42.2	52.9	48.5
SNG_2	54.2	47.6	42.5	53.8	49.5
SNG_3	53.7	47.9	**43.3**	**54.5**	49.9
SNG_4	**54.3**	48.5	43.2	54.4	**50.1**
SNG_5	53.9	48.6	43.2	54.5	50.1
ENT^N	52.1	44.8	40.7	52.4	47.5
ENT^K	53.7	46.7	43.1	53.7	49.3
AGG_5^A	48.4	43.2	37.1	48.4	44.3
AGG_5^S	47.3	48.1	36.1	47.1	44.7
AGG_5^M	46.9	47.8	36.3	47.2	44.6
AGG_5^T	47.1	**48.8**	36.1	46.8	44.7

Table 9: 56 experiments integrated with M2M100 on Schedule *L*.

↑chrF	Frisian	Hmong	Pokomchi	Turkmen	Sesotho	Welsh	Xhosa	Indonesian	Hungarian	Spanish	Average
Baselines:											
Luke	47.5	38.2	37.4	33.8	38.5	38.5	29.2	41.7	31.5	46.3	38.3
Rand	51.3	38.9	41.5	36.4	39.0	43.1	32.1	45.3	34.8	50.2	41.3
Our Models:											
S	48.7	35.8	39.8	27.6	36.1	38.1	29.4	41.5	32.5	47.5	37.7
SN	50.9	38.4	41.5	36.9	38.7	41.1	32.5	44.8	33.1	49.2	40.7
SNG_2	52.9	40.9	42.4	37.3	41.0	44.3	33.4	45.8	35.8	51.2	42.5
SNG_3	53.1	41.8	**43.2**	**38.4**	41.9	45.6	**34.0**	47.0	36.4	52.2	**43.4**
SNG_4	**53.6**	41.8	42.2	38.1	41.7	44.5	33.5	**47.5**	36.7	**52.5**	43.2
SNG_5	53.0	41.5	42.0	38.1	**42.3**	45.1	33.5	47.3	36.4	52.2	43.1
ENT^N	50.7	39.5	34.0	34.8	39.4	42.5	32.4	44.4	33.9	48.6	40.0
ENT^K	52.5	**42.4**	42.3	38.5	41.6	43.4	33.6	47.1	**37.1**	51.7	43.0
AGG_5^L	47.4	38.8	38.9	33.2	37.3	40.1	28.9	41.6	31.7	45.7	38.4
AGG_5^F	44.6	36.0	37.1	30.9	35.8	44.3	27.8	39.2	30.7	43.9	37.0
AGG_5^P	45.2	36.6	36.9	30.8	35.6	44.9	27.9	39.0	30.5	43.8	37.1
AGG_5^N	45.4	36.8	37.1	31.3	35.7	**46.0**	28.0	39.2	30.2	43.8	37.4

Table 10: 140 experiments comparing 14 active learning methods translating into 10 different languages on Schedule F.

Seed Corpus Size	Frisian	Hmong	Pokomchi	Turkmen	Sesotho	Welsh	Xhosa	Indonesian	Hungarian	Spanish	Average
Word count	25695	31249	36763	17354	25642	25786	15017	22318	18619	22831	24127
Line count for each experiment											
Baselines:											
Luke	1151	1151	1151	1151	1151	1151	1151	1151	1151	1151	1151
Rand	1022	1001	1101	1045	976	1117	988	1065	1066	1023	1040
Our Models:											
S	692	654	832	689	657	771	598	634	644	682	685
SN	1522	1399	1522	1524	1434	1595	1501	1601	1545	1488	1513
SNG_2	1484	1350	1490	1454	1369	1557	1418	1513	1468	1463	1457
SNG_3	1385	1319	1468	1416	1317	1439	1368	1451	1415	1365	1394
SNG_4	1327	1295	1419	1367	1279	1409	1309	1426	1374	1310	1352
SNG_5	1289	1289	1397	1311	1280	1381	1256	1359	1334	1273	1317
ENT^N	1796	1721	1769	1840	1761	1914	1839	1967	1884	1805	1830
ENT^K	1340	1287	1507	1266	1132	1405	1128	1358	1264	1327	1301
AGG_5^A	984	1025	1060	998	967	1031	1016	1018	993	958	1005
AGG_5^S	1049	1084	1152	1043	1025	1182	1147	1093	1076	1019	1087
AGG_5^M	1058	1097	1159	1109	1025	1232	1159	1101	1087	1018	1105
AGG_5^T	1048	1094	1153	1101	1020	1274	1141	1101	1087	1014	1103

Table 11: Seed Corpus Size for different target languages. The seed corpus gives rise to both training data and validation data, therefore the training size is smaller than the above. Note that all experiments for a given target language share the same number of words, although they have different number of lines. Since each language use different number of words to express the same meaning of a given text, we choose the number of words in the given book "Luke" as the standard reference for each target language. For example, "Luke" in Xhosa contains 15,017 words while "Luke" in Frisian contains 25,695 words.

Target	System Translation	Reference
Frisian	mar Ruth sei: Ik scil dy net forlitte, en ik scil fen dy net weromkomme; hwent hwer "tstû hinnegeane, den scil ik hinnegean, en dêr scil ik dy fornachtsje. dyn folk is myn folk, en dyn God is myn God.	mar Ruth sei: Sit net tsjin my oan, dat ik jo forlitte en weromtsjen scil; hwent hwer "t jo hinne geane, dêr scil ik hinne gean, en hwer "t jo fornachtsje, dêr scil ik fornachtsje; jins folk is myn folk en jins God is myn God;
Hmong	Lauj has rua nwg tas, "Tsw xob ua le ntawd, kuv yuav moog rua koj lub chaw kws koj moog, hab kuv yuav nyob huv koj haiv tuabneeg. koj yog kuv tug Vaajtswv."	tassws Luv has tas, "Tsw xob has kuas kuv tso koj tseg ncaim koj rov qaab moog. koj moog hovtwg los kuv yuav moog hab, koj nyob hovtwg los kuv yuav nyob hov ntawd hab, koj haiv tuabneeg los yog kuv haiv tuabneeg hab, koj tug Vaajtswv los yog kuv tug Vaajtswv.
Pokomchi	eh je' wili i xq'orarik reh i Rut: Maacanaa' chih taj i hin. re' hin naa nub'anam aweh chupaam i ye'aab' naa nuk'achariik ayu'. re' hin naa nuk'achariik awuuk', eh re' hin naa nukahniik chi nuDios, inki.	re' Rut je' wili i chaq'wik xub'an: Maa pahqaaj aakuyariik weh re' hin ma' jaruuj nee tinukanaa' kahnoq, xa aha' pa' nee tiooj i hat, nee wo' kinooj chawiij, xa aha' pa' nee ti k'achariik i hat ar nee kink'acharik i hin. eh re' aatinamiit re' wo' re' nutinamiit i hin, eh re' aaDios re' wo' re' nuDios i hin.
Turkmen	Rut: oňa: "Sen nirä gitseň, men hem seniň ýanyňa gitmerin. Sen nirä gitseň, men hem seniň halkym bolaryn. Men seniň Hudaýym bolaryn.	emma Rut: "Seni terk edip ýanyňdan gitmegi menden haýyş etme. sen Nirä gitseň, Menem şol ýere gitjek. sen nirede bolsaň, Menem şol ýerde boljak. seniň halkyň - meniň halkym, seniň Hudaýyň meniň Hudaýym bolar.
Sesotho	yaba Ruthe o re ho yena: "O se ke wa tloha ho wena, hobane ke tla ya le wena, ke tla ya le wena, mme ke tla ya hona moo. setjhaba sa ka, le Modimo wa hao."	empa Ruthe a re: "O se ke wa nqobella hore ke kgaohane le wena, kapa hore ke se ke ka tsamaya le wena, hobane" moo o yang teng ke tla ya teng, moo o phelang teng ke tla phela teng; tjhaba sa heno e be tjhaba sa heso, Modimo wa hao e be Modimo wa ka.
Welsh	a Ruth a ddywedodd, Nuw gael arnaf fi, atolwg, atolwg, oddi wrthyt: canys lle yr wyt yn myned, ac yno yr wyt yn myned, y byddaf fy hun. dy bobl yw fy bobl, a'th Dduw yw fy Duw.	a Ruth a ddywedodd, Nac erfyn arnaf fi ymado â thi, i gilio oddi ar dy ôl di: canys pa le bynnag yr elych di, yr af finnau; ac ym mha le bynnag y lletyech di, y lletyaf finnau: dy bobl di fydd fy mhobl i, a'th Dduw di fy Nuw innau:
Xhosa	URute waphendula wathi: "Undiyekeli ukuba ndixhamle, kuba ndiza kuhlala apho uthanda khona. mna ndiza kuba ngabantu bam, abe nguThixo wam."	Waphendula uRute wathi: "Sukundinyanzela usithi mandikushiye. apho uya khona, nam ndiya kuya, ndiye kuhlala nalapho uhlala khona, amawenu abe ngamawethu, noThixo wakho abe nguThixo wam.
Indonesian	tetapi Rut: menjawab: "Janganlah engkau meninggalkan aku dan pulang ke tempat kediamanmu, sebab aku akan pergi dan berdiam di mana engkau diam, sebab orang-orangmu akan menjadi umat-Ku dan Allahmu."	tetapi kata Rut: "Janganlah desak aku meninggalkan engkau dan pulang dengan tidak mengikuti engkau; sebab ke mana engkau pergi, ke situ jugalah aku pergi, dan di mana engkau bermalam, di situ jugalah aku bermalam: bangsamulah bangsaku dan Allahmulah Allahku;
Hungarian	Ruth így felelt: Nem kérlek téged, hogy gondolj meg téged, mert csak hozzád megyek, és én otthagytam, hogy legyenek hozzád. a te népem az én, és az én Istenem az én.	de Ruth azt felelte: Ne unszolj engem, hogy elhagyjalak és visszatérjek tőled. mert ahová te mégy, odamegyek, ahol te megszállsz, ott szállok meg. Néped az én népem, és Istened az én Istenem.
Spanish	y Rut: dijo a David: No me permite de ti, y me quitaré de ti; porque donde vayas, yo iré a donde vayas, y habitaré; y tu pueblo es mi pueblo, y tu Dios es mi Dios.	respondió Rut: No me ruegues que te deje, y me aparte de ti; porque a dondequiera que tú fueres, iré yo, y dondequiera que vivieres, viviré. tu pueblo será mi pueblo, y tu Dios mi Dios.

Table 12: Qualitative evaluation using SNG_5 to translate into each target language.

Multilingual Bidirectional Unsupervised Translation Through Multilingual Finetuning and Back-Translation

Bryan Li[1*], **Mohammad Sadegh Rasooli**[2], **Ajay Patel**[1], **Chris Callison-Burch**[1]
[1]University of Pennsylvania, Philadelphia, PA, USA
[2]Microsoft, Mountain View, CA, USA

Abstract

We propose a two-stage approach for training a single NMT model to translate unseen languages both to and from English. For the first stage, we initialize an encoder-decoder model to pretrained XLM-R and RoBERTa weights, then perform multilingual fine-tuning on parallel data in 40 languages to English. We find this model can generalize to zero-shot translations on unseen languages. For the second stage, we leverage this generalization ability to generate synthetic parallel data from monolingual datasets, then bidirectionally train with successive rounds of back-translation.

Our approach, which we EcXTra (English-centric Crosslingual (X) Transfer), is conceptually simple, only using a standard cross-entropy objective throughout. It is also data-driven, sequentially leveraging auxiliary parallel data and monolingual data. We evaluate unsupervised NMT results for 7 low-resource languages, and find that each round of back-translation training further refines bidirectional performance. Our final single EcXTra-trained model achieves competitive translation performance in all translation directions, notably establishing a new state-of-the-art for English-to-Kazakh (22.9 > 10.4 BLEU).

1 Introduction

Current neural machine translation (NMT) systems owe much of their success to efficient training over large corpora of parallel sentences, and consequently tend to struggle in low-resource scenarios and domains (Kim et al., 2020; Marchisio et al., 2020). This has motivated investigation into the field of zero-resource NMT, in which no parallel sentences are available for the source-target language pair. This is especially valuable for low-resource languages, which by nature have little to no parallel data.

*Correspondence to: bryanli@seas.upenn.edu

There are two mainstream lines of inquiry towards developing models to tackle zero-resource machine translation. *Unsupervised machine translation* learns a model from monolingual data from the source and target languages. Some research involves introducing new unsupervised pre-training objectives between monolingual datasets (Lample and Conneau, 2019; Artetxe et al., 2019). Others devise training schemes with composite loss functions on various objectives (Ko et al., 2021; Garcia et al., 2021). In contrast, *zero-shot machine translation* learns a model by training on other datasets (Liu et al., 2020) or other language pairs (Chen et al., 2021, 2022), then directly employ this model for translating unseen languages.

This work leverages both mainstream approaches in zero-resource translation. We propose a conceptually simple, yet effective, two-stage approach for training a single NMT model to translate unseen languages both to and from English. The first stage model is trained on *real* parallel data from 40 high-resource languages to English. This results in a strong zero-shot model, which we use to translate unseen languages to English. By applying back-translation to flip the order, we obtain English-to-unseen *synthetic* parallel data. In the second stage, we continue training the model on successive rounds of offline back-translation, where each round uses the prior round for both for weight initialization and for synthetic parallel data.

We term our overall unsupervised translation approach EcXTra (English-centric Crosslingual (X) Transfer). EcXTra can be thought of as a data-driven approach, which sequentially leverages auxiliary parallel data then monolingual data. Each stage's model is initialized to an informed pretrained model, before fine-tuning. We initialize the first stage model's encoder and decoder to XLM-RoBERTa (Conneau et al., 2020) and RoBERTa (Liu et al., 2019) respectively, and we initialize the second stage model's weights to those

Proceedings of the The Sixth Workshop on Technologies for Machine Translation of Low-Resource Languages (LoResMT 2023), pages 16–31
May 6, 2023 ©2023 Association for Computational Linguistics

of the first stage. In doing so, EcXTRa importantly avoids the complicated training schemes and custom training objectives of prior work.

As our approach is simple to train and extend to new unseen languages, we release all code, data and pretrained models.[1] Our contributions are:

1. We introduce EcXTra, a two-stage approach for training a single NMT model to translate unseen languages to and from English. In its two stages, EcXTra combines zero-shot NMT and unsupervised NMT: multilingual fine-tuning and back-translation respectively.

2. Our work is an empirical study of an agnostic view towards multilinguality, as we train the zero-shot stage on balanced splits of parallel data from 40 languages to English. In contrast, prior work has largely explored multilinguality by selecting train languages with oracle knowledge of the test languages.

3. We evaluate the bidirectional unsupervised NMT performance of a single EcXTra-trained model on 7 foreign-English test sets (14 total). This final model, trained in two rounds of back-translation, achieves competitive unsupervised performance for most language directions, establishing a new state-of-the-art for English-Kazakh. We are also the first to report, the best of our knowledge, unsupervised results for 3 translation directions: English-Pashto, English-Myanmar, and English-Icelandic.

2 Our Approach

Our training procedure closely follows the standard machine translation task. *Machine translation* involves developing models to output text in a target language $\mathcal{T}$, given text in a source language $\mathcal{S}$. In a typical supervised MT setting, it is assumed there is a parallel corpus $\mathcal{P} = \{(s_i, t_i)\}_{i=1}^{n}$ in which each sentence $t_i \in \mathcal{T}$ is a translation of $s_i \in \mathcal{S}$. A model is then trained on these examples, to minimize the cross-entropy loss given by

$$\mathcal{L}(\mathcal{P};\theta) = \sum_{i=1}^{n} \log p(t_i|s_i;\theta) \qquad (1)$$

where θ is a collection of learned parameters.

Given enough parallel data, this training framework allows contemporary NMT models to achieve strong performance (Dabre et al., 2020). However, in the unsupervised setting arises the fundamental challenge that we no longer have any parallel data between the source and target languages of interest.

Conceptually, we divide the two stages of our training procedure into four steps:

1a. *Zero-shot model transfer* by initializing to pretrained multilingual LMs. We use an XLM-RoBERTa encoder and a RoBERTa decoder.

1b. *Multilingual fine-tuning* for this initialized model, on parallel data from diverse source languages to English.

2a. *Synthetic parallel data creation* using back-translations from the stage 1 model.

2b. *Back-translation training* by initializing to the stage 1 model, then further training on the synthetic parallel data, in both translation directions. Steps 2a and 2b are iterated for several rounds, in each initializing to the prior round model.

Observe that these are are widely-used techniques in the field of machine translation. Our main contribution is in presenting an effective synthesis of the techniques to enable a single model to perform zero-shot and bidirectional translation (while using only a standard loss function).

Terminology It is worthwhile formalizing our exact terminology, given that prior work in this field uses terms rather inconsistently.[2] Our setting is *English-centric*, as the language pairs include English as either the source or target[3] Our final model is *bidirectional*, in that it can translate $\mathcal{S}$ to $\mathcal{T}$ and also translate $\mathcal{T}$ to $\mathcal{S}$. We call the non-English side of a pair a *foreign* language. Therefore, we use the terms foreign-English and many-to-English interchangeably (likewise with English-foreign and English-to-any). Languages seen during training on parallel datasets are *auxiliary* languages.

2.1 Zero-shot Model Transfer

There are many structural as well as lexical similarities across different languages, especially within language families. By training a multilingual translation model on gold-standard parallel datasets for auxiliary higher-resource languages, we aim to exploit these similarities. Specifically, we train model

[1] `https://github.com/manestay/EcXTra`

[2] See Section 2.1 of Garcia et al. (2021) for further discussion on this inconsistency.

[3] We focus on the English-centric setting because it is the language with the most parallel data to other languages.

parameters θ on parallel data between n auxiliary languages $\mathcal{S} = \mathcal{S}_1 \dots \mathcal{S}_n$ and some target language $\mathcal{T}$ (for us, English). The goal is to have the model learn to generalize to translating m unseen language data $\mathcal{U} = \mathcal{U}_1 \dots \mathcal{U}_m$ to $\mathcal{T}$. In other words, in the absence of gold-standard parallel data $\mathcal{P}$ in our zero-resource languages, we make use of knowledge transfer from larger parallel datasets with auxiliary source languages. Looking back at Equation 1, we redefine its objective function as

$$\sum_{i=1}^{n} \mathcal{L}(D(\mathcal{S}_i, \mathcal{T}); \theta) \tag{2}$$

where $D(\mathcal{S}_i, \mathcal{T})$ is the gold-standard parallel dataset for language $\mathcal{S}_i$ and English ($\mathcal{T}$).

EcXTRA: Multilingual fine-tuning Multilinguality, namely having diverse auxiliary languages is key to good zero-resource NMT performance (Garcia et al., 2021). In this setting, because there are no true (s_i, t_i) examples until inference time, performance becomes especially sensitive to the initialization of parameters θ. We do so by initializing the encoder with XLM-RoBERTa and decoder with RoBERTa. The former allows for transfer learning from strong pretrained models that are already trained on monolingual data in languages (including the unseen languages of interest), whereas the latter allows for a good understanding of fluent English sentences. Initializing the encoder and decoder to pretrained LMs follows prior work (Rothe et al., 2020; Ma et al., 2020).

From this initialization, we then fine-tune the model on parallel data from many high-resource languages to English. The resulting model is able to translate from unseen language to English, but not the other way. We next discuss how we extend our approach to develop a bidirectional model.

2.2 Synthetic Parallel Data Creation

We assume in this step that we have monolingual data in the unseen languages, which are typically collected by crawling web data. We make use of the model trained in the previous stage to translate all the monolingual sentences $(s_j)_{j=1}^{k}$ to English, thereby having synthetic parallel data $(s_j, \hat{t}_j)_{j=1}^{k}$ where $\hat{t}_i$ is the translation output from the zero-shot model. We then flip the order in each pair to produce examples $\hat{\mathcal{P}} = (\hat{t}_j, s_j)_{j=1}^{k}$, then continue training. This process of bootstrapping additional data is called (offline) *back-translation*.

While back-translation is typically used in low-resource settings, our approach extends it towards the zero-resource setting. We perform back-translation for all unseen languages, and concatenating together all synthetic parallel data $(\hat{\mathcal{P}}_i)_{i=1}^{m}$.

EcXTRA: Training on Synthetic Data In this step, we train a bidirectional English-centric model. We ensure bidirectionality by training on both the English-foreign synthetic parallel data, and the foreign-English auxiliary parallel data. Our new objective function is thus a combination of the two cross-entropy losses:

$$\sum_{i=1}^{n} \mathcal{L}(D(\mathcal{S}_i, \mathcal{T}); \theta) + \sum_{i=1}^{m} \mathcal{L}(\hat{\mathcal{P}}_i; \theta)$$

Just as we initialized the zero-shot model to pretrained multilingual LMs, so too do we initialize the unsupervised model to the zero-shot model. After training an initial unsupervised bidirectional model, we further refine performance by running iterative rounds of the synthetic parallel data creation and training process.

3 Datasets Used

Here we succinctly describe the data, providing further details in Appendix B.

Training For the zero-shot stage, we use parallel corpora from higher-resource auxiliary languages to English. We utilize a subset of the Many-to-English v1 dataset (Gowda et al., 2021). We consider only the 40 largest foreign-English pairs,[4] and equally sample 2 million examples from each.[5]

The resulting dataset, which we term *m2e-40*, consists of 80 million sentence pairs from 40 source languages. Note that unlike most prior work, we have taken an agnostic view towards multilinguality — we do not choose the training languages with reference to the testing languages.

For the unsupervised stage, we use monolingual corpora in the 7 test languages (below) from CommonCrawl and CC-100.

Testing We evaluate our approach on 7 languages: Kazakh (kk), Gujarati (gu), Sinhala (si), Nepali (ne), Pashto (ps), Icelandic (is), and Burmese (my). Test sets are taken from WMT21,

[4]Codes for training languages (with those used for validation in bold): **tr**, sr, **fr**, he, **ru**, ar, **zh**, bs, nl, **de**, pt, no, **it**, **es**, pl, **fi**, fa, sv, da, el, **hu**, sl, vi, **et**, sk, ja, **lt**, **lv**, uk, th, **cs**, ko, id, ca, mt, **ro**, bg, hr, **hi**, eu

[5]The rationale is further discussed in Section A.

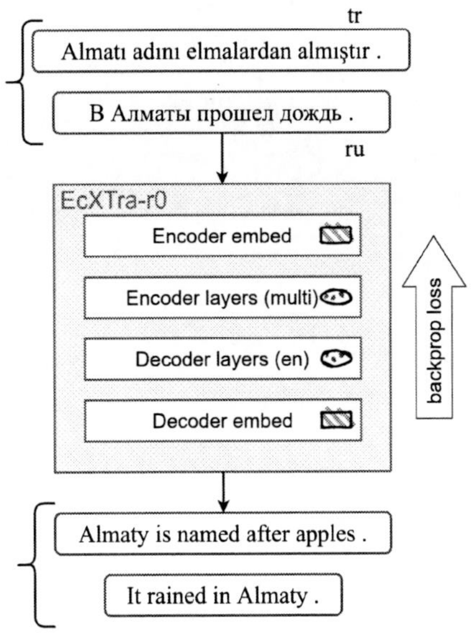

Figure 1: An illustration of the first stage of training (or EcXTra-r_0). The model learns to translate foreign sentences to English. The encoder is initialized to XLM-RoBERTa, and the decoder is initialized to RoBERTa. Both embeddings are frozen (blue rectangle), while layers are finetuned (red ellipse).

FLORES-101 and WAT21. The languages were chosen for both their diversity and for comparison to prior unsupervised NMT work.

Validation To validate the zero-shot stage, we select 15 foreign-English parallel datasets from WMT19 development data; these languages are seen during training.

In the unsupervised stage we only have access to monolingual data. For validation purposes, we thus reserve a small number of synthetic sentence pairs (250 per direction * 14 directions).

4 Experimental Setup

We move from the overall EcXTra approach, to the specifics of using EcXTra to train an NMT model.

4.1 Stage 1: Multilingual Fine-Tuning

Multilingual fine-tuning is the process of training a many-to-English zero-shot NMT model on parallel data from auxiliary languages to English. Figure 1 depicts the multilingual fine-tuning process.

Architecture We use an encoder-decoder, Transformer-based NMT model. Encoder layers and embeddings are initialized to XLM-R large, and decoder layers and embeddings are initialized to RoBERTa-large. These models were pretrained on a large multilingual corpora with various self-supervised language objectives. The encoder vocabulary is from XLM-R, and the decoder vocabulary is from RoBERTa.

Setup In the multilingual fine-tuning stage, we fine-tune our initialized model on WikiMatrix-25en. We freeze both the encoder and decoder embeddings and fine-tune both the encoder and decoder layers. This model thus has 0.76B trainable parameters (1.1B total). We select the best model checkpoint using early stopping.

Our training scheme uses the same supervised training objective of standard supervised NMT models. We hypothesize that this training scheme unlocks the cross-lingual transferability of XLM-R to zero-shot settings, with the same reasoning as Chen et al. (2022).

4.2 Stage 2: Back-Translation

In the unsupervised stage, we perform offline back-translation to bootstrap from foreign-English translation to English-foreign (and back). Figure 2 depicts the back-translation and training process.

Architecture Most of the architecture is transferred directly from the stage 1 model: encoder embeddings, encoder layers, and decoder layers. We cannot transfer the decoder embeddings, since the model now needs to output multiple languages. Instead, the decoder embeddings are tied to the encoder embeddings, which are frozen XLM-R embeddings. The resulting model thus has 0.96B trainable parameters (1.2B total parameters).

Notation Recall the zero-shot stage can be thought of as a pre-training step for the unsupervised stage. We thus designate the zero-shot model as EcXTra-r_0, and the unsupervised models as EcXTra-r_i, where i denotes the current round of back-translation (or simply r_i for brevity). We denote the *m2e-40* dataset as $\mathcal{D}_0$, the concatenation of all foreign monolingual corpora as $\mathcal{D}_{(l)}$, and the English monolingual corpus as $\mathcal{D}_{(e)}$. Synthetic parallel data are $\hat{\mathcal{D}}_{(l)\leftarrow(e)_i}$ or $\hat{\mathcal{D}}_{(e)\leftarrow(l)_i}$.

Training Data As 25M parallel sentences were used to train r_0, we generate about the same amount (3M per language * 8 languages = 24M) of back-translation data. Each r_i therefore is trained on ~50M sentences, given the bidirectional training.

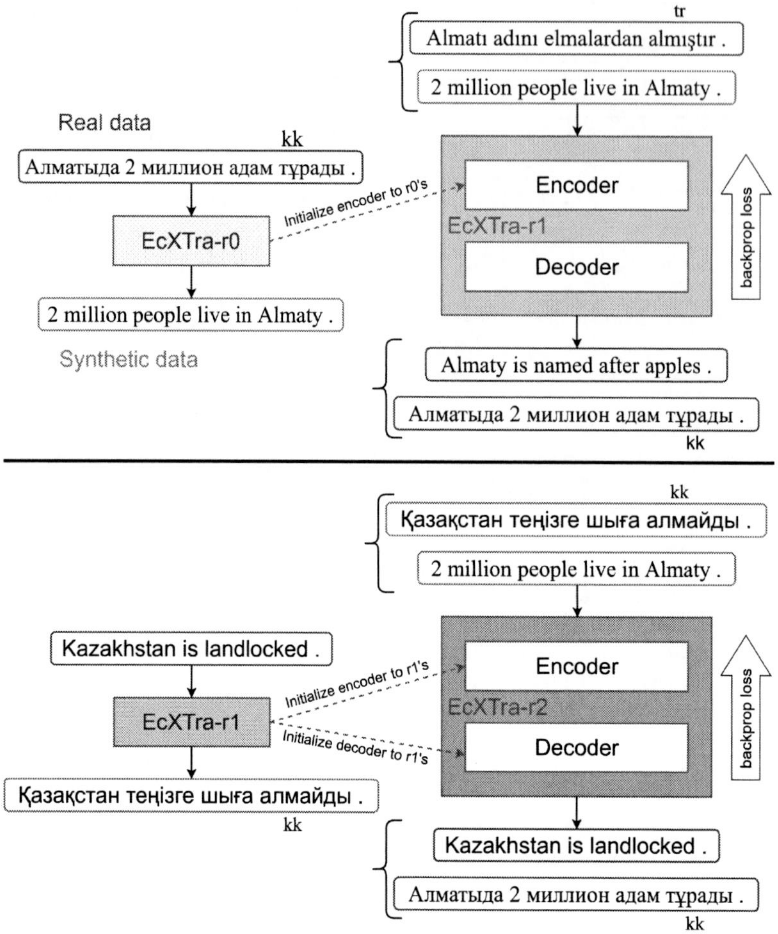

Figure 2: An illustration of the second stage of training, split into 2 rounds. Each round n is trained on a concatenation of back-translations from round $n-1$, and the the opposite direction training data from round $n-1$. Round 1 uses English-foreign synthetic data and transfers only the encoder, while round 2 uses synthetic data for both directions and transfers both encoder and decoder. Note that EcXTra blocks are abbreviated from Figure 1.

For each source language sentence, we add a special start token to indicate the desired target language, following the trick of Johnson et al. (2017). An example is <2kk> to target Kazakh.[6]

Setup Back-translation proceeds in successive stages. The main idea is that, for the current round r_i, we use r_{i-1} to generate synthetic parallel data by translating the monolingual corpus—$\mathcal{D}_{(l)}$ for odd rounds, $\mathcal{D}_{(e)}$ for even rounds. The source and target directions are then flipped before being used as training data. We also use r_{i-1} to intialize weights for r_i.

In our approach we aim to train bidirectional models. Therefore, the training data of r_i consists of both back-translations from r_{i-1}, as well as the opposite direction training data used for r_{i-1} itself. Thus the training data for round 1 is $\hat{\mathcal{D}}_{(l)\leftarrow(e)_1} + \mathcal{D}_0$, and for round 2 is $\hat{\mathcal{D}}_{(e)\leftarrow(l)_2} + \hat{\mathcal{D}}_{(l)\leftarrow(e)_1}$.

We ensure that for synthetic parallel data, the target side is always fluent monolingual text. As observed by Niu et al. (2018), this avoids the possible degradation from training to produce MT output.

For our experiments, we set $m = 2$, performing two rounds of back-translation – consistent with prior findings that improvement tapers off after two rounds (Hoang et al., 2018). The final model, EcXTra-r_2, will have learned from back-translated data in both directions.

[6] Our specific implementation is detailed in Appendix D.

Round	kk-en →	kk-en ←	gu-en →	gu-en ←	si-en →	si-en ←	ne-en →	ne-en ←	ps-en →	ps-en ←	is-en →	is-en ←	my-en →	my-en ←	Avg. →	Avg. ←
r_0	19.6	n/a	23.2	n/a	17.5	n/a	20.9	n/a	9.8	n/a	26.0	n/a	16.5	n/a	19.1	n/a
r_1	**18.5**	20.7	21.1	13.1	14.8	6.6	18.0	8.3	9.0	8.0	24.4	23.4	**14.3**	8.3	17.2	12.6
r_2	18.2	**22.9**	**21.5**	**13.9**	**17.8**	**7.1**	**19.7**	**9.3**	**13.0**	**8.1**	**30.6**	**25.4**	12.9	**8.8**	**19.1**	**13.6**

Table 1: BLEU scores for various rounds of EcXTra models on several low-resource translation test sets. The row divisions indicate groups by approach: zero-shot (no synthetic parallel data), unsupervised (synthetic parallel data). Foreign-English translation (→) columns are in white, while English-foreign (←) columns are in grey. 'Avg.' is the unweighted average BLEU scores across that translation direction. 'n/a' indicates unsupported directions. For the second group, the best BLEU score per column is **bolded**.

5 Results

We evaluate our models on test sets for 7 low-resource-to-English pairs in both translation directions (14 directions total). We use evaluation metrics with are consistent with prior work. By default, we report detokenized sacreBLEU (Post, 2018).[7] For the Indic languages (gu, si, ne), we report tokenized BLEU with the Indic-NLP library (Kunchukuttan, 2020). For Burmese (my), we report SPM-BLEU (Goyal et al., 2022) to handle the language's optional spacing.

5.1 Main Results

Table 1 shows results for each EcXTra round.

Foreign-English Results (→) EcXTra-r_0 (or r_0) is indeed able to perform zero-shot foreign-English translations. The unsupervised r_1 has lower scores, this is likely because this model is now tasked with performing 7 additional tasks on top of the original many-to-English task. r_2 recovers the overall performance, with the same average BLEU as r_0. While r_2 underperforms r_1 for a few individual pairs, it handily beats r_0 for ps-en (13.0 > 9.8) and for is-en (30.6 > 26.0), underscoring the overall quality of the back-translations.

English-Foreign Results (←) Similarly for English-foreign, we observe that r_2 matches or exceeds r_1 overall across language pairs (13.6 > 12.6). This is in spite of r_1 and r_2 sharing the same English-foreign training data $\mathcal{D}_{(l)\leftarrow(e)_1}$.

5.2 Comparisons with Prior Work

Table 2 compares the best EcXtra-trained model, r_2, with prior work (as well as the zero-shot r_0).[8]

We emphasize that these results are *not fully comparable*, given the differing training datasets, models, and number of languages supported.[9] However, the comparisons can still illustrate the effectiveness of the language-agnostic nature and simplicity of EcXTra. We compare to:

SixT (Chen et al., 2021): trained on a German-English parallel dataset.

SixT+ (Chen et al., 2022): trained on AUX6, a parallel dataset in 6 high-resource languages. This is concurrent to our work.

mBART-ft (Tang et al., 2021): mBART-ft is an mBART model further fine-tuned on AUX6.

Garcia et al. (2021) : a single bidirectional unsupervised NMT model trained in 3 stages using combinations of various training objectives on parallel data, real and synthetic (from back-translation).

Zero-Shot NMT Results Considering the first four rows of Table 2 we see that EcXTra-r_0 outperforms mBART-ft and SixT for all translation pairs. Overall, it underperforms SixT+ (a concurrent work), but ties for si-en, and bests it for my-en (16.5 > 15.3).[10]

Unsupervised NMT Results We next compare our best unsupervised model, EcXTra-r_2 to Garcia et al. (2021), the only prior work, to the best of our knowledge, that also trains a single bidirectional unsupervised NMT model. r_2 notably achieves a new state-of-the-art for unsupervised en-kk (22.9 > 10.4), and also improves on kk-en (18.2 > 16.4) and si-en (17.8 > 16.2). r_2 underperforms for gu-en (13.9 < 16.4) and ne-en (19.7 < 21.7).

[7] `BLEU|nrefs:1|case:mixed|eff:no|tok:13a|smooth:exp|version:2.0.0`

[8] Confidence intervals for our results are not shown, but fall between ±0.4 to ±1.0.

[9] More discussion can be found in Section A.

[10] Chen et al. (2022) did not provide is-en results, but their model should support it.

Round	kk-en		gu-en		si-en		ne-en		ps-en		is-en		my-en	
	→	←	→	←	→	←	→	←	→	←	→	←	→	←
mBART-ft	19.6	n/a	17.3	n/a	12.2	n/a	14.4	n/a	0.9	n/a	...	n/a	3.6	n/a
SixT	19.0	n/a	17.3	n/a	12.2	n/a	14.4	n/a	11.4	n/a	...	n/a	5.4	n/a
SixT+	**27.3**	n/a	**27.5**	n/a	**17.5**	n/a	**23.7**	n/a	**12.9**	n/a	...	n/a	15.3	n/a
EcXTra-r_0	19.6	n/a	23.2	n/a	**17.5**	n/a	20.9	n/a	9.8	n/a	26.0	n/a	**16.5**	n/a
Garcia et al. (2021)	16.4	10.4	**22.2**	**16.4**	16.2	**7.9**	**21.7**	8.9	n/a	n/a	n/a	n/a	n/a	n/a
EcXTra-r_2	**18.2**	**22.9**	21.5	13.9	**17.8**	7.1	19.7	**9.3**	13.0	8.1	30.6	25.4	12.9	8.8
Supervised[1234567]	...	12.1	...	28.2	...	6.5	...	26.3	...	11.0	...	23.6	...	13.9

Table 2: BLEU scores comparing various models to EcXTra. The row divisions indicate groups by approach: zero-shot (no synthetic parallel data), unsupervised (synthetic parallel data), and supervised (real parallel data). 'n/a' indicates unsupported directions, while '...' indicates results not provided. Within a row group, the best BLEU score per column is **bolded**. Supervised results, from left to right: [1]Rasooli et al. (2021) [2]Li et al. (2019) [3]Bei et al. (2019) [4]Ko et al. (2021) [5]Shi et al. (2020) [6]Símonarson et al. (2021) [7]Hlaing et al. (2021)

Our work is the first to report unsupervised NMT on en-ps, en-is, and en-my. For an upper bound we cite prior results from supervised NMT systems; these are for reference only (and not even necessarily bidirectional nor multilingual). As expected, r_2 underperforms for most tasks. However, r_2 notably exceeds supervised results for en-is (25.4 > 23.6), showing the strength of our approach.

6 Discussion and Analysis

Enabling English-foreign translation in the second stage seems to come at the cost of some foreign-English performance. This may be an instance of the insufficient modeling capacity problem of multilingual NMT models (Zhang et al., 2020). Still, r_2 improves over r_1, while training on entirely synthetic parallel data generated from back-translations in both directions. This finding underscores the effectiveness of successive rounds of back-translation.

The EcXTra-trained model r_0 underperforms SixT+ (Chen et al., 2022) for foreign-English translations. Because EcXTra is a training approach, we can use SixT+ as a drop-in replacement for r_0 for both weight initialization, and for its back-translations. We suspect that training such a combined model would achieve even better English-foreign performance, and leave this to future work.

The EcXTra-trained model r_2 underpeforms Garcia et al. (2021) for English-Indic translations. This is likely a function of our *m2e-40* dataset having a much lower proportion of Hindi that the dataset of Garcia et al. (2021).[11] While we take an agnostic view of multilinguality, our training data is by no means writing script-centric; possibly making our model worse at outputting Indic texts. The exceeding en-kk and high en-is scores of r_2 provide some evidence for this.

Overall, the r_2 achieves competitive unsupervised translation results. Our model supports 3 additional language pairs over prior bidirectional unsupervised translation models, and the EcXTra approach makes it simple to extend to even more translation pairs. We underscore the overall appeal of our approach, in that we can use the zero-shot model to bootstrap back-translations for any unseen language, and train a bidirectional translation system from there.

6.1 Many-to-English Performance of Unsupervised Models

Unlike for the zero-shot r_0, the unsupervised r_2 has seen text in the text languages, albeit as synthetic parallel sentences with English. A natural question to ask is whether r_2 is able to maintain many-to-English performance for non-test languages.

We perform the following experiment to examine this. The models are tasked with *supervised* translation from 4 train languages (zh, hi, tr, ru) to English. r_0 and r_1 directly see these in their training parallel data, whereas r_2 has only indirectly seen them through the prior rounds.

The results are shown in Table 3. As was found for the test languages, r_1 performs worse than r_0. r_2 has the same average BLEU across language pairs as r_1. From this short experiment we have

[11]This is not explicitly specified in their paper, but is clear given their 4 auxiliary languages, vs our 40.

Round	zh-en	hi-en	tr-en	ru-en	Avg.
r_0	19.2	21.9	28.5	34.0	25.9
r_1	17.0	17.6	26.2	32.5	23.3
r_2	17.4	16.0	27.1	32.9	23.3

Table 3: BLEU scores for each EcXtra training round on several supervised foreign-English translations.

shown that the unsupervised models r_1 and r_2 do retain reasonable Many-to-English performance. We leave future work to investigate mitigation of the forgetting of prior learned tasks, endemic to (almost) all deep learning-based models.

7 Related Work

The field of low-resource and zero-resource neural machine translation is an area of continued interest. Below, we describe related works those which follow our data constraint: parallel foreign-English data in auxiliary languages, and monolingual data in unseen languages.

7.1 Many-to-English zero-shot NMT Models

Chen et al. (2021) propose SixT, a fine-tuning method for foreign-English zero-shot NMT. They initialize both the encoder and decoder to XLM-R. They follow a two-stage fine-tuning approach, first only fine-tuning the decoder layers, then continuing training by unfreezing the encoder layers and decoder embeddings. The model is trained on a parallel corpora in only de-en, and they report zero-shot to-English performance for 10 languages.

Chen et al. (2022) propose SixT+, which builds upon the authors' prior work, and is trained on a parallel corpus in 6 source languages. This is concurrent to the first submission of our work. They show their model can address zero-shot tasks from NMT to cross-lingual abstractive summarization. This work has the same goal as our first stage of training.[12] The main differences are in our training data (40 vs 6 source languages, 80M vs 120M pairs), and our simpler zero-shot training stage (no unfreezing, no position disentangled encoder).

7.2 Unsupervised MT Models

Utilizing Both Parallel and Monolingual Data Ko et al. (2021) propose NMT-Adapt, a method which follows the same data constraints as our work. Their method jointly optimizes four tasks: denoising autoencoder, adversarial training, high-resource translation, and low-resource back-translation – the latter two of which we also use. However, their work trains individual models for each direction, and furthermore for each model explicitly trains on related high-resource language datasets. This approach is thus more expensive and less adaptable to new languages as ours.

Bidirectional Multilingual NMT Garcia et al. (2021) train a single model to translate unseen languages to and from English, under the same data constraints as our work. They proceed in 3 stages, each of which uses a mixture of training data and objectives: *MASS* (Song et al., 2019) for monolingual data, *cross-entropy* for auxiliary parallel data, and both *iterative back-translation* (Hoang et al., 2018) and *cross-translation* (Garcia et al., 2020) for synthetic parallel data. This work shares our goal of developing a single bidirectional UNMT model for unseen languages. There are two main differences. First, their aforementioned training scheme is fairly involved. Second, their approach relies on cross-translation, which explicitly ties individual auxiliary languages to unseen languages, limiting their model's cross-lingual generalizability.

8 Conclusion

We have described a two-stage training approach for developing a single bidirectional, unsupervised NMT model, which we term EcXTra. The main contribution of EcXTra is in its effective synthesis of techniques from both zero-shot NMT, multilingual fine-tuning, and from unsupervised NMT, back-translation. While prior work also uses similar underlying techniques, they have much more involved training processes, either to consider the bidirectional and zero-shot direction, or introduce additional loss functions (which make training more involved). Furthermore, in this work we have taken an agnostic view towards multilinguality.

We trained a single NMT model through EcXTra, and find that each round of back-translation training further refines bidirectional translation performance. This gives rise to the view of EcXTra as successive rounds of informed initialization into further fine-tuning. The final, unsupervised EcXTra-trained model achieves competitive performance on 7 foreign-English tasks, in both directions. The straightforward nature of EcXTra allows it to be easily extended to new unseen languages.

[12] Chen et al. (2022) does perform a small-scale study on back-translation for translating English-foreign, but these models are neither multilingual nor bidirectional.

References

Mikel Artetxe, Gorka Labaka, and Eneko Agirre. 2019. An effective approach to unsupervised machine translation. *arXiv preprint arXiv:1902.01313*.

Chao Bei, Hao Zong, Conghu Yuan, Qingming Liu, and Baoyong Fan. 2019. GTCOM neural machine translation systems for WMT19. In *Proceedings of the Fourth Conference on Machine Translation (Volume 2: Shared Task Papers, Day 1)*, pages 116–121, Florence, Italy. Association for Computational Linguistics.

Guanhua Chen, Shuming Ma, Yun Chen, Li Dong, Dongdong Zhang, Jia Pan, Wenping Wang, and Furu Wei. 2021. Zero-shot cross-lingual transfer of neural machine translation with multilingual pretrained encoders. In *Proceedings of the 2021 Conference on Empirical Methods in Natural Language Processing*, pages 15–26, Online and Punta Cana, Dominican Republic. Association for Computational Linguistics.

Guanhua Chen, Shuming Ma, Yun Chen, Dongdong Zhang, Jia Pan, Wenping Wang, and Furu Wei. 2022. Towards Making the Most of Multilingual Pretraining for Zero-Shot Neural Machine Translation. *arXiv:2110.08547 [cs]*.

Alexis Conneau, Kartikay Khandelwal, Naman Goyal, Vishrav Chaudhary, Guillaume Wenzek, Francisco Guzmán, Édouard Grave, Myle Ott, Luke Zettlemoyer, and Veselin Stoyanov. 2020. Unsupervised cross-lingual representation learning at scale. In *Proceedings of the 58th Annual Meeting of the Association for Computational Linguistics*, pages 8440–8451.

Raj Dabre, Chenhui Chu, and Anoop Kunchukuttan. 2020. A Survey of Multilingual Neural Machine Translation. *ACM Computing Surveys*, 53(5):1–38.

Jacob Devlin, Ming-Wei Chang, Kenton Lee, and Kristina Toutanova. 2019. Bert: Pre-training of deep bidirectional transformers for language understanding. In *NAACL*.

Xavier Garcia, Pierre Foret, Thibault Sellam, and Ankur Parikh. 2020. A Multilingual View of Unsupervised Machine Translation. In *Findings of the Association for Computational Linguistics: EMNLP 2020*, pages 3160–3170, Online. Association for Computational Linguistics.

Xavier Garcia, Aditya Siddhant, Orhan Firat, and Ankur Parikh. 2021. Harnessing multilinguality in unsupervised machine translation for rare languages. In *Proceedings of the 2021 Conference of the North American Chapter of the Association for Computational Linguistics: Human Language Technologies*, pages 1126–1137, Online. Association for Computational Linguistics.

Thamme Gowda, Zhao Zhang, Chris Mattmann, and Jonathan May. 2021. Many-to-English machine translation tools, data, and pretrained models. In *Proceedings of the 59th Annual Meeting of the Association for Computational Linguistics and the 11th International Joint Conference on Natural Language Processing: System Demonstrations*, pages 306–316, Online. Association for Computational Linguistics.

Naman Goyal, Cynthia Gao, Vishrav Chaudhary, Peng-Jen Chen, Guillaume Wenzek, Da Ju, Sanjana Krishnan, Marc'Aurelio Ranzato, Francisco Guzman, and Angela Fan. 2022. The flores-101 evaluation benchmark for low-resource and multilingual machine translation. *Transactions of the Association for Computational Linguistics*, 10:522–538.

Zar Zar Hlaing, Ye Kyaw Thu, Thazin Myint Oo, Mya Ei San, Sasiporn Usanavasin, Ponrudee Netisopakul, and Thepchai Supnithi. 2021. NECTEC's participation in WAT-2021. In *Proceedings of the 8th Workshop on Asian Translation (WAT2021)*, pages 74–82, Online. Association for Computational Linguistics.

Vu Cong Duy Hoang, Philipp Koehn, Gholamreza Haffari, and Trevor Cohn. 2018. Iterative back-translation for neural machine translation. In *Proceedings of the 2nd Workshop on Neural Machine Translation and Generation*, pages 18–24.

Melvin Johnson, Mike Schuster, Quoc V. Le, Maxim Krikun, Yonghui Wu, Zhifeng Chen, Nikhil Thorat, Fernanda Viégas, Martin Wattenberg, Greg Corrado, Macduff Hughes, and Jeffrey Dean. 2017. Google's Multilingual Neural Machine Translation System: Enabling Zero-Shot Translation. *Transactions of the Association for Computational Linguistics*, 5:339–351.

Yunsu Kim, Miguel Graça, and Hermann Ney. 2020. When and Why is Unsupervised Neural Machine Translation Useless? In *Proceedings of the 22nd Annual Conference of the European Association for Machine Translation*, pages 35–44, Lisboa, Portugal. European Association for Machine Translation.

Wei-Jen Ko, Ahmed El-Kishky, Adithya Renduchintala, Vishrav Chaudhary, Naman Goyal, Francisco Guzmán, Pascale Fung, Philipp Koehn, and Mona Diab. 2021. Adapting high-resource NMT models to translate low-resource related languages without parallel data. In *Proceedings of the 59th Annual Meeting of the Association for Computational Linguistics and the 11th International Joint Conference on Natural Language Processing (Volume 1: Long Papers)*, pages 802–812, Online. Association for Computational Linguistics.

Julia Kreutzer, Isaac Caswell, Lisa Wang, Ahsan Wahab, Daan van Esch, Nasanbayar Ulzii-Orshikh, Allahsera Tapo, Nishant Subramani, Artem Sokolov, Claytone Sikasote, Monang Setyawan, Supheakmungkol Sarin, Sokhar Samb, Benoît Sagot, Clara Rivera, Annette Rios, Isabel Papadimitriou, Salomey Osei, Pedro Ortiz Suarez, Iroro Orife, Kelechi Ogueji, Andre Niyongabo Rubungo, Toan Q. Nguyen, Mathias Müller, André Müller, Shamsuddeen Hassan

Muhammad, Nanda Muhammad, Ayanda Mnyakeni, Jamshidbek Mirzakhalov, Tapiwanashe Matangira, Colin Leong, Nze Lawson, Sneha Kudugunta, Yacine Jernite, Mathias Jenny, Orhan Firat, Bonaventure F. P. Dossou, Sakhile Dlamini, Nisansa de Silva, Sakine Çabuk Ballı, Stella Biderman, Alessia Battisti, Ahmed Baruwa, Ankur Bapna, Pallavi Baljekar, Israel Abebe Azime, Ayodele Awokoya, Duygu Ataman, Orevaoghene Ahia, Oghenefego Ahia, Sweta Agrawal, and Mofetoluwa Adeyemi. 2022. Quality at a Glance: An Audit of Web-Crawled Multilingual Datasets. *Transactions of the Association for Computational Linguistics*, 10:50–72.

Anoop Kunchukuttan. 2020. The Indic-NLP Library. `https://github.com/anoopkunchukuttan/indic_nlp_library/blob/master/docs/indicnlp.pdf`.

Guillaume Lample and Alexis Conneau. 2019. Cross-lingual language model pretraining. *arXiv preprint arXiv:1901.07291*.

Guillaume Lample, Alexis Conneau, Ludovic Denoyer, and Marc'Aurelio Ranzato. 2018. Unsupervised Machine Translation Using Monolingual Corpora Only. *arXiv:1711.00043 [cs]*.

Bei Li, Yinqiao Li, Chen Xu, Ye Lin, Jiqiang Liu, Hui Liu, Ziyang Wang, Yuhao Zhang, Nuo Xu, Zeyang Wang, Kai Feng, Hexuan Chen, Tengbo Liu, Yanyang Li, Qiang Wang, Tong Xiao, and Jingbo Zhu. 2019. The NiuTrans machine translation systems for WMT19. In *Proceedings of the Fourth Conference on Machine Translation (Volume 2: Shared Task Papers, Day 1)*, pages 257–266, Florence, Italy. Association for Computational Linguistics.

Yinhan Liu, Jiatao Gu, Naman Goyal, Xian Li, Sergey Edunov, Marjan Ghazvininejad, Mike Lewis, and Luke Zettlemoyer. 2020. Multilingual denoising pre-training for neural machine translation. *Transactions of the Association for Computational Linguistics*, 8:726–742.

Yinhan Liu, Myle Ott, Naman Goyal, Jingfei Du, Mandar Joshi, Danqi Chen, Omer Levy, Mike Lewis, Luke Zettlemoyer, and Veselin Stoyanov. 2019. RoBERTa: A Robustly Optimized BERT Pretraining Approach. *arXiv:1907.11692 [cs]*.

Shuming Ma, Jian Yang, Haoyang Huang, Zewen Chi, Li Dong, Dongdong Zhang, Hany Hassan Awadalla, Alexandre Muzio, Akiko Eriguchi, Saksham Singhal, et al. 2020. Xlm-t: Scaling up multilingual machine translation with pretrained cross-lingual transformer encoders. *arXiv preprint arXiv:2012.15547*.

Kelly Marchisio, Kevin Duh, and Philipp Koehn. 2020. When does unsupervised machine translation work? In *Proceedings of the Fifth Conference on Machine Translation*, pages 571–583, Online. Association for Computational Linguistics.

Xing Niu, Michael Denkowski, and Marine Carpuat. 2018. Bi-directional neural machine translation with synthetic parallel data. In *Proceedings of the 2nd Workshop on Neural Machine Translation and Generation*, pages 84–91.

Adam Paszke, Sam Gross, Francisco Massa, Adam Lerer, James Bradbury, Gregory Chanan, Trevor Killeen, Zeming Lin, Natalia Gimelshein, Luca Antiga, et al. 2019. Pytorch: An imperative style, high-performance deep learning library. *Advances in neural information processing systems*, 32.

Ajay Patel, Bryan Li, Mohammad Sadegh Rasooli, Noah Constant, Colin Raffel, and Chris Callison-Burch. 2022. Bidirectional language models are also few-shot learners. *arXiv preprint arXiv:2209.14500*.

Matt Post. 2018. A call for clarity in reporting BLEU scores. In *Proceedings of the Third Conference on Machine Translation: Research Papers*, pages 186–191, Brussels, Belgium. Association for Computational Linguistics.

Mohammad Sadegh Rasooli, Chris Callison-Burch, and Derry Tanti Wijaya. 2021. "wikily" supervised neural translation tailored to cross-lingual tasks. In *Proceedings of the 2021 Conference on Empirical Methods in Natural Language Processing*, pages 1655–1670, Online and Punta Cana, Dominican Republic. Association for Computational Linguistics.

Sascha Rothe, Shashi Narayan, and Aliaksei Severyn. 2020. Leveraging pre-trained checkpoints for sequence generation tasks. *Transactions of the Association for Computational Linguistics*, 8:264–280.

Tingxun Shi, Shiyu Zhao, Xiaopu Li, Xiaoxue Wang, Qian Zhang, Di Ai, Dawei Dang, Xue Zhengshan, and Jie Hao. 2020. OPPO's machine translation systems for WMT20. In *Proceedings of the Fifth Conference on Machine Translation*, pages 282–292, Online. Association for Computational Linguistics.

Aditya Siddhant, Ankur Bapna, Orhan Firat, Yuan Cao, Mia Xu Chen, Isaac Caswell, and Xavier Garcia. 2022. Towards the next 1000 languages in multilingual machine translation: Exploring the synergy between supervised and self-supervised learning. *arXiv preprint arXiv:2201.03110*.

Haukur Barri Símonarson, Vésteinn Snæbjarnarson, Pétur Orri Ragnarson, Haukur Jónsson, and Vilhjalmur Thorsteinsson. 2021. Miðeind's WMT 2021 submission. In *Proceedings of the Sixth Conference on Machine Translation*, pages 136–139, Online. Association for Computational Linguistics.

Kaitao Song, Xu Tan, Tao Qin, Jianfeng Lu, and Tie-Yan Liu. 2019. Mass: Masked sequence to sequence pre-training for language generation. *arXiv preprint arXiv:1905.02450*.

Yuqing Tang, Chau Tran, Xian Li, Peng-Jen Chen, Naman Goyal, Vishrav Chaudhary, Jiatao Gu, and Angela Fan. 2021. Multilingual translation from denoising pre-training. In *Findings of the Association for Computational Linguistics: ACL-IJCNLP 2021*, pages 3450–3466, Online. Association for Computational Linguistics.

Thomas Wolf, Lysandre Debut, Victor Sanh, Julien Chaumond, Clement Delangue, Anthony Moi, Pierric Cistac, Tim Rault, Rémi Louf, Morgan Funtowicz, et al. 2020. Transformers: State-of-the-art natural language processing. In *Proceedings of the 2020 conference on empirical methods in natural language processing: system demonstrations*, pages 38–45.

Biao Zhang, Philip Williams, Ivan Titov, and Rico Sennrich. 2020. Improving massively multilingual neural machine translation and zero-shot translation. *arXiv preprint arXiv:2004.11867*.

Shiyue Zhang, Vishrav Chaudhary, Naman Goyal, James Cross, Guillaume Wenzek, Mohit Bansal, and Francisco Guzman. 2022. How robust is neural machine translation to language imbalance in multilingual tokenizer training? In *Proceedings of the 15th biennial conference of the Association for Machine Translation in the Americas (Volume 1: Research Track)*, pages 97–116, Orlando, USA. Association for Machine Translation in the Americas.

A Limitations

The notable limitations are the datasets used, the compute required for training, and a want for further ablation studies.

Our training dataset *m2e-40* is a subset of the Many-English dataset (Gowda et al., 2021). This is a collection of various datasets, many of which contain mined parallel sentences. While we have assumed in our paper, like prior work, that these datasets are "real" parallel data, they are in fact quite noisy, and contain many low-quality sentence pairs that likely harm downstream system performance (Kreutzer et al., 2022).

Another potential limitation is that when we select only 2 million samples for each training language pair, instead of using all samples, we limit performance. This is possible, but our work explores a language-agnostic multilingual setting. We refer the interested reader to (Zhang et al., 2022), which finds through an empirical study that overall multilingual translation performance is best when languages are balanced.

Our method requires a solid amount of computing resources in order to train the entire NMT system (see details in Appendix C). Unlike several other works, we train a single model for all directions, which allows us to be more resource-efficient. However, very recent work has found that even without fine-tuning, multilingual pretrained LMs are able to perform zero-shot translations to and from low-resource languages (Patel et al., 2022) – so long as they are given few-shot examples (which can even be synthetic). We suspect such in-context learning based approaches will be soon popular in machine translation, as they have become in many other NLP fields.

We also note that in our work, we evaluated using only BLEU scores. BLEU, of course, is widely-used and understood in the MT community. However, over the decades, researchers have called into question relying solely on BLEU results for MT evaluation. We acknowledge this point, and keep our work as-is given our resource limitations, and given our consistency with prior unsupervised NMT work on reporting results.

A.1 Preliminary Ablations

We understand that ablation studies are useful to ascertain the contribution of various parts of the training approach. Unfortunately, we were unable to pursue this in detail because of resource limitations on our end. Therefore, we enumerate several possible ablations here, and provide preliminary observations from some small-scale experiments:

Model Size We found the large models for XLM-R and RoBERTa, instead of the base models, significantly increased performance for all language pairs and directions.

Our Dataset vs. Prior Work Datasets In the unsupervised and zero-shot NMT literature, because of the variety of task formulations and setups, works do not use consistent datasets for training. This is true for the models we provide reference comparisons to, Chen et al. (2022) and Garcia et al. (2021). These works, like ours, provide comparisons to prior work, with a disclaimer that these results cannot be completely fair. To some extent, the multilinguality agnostic dataset is a key part of the full EcXTra approach. Still, an elucidating ablation experiment could be to train our first stage model using the AUX6 dataset of Chen et al. (2022), then run back-translations using the monolingual datasets specified by Garcia et al. (2021). However, this would require additional computational resources that we unfortunately lack.

Unidirectional Unsupervised NMT We found a unidirectional English-foreign second stage model achieves similar BLEU to the bidirectional second stage models. This suggests that this MT system has no issue with bidirectionality, affirming the findings of Niu et al. (2018).

Bilingual vs. Multilingual NMT Models We found a second stage model trained to only translate a single bilingual pair, kk-en, performs quite a bit better for those translation directions than a multilingual model. This suggests that the model has difficulty with maintaining performance given all the different translation tasks, especially those with unique scripts such as Burmese and Nepali.

Training models for individual language pairs (with their own limited vocabularies), and tailoring the datasets specifically to relevant high-resource languages, is one approach as performed by (Ko et al., 2021). For example, their ne-en specific model achieves 26.3 BLEU vs. EcXTra's 8.8.[13]. However, this approach is still someone unsatisfying, as our ultimate goal is still to train a single

[13]Still, in the ne-en direction their models achieves only 18.8 BLEU (vs. EcXTra's 19.9) This suggests the multilingual similarities are currently better exploited for to-English translation, than from-English.

multilingual NMT system. We hope for continued research to close this gap between multilingual and bilingual NMT systems.

Initializing Stage 2 to Stage 1 Model In this experimental setting, we use the trained stage 1 model only to create English-foreign synthetic parallel data, but initialize to RoBERTa and XLM-R (instead of the stage 1 model). We ran this model for a few epochs, before stopping it because we found the validation BLEU increased very slowly relative to the original stage 2 training. This affirms our earlier claim that the stage 1 model is an informed initialization for the stage 2 model.

B Details on Datasets Used

Here, we expand upon Section 3 and provide further detail on the datasets used in this paper.

B.1 Zero-Shot NMT Datasets

Test We consider translation of 7 low-resource languages, which come from 6 language families. We draw these test sets from publicly available datasets from WMT21[14], FLoRes v1[15], and WAT21[16]. Where possible, we use the same test sets as specified by prior unsupervised NMT work.

Training Our first stage model is trained on a parallel dataset we term *m2e-40*. This is a subset of the Many-English[17] dataset (Gowda et al., 2021), which itself is a collection of other publicly available datasets. Of the 500 language pairs in this dataset, we choose the 40 languages with the most parallel sentences[18]. This criterion contrasts with prior work (Siddhant et al., 2022; Chen et al., 2022), which specifically select language pairs based on coverage and/or similarity to the unseen test languages. Table 5 shows more information for the training languages.

Prior work has handled the imbalance in auxiliary language pairs through temperature sampling (Devlin et al., 2019). Essentially, this is a simple trick to up-sample high-resource languages and down-sample low-resource once. In our work we take the even simpler trick of equally sampling 2 million sentences from each training language. This follows the finding of Zhang et al. (2022) that more equal sampling of languages results in the relatively best multilingual performance.

The Many-English dataset is provided as pre-tokenized and pre-processed. For our use-case, we are fine-tuning the encoder of XLM-R, which was pretrained on untokenized text. Therefore, we detokenize both the English and the foreign sides of our subset using `sacremoses`[19].

Validation The validation data comes from the development tarball of WMT19[20]. Of the 40 training languages, 15 of them are found in this tarball. As some translation directions appear multiple times (e.g. fr-en), we choose just 1 per task. Table 6 shows more information. For the supervised NMT experiment of Section 6.1, we utilize the same development datasets for the languages {zh, hi, tr, ru}.

B.2 Unsupervised NMT Datasets

Training We use several monolingual datasets for training our unsupervised NMT model. For the 7 test languages we draw from Common Crawl[21] for {kk, gu, is} and CC-100[22] for {my, ps, ne, si}.

We take the first 4M sentences of each monolingual dataset–except for Burmese (my), which has only 2M sentences. We then filter out duplicated lines, and empty lines. We thus have 26M test language sentences.

For the English-to-many direction, we require monolingual English data, which we draw from News crawl[23]. As above, we take the first 4M sentences, then filter out duplicated and empty lines. The English monolingual sentences are then translated in the 7 languages, resulting in 7 * 4M = 28M synthetic sentence pairs total.

Validation For each round of back-translation training, we use datasets in 14 directions – from/to the 7 translation directions. We withhold the first 250 sentence pairs of each translation direction (14

[14] `https://www.statmt.org/wmt21/index.html`

[15] `https://github.com/facebookresearch/flores/tree/main/floresv1`

[16] `http://lotus.kuee.kyoto-u.ac.jp/WAT/my-en-data/`

[17] `http://rtg.isi.edu/many-eng/data-v1.html`

[18] The motivation for choosing 40 languages is largely because of resource limitations on our end. Ideally, we would have liked to train on all languages with 1M+ sentence pairs.

[19] `https://github.com/alvations/sacremoses`

[20] `http://data.statmt.org/wmt19/translation-task/dev.tgz`

[21] `https://data.statmt.org/ngrams/`

[22] `https://data.statmt.org/cc-100/`

[23] `https://data.statmt.org/news-crawl/en/`

directions, so 3500 pairs total) to serve as validation. The early stopping criteria is standard BLEU. We tried as an alternative the round-trip BLEU proposed by Lample et al. (2018), but found this made little difference in final evaluation results.

C Modeling and Training Setup

Our research was pursued in a resource-limited setting. For training, we used 4 NVIDIA RTX A6000 GPUs (48GB vRAM each). For inference, we used the above, and additionally had access to 16 NVIDIA GeForce RTX 2080 Ti GPUs (11GB vRAM each).

Given the above resource-limited training and inference setup, we provide some rough estimates of runtime. Training a stage 1 model takes about 1 week. Training a stage 2 model takes about 6 weeks, given the steps: a) run xx->en back-translations on 26m sentences (2 weeks), b) train the round 1 model (1 week), c) run en->xx back-translations on 28M sentences (2 week), d) train the round 2 model (1 week). Given more standard GPU resources, we would expect at least a 3-4x speedup in the whole training process.

We use the `transformers` package (Wolf et al., 2020) as the backbone for our modeling work. Specifically, we use it to load pretrained model weights and tokenizers. The rest of the code is implemented in PyTorch (Paszke et al., 2019).

Hyperparameters The most up-to-date version of the hyperparameters can be found in the repository.[24] For training, the batch size = 20000 for round 0, and 11500 for rounds 1 and 2. We use an Adam optimizer, with learning rate = 1e-3, and warmup steps = 12500. The learning rate decay schedule is based on the inverse square root of the update number. The dropout probability = 0.1, and the random mask probability = 0.4. For inference, the batch size = 1500, and beam size = 5.

D Start Tokens to Indicate Target Language

Following Johnson et al. (2017), we add special start tokens to each source sentence, to indicate the desired target language. This only applies to stage 2, because stage 1 always targets English. The default implementation directly adds these tokens, of the form `<2xx>` to the target vocabulary. Our setting requires adapting the implementation because as we have frozen the target embeddings (and source embeddings), we cannot increase the vocabulary size. We therefore indicate the target language with a two-token sequence, which consists of the usual start token `<s>`, and another token $\texttt{TOK}_\texttt{i}$ drawn from the long tail of the vocabulary. The model then must learn that `<s> + ` $\texttt{TOK}_\texttt{i}$ means to translate to a given language.

To be concrete, we use XLM-R tokenization, which consists of 250,002 SentencePiece tokens. For this paper, in which the model supports 8 languages, we arbitrary select indices 202201 to 202208, and assign each to a language.

E How Zero-Resource is Zero-Resource?

In this work, we have defined zero-resource as the setting in which no parallel sentences are available for a language pair of interest. This definition follows the general usage in the field. To be exactly precise, though, the pretrained multilingual model used, XLM-RoBERTa, has indeed seen monolingual text in each of the 7 low-resource languages.

F Sample Output

Sample output for the EcXTra NMT models are shown in Tables 7 and 8.

[24] `https://github.com/manestay/EcXTra/`

Code	Language	Family	Script	Source	# Pairs
kk	Kazakh	Turkic	Cyrillic	newstest2019	1000
gu	Gujarati	Indic	Gujarati	newstest2019	1016
si	Sinhala	Indic	Sinhala	FLoRes v1	2905
ne	Nepali	Indic	Devanagari	FLoRes v1	2924
ps	Pashto	Iranian	Arabic	newstest2020	2719
is	Icelandic	Germanic	Latin	newstest21	1000
my	Burmese	Burmese-Lolo	Burmese	WAT21	1018

Table 4: Information for the **test** languages, and the foreign-English datasets used. The columns are, from left to right, the ISO 639-1 language code, the name of the language, the language family at the Genus level, the data source, and the number of sentence pairs.

Code	Language	Code	Language
tr	Turkish	hu	Hungarian
sr	Serbian	sl	Slovenian
fr	French	vi	Vietnamese
he	Hebrew	et	Estonian
ru	Russian	sk	Slovak
ar	Arabic	ja	Japanese
zh	Chinese	lt	Lithuanian
bs	Bosnian	lv	Latvian
nl	Dutch	uk	Ukrainian
de	German	th	Thai
pt	Portuguese	cs	Czech
no	Norwegian	ko	Korean
it	Italian	id	Indonesian
es	Spanish	ca	Catalan
pl	Polish	mt	Maltese
fi	Finnish	ro	Romanian
fa	Persian	bg	Bulgarian
sv	Swedish	hr	Croatian
da	Danish	hi	Hindi
el	Greek	eu	Basque

Table 5: Information for the **train** languages. The columns are, from left to right, the ISO 639-1 language code, and the name of the language.

Code	Language	Source	# Pairs
tr	Turkish	newsdev2016	1001
fr	French	newstest2009	2525
ru	Russian	newstest2012	3003
zh	Chinese	newsdev2017	2002
de	German	newstest2009	2525
it	Italian	newstest2009	2525
es	Spanish	newstest2009	2525
fi	Finnish	newsdev2015	1500
hu	Hungarian	newstest2009	2525
et	Estonian	newsdev2017	2000
lt	Lithuanian	newsdev2019	2000
lv	Latvian	newsdev 2017	2003
cs	Czech	newstest2009	2525
ro	Romanian	newsdev2016	1999
hi	Hindi	newsdev2014	520

Table 6: Information on the **validation** languages, and the foreign-English datasets used. The columns are, from left to right, the ISO 639-1 language code, the name of the language, the source (from WMT development set), and the number of sentence pairs.

Model	Translation (kk-en)
Reference	The first medal place was given to Dastan Aitbay from Kyzylorda and his project on "Safe Headphones" Innovative headphones".
EcXTra-r_0	The winning first place was won by Dastan Aitbay's innovative earpiece "Safe headphones" from the city of Kyushu.
EcXTra-r_1	First place was won by Dastan Attbay of the city of Kyrgyzlord "Innovative earphones "Safe headphones."
EcXTra-r_2	The cool first place was won by Dastan Aitbay, from the city of Kyrgyzstan, the "Inventive earcap Safe Headphones."

Table 7: Sample kk-en unsupervised translations for the input: Жүлделі бірінші орынды Қызылорда қаласынан Дастан Айтбайдың "Инновациялық құлаққап "Safe headphones"жобасы жеңіп алды.

Model	Translation (en-is)
Reference	Markmiðið er að fegra svæðið og leyfa mósaíkverki Gerðar Helgadóttur á Tollhúsinu að njóta sýn betur.
EcXTra-r_0	N/A
EcXTra-r_1	Markmið er að fagna svæðið og gera mosaík Gerður Helgadóttir á Tollhúsinu áberandi.
EcXTra-r_2	Tilgangurinn er að fallega svæðið og gera mosamynd Gerður Helgadóttir á tollhúsinu meira áberandi.

Table 8: Sample en-is unsupervised translations for the input: The aim is to beautify the area and make Gerður Helgadóttir's mosaic on the Customs House more prominent.

PEACH: Pre-Training Sequence-to-Sequence Multilingual Models for Translation with Semi-Supervised Pseudo-Parallel Document Generation

Alireza Salemi[1]*, **Amirhossein Abaskohi**[1]*, **Sara Tavakoli**[1], **Yadollah Yaghoobzadeh**[1], **Azadeh Shakery**[1,2]

[1]School of Electrical and Computer Engineering
College of Engineering, University of Tehran, Tehran, Iran
[2]School of Computer Science
Institute for Research in Fundamental Sciences (IPM), Iran
{alireza.salemi,amir.abaskohi,saratavakoli77,y.yaghoobzadeh,shakery}@ut.ac.ir

Abstract

Multilingual pre-training significantly improves many multilingual NLP tasks, including machine translation. Most existing methods are based on some variants of masked language modeling and text-denoising objectives on monolingual data. Multilingual pre-training on monolingual data ignores the availability of parallel data in many language pairs. Also, some other works integrate the available human-generated parallel translation data in their pre-training. This kind of parallel data is definitely helpful, but it is limited even in high-resource language pairs. This paper introduces a novel semi-supervised method, SPDG, that generates high-quality pseudo-parallel data for multilingual pre-training. First, a denoising model is pre-trained on monolingual data to reorder, add, remove, and substitute words, enhancing the pre-training documents' quality. Then, we generate different pseudo-translations for each pre-training document using dictionaries for word-by-word translation and applying the pre-trained denoising model. The resulting pseudo-parallel data is then used to pre-train our multilingual sequence-to-sequence model, PEACH. Our experiments show that PEACH outperforms existing approaches used in training mT5 (Xue et al., 2021) and mBART (Liu et al., 2020) on various translation tasks, including supervised, zero- and few-shot scenarios. Moreover, PEACH's ability to transfer knowledge between similar languages makes it particularly useful for low-resource languages. Our results demonstrate that with high-quality dictionaries for generating accurate pseudo-parallel, PEACH can be valuable for low-resource languages.

1 Introduction

Machine Translation (MT) involves transferring a text from one language to another. Recent investigations have revealed that multilingual pre-training on a large corpus is profitable for NLP systems' performance on multilingual downstream tasks (Liu et al., 2020; Lample and Conneau, 2019; Conneau et al., 2020; Xue et al., 2021; Devlin et al., 2019) and knowledge transferability between languages (Wu and Dredze, 2019; K et al., 2020; Liu et al., 2020). Furthermore, using parallel data in pre-training encoder and encoder-decoder models effectively increases the models' performance in downstream tasks (Lample and Conneau, 2019; Chi et al., 2021). The existing pre-training approaches are mainly based on Masked Language Modeling (MLM) and its variations (Liu et al., 2020; Raffel et al., 2020; Xue et al., 2021; Lewis et al., 2020).

Although using parallel data in pre-training multilingual models improves their performance on downstream tasks, the amount of available parallel data is limited (Tran et al., 2020). Moreover, MLM-based objectives for sequence-to-sequence (seq2seq) models usually ask the model to generate an output in the same language as input, which is not in the interests of translation tasks. Additionally, MLM-based objectives use shared subwords or alphabets between different languages to learn shared embedding spaces across them (Lample and Conneau, 2019; Lample et al., 2017; Smith et al., 2017); this would not be possible for languages without shared alphabets.

Using dictionaries to define anchor points between different languages in cross-lingual pre-training of the encoder of seq2seq models has been investigated and shown to be effective for unsupervised translation (Duan et al., 2020). Still, it never has been used as a method for pre-training multilingual seq2seq models.

Our proposed method, Semi-Supervised Pseudo-Parallel Document Generation (SPDG), addresses the challenge of limited parallel data for low-resource languages by leveraging dictionaries to generate pseudo-parallel documents. SPDG adopts unsupervised translation techniques (Kim et al., 2018; Lample et al., 2017) to generate a high-

*Equal contribution

Proceedings of the The Sixth Workshop on Technologies for Machine Translation of Low-Resource Languages (LoResMT 2023), pages 32–46
May 6, 2023 ©2023 Association for Computational Linguistics

quality translation for each pre-training document. We use a pre-trained denoising seq2seq model with word reordering, adding, removing, and substituting to enhance the quality of the word-by-word translated document. The improved unsupervised translated text is used as the target text for training our multilingual seq2seq model, PEACH, using SPDG as a new pre-training method. SPDG enables transfer of knowledge between similar languages, making it particularly useful for low-resource languages.

Our experiments show that PEACH outperforms the pre-trained models with mT5's MLM and mBART's MLM with Reordering objectives in English, French, and German. Additionally, PEACH demonstrates strong performance in zero- and few-shot scenarios. Moreover, we test our model for other multilingual tasks, such as natural language inference, to investigate the model's ability in this task. Our results show that our model achieves a higher score in this task than other objectives, which shows PEACH's ability to transfer knowledge between languages. The main contribution of this paper is twofold:

- We propose a novel semi-supervised pre-training method using bilingual dictionaries and pre-trained denoising models for seq2seq multilingual models.
- We show the benefits of SPDG objective in translation, supervised and zero- and few-shot cases, and knowledge transfer between languages.

2 Related Work

Among the first endeavor for MT, dictionary and rule-based methods were popular (Dolan et al., 1993; Kaji, 1988; Meyers et al., 1998), followed by Knowledge-Based Machine Translation (KBMT) and statistical methods (Mitamara et al., 1993; Carbonell et al., 1981; Koehn, 2009; Al-Onaizan et al., 1999). The popularity of neural machine translation has only grown in the recent decade with the introduction of the first deep neural model for translation (Kalchbrenner and Blunsom, 2013).

While the RNN-based seq2seq models seemed to be promising in neural machine translation (Wu et al., 2016; Bahdanau et al., 2015; Sutskever et al., 2014), the advent of the transformer architecture (Vaswani et al., 2017) plays an integral role in modern MT. With the introduction of the transformer architecture, pre-training general-purpose language models seemed to be an effective way to improve different NLP tasks (Devlin et al., 2019; Liu et al., 2019). In most cases, transformer models were asked to denoise a noisy input to learn a language (Lewis et al., 2020; Devlin et al., 2019; Raffel et al., 2020). One of the most popular pre-training objectives for both encoder-only and encoder-decoder models is called Masked Language Modeling (MLM), in which the model should predict the masked part of a document and generate it in its output (Raffel et al., 2020). However, many other objectives were also developed for encoder-decoder and encoder-only models (Song et al., 2019; Clark et al., 2020).

Meanwhile, unsupervised methods for neural machine translation (NMT) using monolingual corpora based on adversarial learning (Lample et al., 2017) and transformer-based text denoising (Kim et al., 2018) was tested and demonstrated promising outcomes. Using bilingual dictionaries for defining anchors in pre-training unsupervised translation models was successful (Duan et al., 2020) but never has been used for generating data for supervised translation on a large scale. Our work differs from using dictionaries as anchor points for learning a better representation for tokens in encoder (Duan et al., 2020). We use dictionaries to generate a pseudo translation of the source language in the target language instead of just defining some anchor points. Thus, the model in pre-training steps learns to generate a text in the target language based on input in the source language using only monolingual data and dictionaries on a large scale.

Pre-training task-specific models by generating pseudo-summaries was successful in some cases for summarization (Salemi et al., 2021; Zhang et al., 2020), but it has not been performed for pre-training encoder-decoder seq2seq models for supervised translation according to the best of our knowledge. On the other hand, the endeavors for pre-training specific models for translation ended up in training multilingual language models (Xue et al., 2021; Liu et al., 2020). mT5 (Xue et al., 2021) is trained with the MLM objective of T5 (Raffel et al., 2020). In its pre-training objective, some spans of the input document are masked by specific tokens, and the model has to predict those spans by generating them in its output. mBART (Liu et al., 2020) is another multilingual model based on the BART (Lewis et al., 2020) model, pre-trained with MLM with Reordering objective. In mBART's pre-training objective, the order of sentences in the input document is corrupted while a specific token masks some spans of the document. The model has to generate the original document in its output.

PEACH is different from both mentioned models because we use a semi-supervised method to generate several pseudo-translations (one for each selected language) of each pre-training document. These translations are then fed to pre-train PEACH. Furthermore, in the mentioned models, the inputs and outputs are from the same language while we ask the model to translate texts from one language to another in our pre-training phase.

3 PEACH

PEACH is a new sequence-to-sequence multilingual transformer model trained with SPDG, a semi-supervised pseudo-parallel document generation method. This section explains the pre-training objective and the model architecture.

3.1 Semi-Supervised Pseudo-Parallel Document Generation (SPDG)

Our proposed pre-training objective, SPDG, generates a pseudo-translation of the input document. For generating pseudo-translations, we use Kim et al. (2018)'s approach for unsupervised translation with some modifications. Our pipeline for pre-training a model based on SPDG is shown in Figure 2. We pre-train a seq2seq denoising model for the target language using the pre-training corpus of that language. Next, for each pre-training document in the source language, we translate it to the target language word-by-word using dictionaries. Then, we give this word-by-word translated document to the pre-trained model with denoising objectives to improve its quality and restore missing words.

Using this method, we can generate the pseudo-translation of each pre-training document from the source language to the target language. We use these pseudo-translations as gold translations for each pre-training document to pre-train a new language model for translation tasks. Since this pre-training objective is similar to translation, we hypothesize that the pre-trained model learns the translation task faster than the models trained using monolingual data.

Word-by-Word Translation Using Dictionaries The first step to generate pseudo-parallel documents is to map sentences from one language to another using dictionaries. We used bilingual dictionaries provided by Conneau et al. (2017) for our work. To map sentences word-by-word from one language to another, we first tokenize sentences using the NLTK[1] library. Then, for each token, we find a translation for the token in the target language using a dictionary from the source to the target language. Some tokens, such as punctuations and numbers, do not need to be translated to the target language because they are shared between them. Therefore, we just put them in the translated words set. Furthermore, we can not find any translation for named entities in dictionaries. To solve this issue, spaCy[2] small (<lang>_core_news_sm) models for named entity recognition for each language are used to extract named entities. We transliterate the named entities and put them in the translated words set. Tokens without translation in dictionaries that are not named entities, punctuations, or numbers are skipped. We hope denoising objectives could find an appropriate substitute for these tokens in the next step. The implementation details of word-by-word translation can be found in Appendix B.

Improving Word-by-Word Translations with Denoising Objectives A critical problem with word-by-word translation is that the word order in the target language is not usually the same as the source. Furthermore, some words in the source language might not have any translation in the target language or vice versa. Additionally, since many words have multiple meanings, word-by-word translation might select the wrong translation for a word.

We define four denoising objectives to overcome the mentioned challenges, and train a denoising model for each language. The pipeline is shown in Figure 1. First, we shuffle the words in each sentence in a document while keeping the relative order of shuffled words in different sentences in the document. Next, we remove, add, and replace some of the words in each sentence to encourage the model to resolve the aforementioned issues in word-by-word translation. We use the corrupted document as the model's input and ask the model to generate the original one as its output.

The deshuffling objective aims to improve the

[1]https://www.nltk.org/

[2]https://spacy.io/

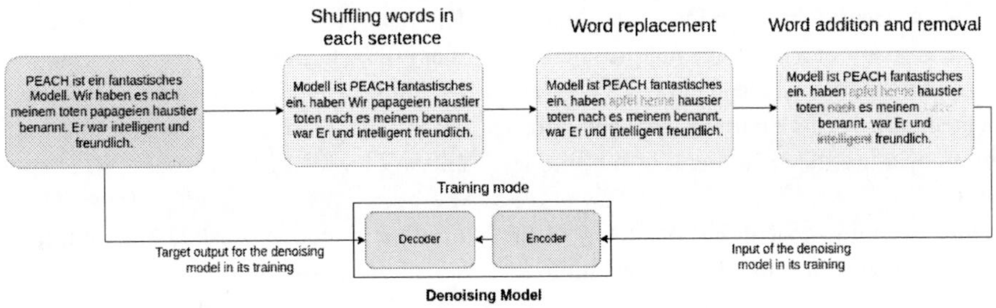

Figure 1: An overview of denoising objectives used for training denoising models. We use word shuffling, addition, substitution, and removing based on the values in Table 7 in Appendix C.

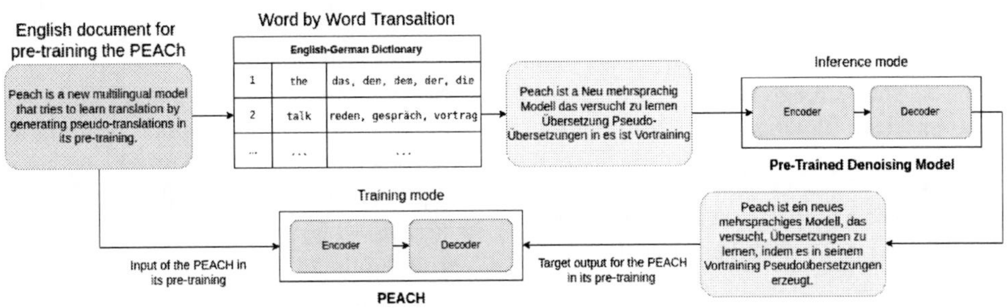

Figure 2: An overview of our pre-training pipeline for training a model based on SPDG. The method uses the output of the word-by-word translation of a pre-training document as the input of the trained denoising model based on Figure 1 to improve its quality.

ability of the model to reorder word-by-word translated documents. Removing and adding words help the model to correct some translations. Moreover, replacing is beneficial especially for correcting the word-by-word translation of ambiguous words.

Figure 2 depicts our pipeline for pre-training with SPDG on a single example. In the mentioned example, after word-by-word translation, some of the words in the pre-training document cannot be translated into German because they do not exist in the dictionary. Furthermore, the relative order of words in the word-by-word translated text is not grammatically correct, and some words can be substituted with more suitable ones. It can be seen that after applying the denoising model to the word-by-word translated text, the mentioned problems are resolved.

3.2 Pre-Training with Multilingual SPDG

Most common multilingual models, such as mT5 (Xue et al., 2021) and mBART (Liu et al., 2020), use MLM and MLM with Reordering as their pre-training objectives. Despite their success, these objectives are not perfectly aligned with the goal of MT. Specifically, these objectives are designed to work on monolingual inputs; they denoise the input document in a specific language and produce the denoised version in the same language. Here, we design Algorithm 1, in which the pre-training task's input is in one language, and its output is in another language. The algorithms' inputs are the corpora of all languages that the model should be trained on as well as their names. The algorithm generates the input-output pairs for pre-training the multilingual model.

Algorithm 1: Multilingual SPDG

Input : Corpora, Langs
Output : MInputs,Moutputs
$MInputs := \emptyset$
$MOutputs := \emptyset$
for $corpus$ **in** $Corpora$ **do**
  for doc **in** $corpus$ **do**
    for $lang$ **in** $Langs - Lang(doc)$ **do**
      $pst := SPDG(doc, Lang(doc), lang)$
      $MInputs := MInputs \cup \{doc\}$
      $MOutputs := MOutputs \cup \{pst\}$
    end for
  end for
end for

In Algorithm 1, given a pre-training document, we generate a pseudo-translation of it to each of the other languages. So, the model can observe translations in different languages for a single document.

This helps the model in learning cross-lingual knowledge even about a language not present in a specific training instance. The mentioned claim is because the model learns about the language differences by translating the same input into multiple languages.

It should be noted that based on the goal of pre-training a language model for translation, it is possible to change Algorithm 1. For example, if the multilingual model is going to be used to just translate from or to English, there is no need to pre-train the model with the task of generating pseudo-translation from German to French. Since we are interested in evaluating our model on all pairs of the pre-training languages, we generate pseudo-translation for all pairs in Algorithm 1.

Architecture Our model, PEACH, and the other presented denoising models are all based on transformer (Vaswani et al., 2017) encoder-decoder architecture with a 12 layer encoder and a 12 layer decoder with 768 hidden size, 3072 feed-forward filter size, and 12 self-attention heads.

4 Experiments

In this section, we compare the results of PEACH, trained with SPDG, with other common objectives utilized for pre-training multilingual models. To investigate the effectiveness of SPDG in comparison with common objectives, we pre-trained two other models based on mT5's MLM objective (Xue et al., 2021) and mBART's MLM with Reordering objective (Liu et al., 2020) in the same setup.

The codes for pre-training and fine-tuning of all models are publicly available on GitHub[3].

4.1 Pre-Training Data and Configuration

We pre-train PEACH on English, French, and German with the CC100 corpora (Wenzek et al., 2020; Conneau et al., 2020). Due to the lack of computing power, we cannot use more than around $550M$ words of text from each language. So, we train our model on around $1.6B$ total words. Our pre-training batch size is 96, with a maximum of 512 input and output tokens, and we train it for 500K steps on Google Colab TPUs (v2-8). The AdaFactor (Shazeer and Stern, 2018) optimizer with a decay rate of 0.8 and a dropout rate of 0.1 is used in pre-training and fine-tuning. Furthermore, we use the SentencePiece BPE algorithm (Gage, 1994; Kudo and Richardson, 2018) to generate a vocabulary of 32K words for denoising models and 96k for multilingual models. We pre-train PEACH with Multilingual SPDG for 75% of its pre-training steps and mT5's MLM (Xue et al., 2021) approach for the other 25% pre-training steps. The latter pre-training objective is used because it increases the scope of the fine-tuning tasks that our model can do well. Indeed, multilingual SPDG teaches the model to transform a text from one language to another, but it does not help the model in tasks where their inputs and outputs are in the same language. Therefore, pre-training the model with MLM for a few steps is helpful.

We train the denoising models with the same setup as PEACH. An important factor in training denoising models is the rate of corruption for training documents. We shuffle all words in sentences while removing, adding, and replacing a small proportion of them. We use the word-by-word translation script outputs to decide on these rates. First, we calculate the rate of missing words in word-by-word translation using dictionaries for all languages to a specific language on around 1GB of text of each language. Then, we use a normal distribution with mean and standard deviation of the same as the calculated numbers to define the rate of words that should be removed from a sentence. The values of corruption rates for each language are reported in Table 7 in Appendix C, in which we explain the method to find the best values for rates.

Due to the lack of computing power, we cannot train a large-scale PEACH and compare it with pre-trained models like mT5 or mBART. Instead, we train two models based on mT5 (Xue et al., 2021) objective, which we call MLM, and mBART (Liu et al., 2020) objective, which we call MLM with Reordering, with the same setup as PEACH. Also, we fine-tune a Transformer model with randomly initialized weights on downstream tasks.

4.2 Results

This section evaluates PEACH in various translation scenarios, including supervised, zero- and few-shot. We also evaluate PEACH's ability for cross-lingual knowledge transfer in translation and natural language inference tasks.

Supervised Translation In order to evaluate PEACH on translation tasks, we fine-tune it on the EN-DE and EN-FR parts of the WMT14 dataset (Bojar et al., 2014). Additionally, we fine-tune our

[3]https://github.com/AmirAbaskohi/PEACH

Model	WMT14		WMT19
	FR↔EN	DE↔EN	DE↔FR
MLM	$21.38 \leftrightarrow 21.64$	$17.88 \leftrightarrow 19.54$	$16.59 \leftrightarrow 16.54$
MLM with Reordering	$29.02 \leftrightarrow 28.71$	$22.80 \leftrightarrow 25.53$	$21.39 \leftrightarrow 22.45$
Transformer	$9.15 \leftrightarrow 9.17$	$10.02 \leftrightarrow 9.79$	$9.16 \leftrightarrow 10.31$
PEACH	**31.25 ↔ 29.98**	**23.61 ↔ 26.97**	**23.13 ↔ 25.25**

Table 1: The supervised translation results evaluated with BLEU score.

Model	WMT14		WMT19
	FR↔EN	DE↔EN	DE↔FR
SPDG$_{EN \leftrightarrow FR}$ **(200k steps)**	$25.98 \leftrightarrow 25.42$	–	–
SPDG$_{EN \leftrightarrow DE}$ **(200k steps)**	–	$17.75 \leftrightarrow 22.97$	–
SPDG$_{FR \leftrightarrow DE}$ **(200k steps)**	–	–	$16.24 \leftrightarrow 18.77$
SPDG$_{EN \leftrightarrow FR \leftrightarrow DE}$ **(100k steps)**	$27.40 \leftrightarrow 26.60$	$21.21 \leftrightarrow 23.89$	$20.49 \leftrightarrow 22.32$
SPDG$_{EN \leftrightarrow FR \leftrightarrow DE}$ **(200k steps)**	**29.04 ↔ 28.08**	**22.33 ↔ 25.29**	**21.67 ↔ 23.29**

Table 2: Results of different models trained with SPDG on either two or three indicated languages. The number of pre-training steps is shown in parenthesis.

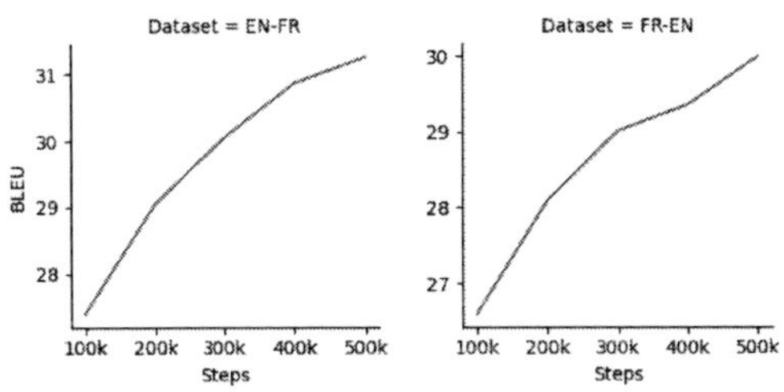

Figure 3: PEACH's performance in pre-training steps on WMT14's EN-FR section. Results for EN-DE and DE-FR are reported in Table 14 in Appendix E.

model on the FR-DE part of the WMT19 dataset (Barrault et al., 2019) in the same setup. Since the test set of WMT19 DE-FR datasets is not available publicly to the best of our knowledge, we evaluated the models on its validation set. The model is fine-tuned for 50K steps with a batch size of 96, a learning rate of 5×10^{-5}, and the same optimizer as pre-training. We use 10K warmup steps for fine-tuning. More information about the experiments' setup is reported in Appendix D. It should be noted that while translation downstream datasets usually have millions of samples, we at most use 50000×96 samples of them due to the lack of computing power. To support the selected number of samples for the downstream task, we report pre-training and fine-tuning time on the whole datasets for an epoch in Appendix D. This sample count is less than 15% of samples for the WMT14 English-French dataset. Additionally, since the primary purpose of this paper is to introduce a new method for pre-training multilingual models and the comparisons happen in the same setup for all objectives, the results are fair and valid.

The results of our model and other trained models on translation tasks are reported in Table 1. Additionally, the results of our model on EN-FR downstream dataset in some pre-training steps are shown in Figure 3. Also, the results for other downstream datasets are reported in Table 14 in Appendix E. The presented results show that PEACH outperforms other models, not only with 500K steps of pre-training but also even with its 200K steps pre-training checkpoint. Furthermore, the MLM method used in mT5 achieves worse results than MLM with Reordering objective that mBART used. We believe this is because the MLM objective of mT5 just asks the model to generate the masked spans in the output, while mBART's objective asks the model to reorder and predict the masked spans of the input document simultaneously. Indeed, the objective of mBART asks the model to generate complete sentences in its output, and that is why it can generate better translations. On the other hand, mT5 just predicts spans of text, which are not complete sentences in many cases.

We believe that the better results of our model stem from its pre-training objective which is similar to translation tasks. Indeed, we pre-trained our model on a massive amount of pre-training data with a task similar to translation, which increases the model's ability in translation when it is fine-tuned with a smaller amount of translation samples.

To investigate the effect of pre-training on more than two languages on the performance of our model on translation tasks, we pre-train a model based on SPDG for 200K steps for each pair of languages, and fine-tune them for 50k steps, with the same setup as PEACH. The results are reported in Table 2. We show that our multilingual model with three languages outperforms other models not only with full pre-training for 200K steps but also with 100K steps of pre-training. We believe this is because we perform the SPDG objective between each pair of languages in its pre-training. Indeed, this approach for pre-training multilingual models helps the model simultaneously gain knowledge about other languages than the pair of languages in each pre-training example because it observes the same input with different outputs for each language. These results support our claim in section 3.2.

Zero- and Few-Shot Translation We evaluate the pre-trained models in a zero-shot setting to investigate our model's ability in low-resource scenarios. Each pre-trained model is evaluated on the test set of WMT14 EN-FR dataset without fine-tuning. The results of this experiment are reported in Figure 4. The results for EN-DE and DE-FR section of WMT14 and WMT19 are reported in Table 15 in Appendix E. The results in Figure 4 and Table 15 show that our model, PEACH, outperforms other models in zero-shot translation. We believe this stems from the similarity of its pre-training objective with actual translation tasks.

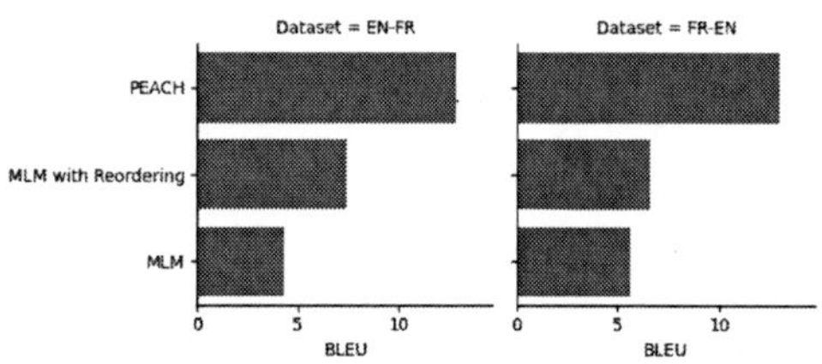

Figure 4: Comparing the pre-trained models in zero-shot setting on WMT14 EN-FR section. Results for EN-DE and DE-FR are reported in Table 15 in Appendix E.

For few-shot experiments, we fine-tuned PEACH on 50K samples from the English-French section of the WMT14 dataset at a maximum of 50K steps. The results are shown in Figure 5. Accordingly, PEACH outperforms MLM with Reordering model trained in the same setup. Additionally, PEACH surpasses MLM and MLM with Reordeing models' checkpoints in 50K fine-tuning steps on around 5M samples, after only 10K and 25K steps of fine-tuning on 50K samples. We conclude that PEACH performs well in low-resource scenarios because it is trained on a massive amount of psuedo-translation data.

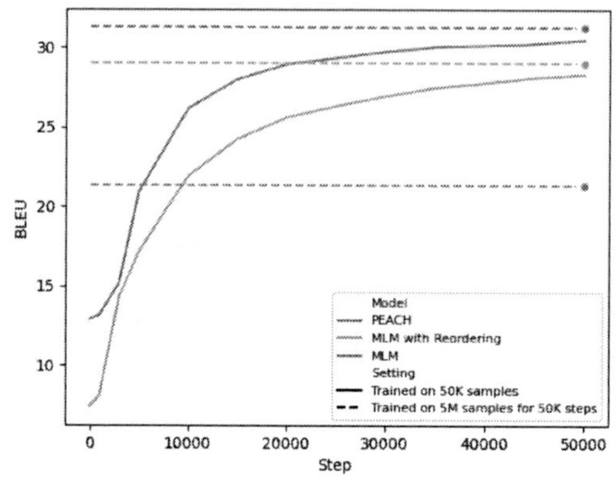

Figure 5: Results of fine-tuning PEACH with 50K samples of WMT14 EN-FR dataset for 0 to 50k steps, and its comparison with MLM and MLM with Reordering objectives on 50000×96 data points. PEACH outperforms the fully-trained MLM models after only 25K fine-tuning steps.

Cross-Lingual Transfer for Translation Here we evaluate each fine-tuned model on a language pair on how it performs for other pairs and directions. We use the fine-tuned models in Table 1 for these experiments.

The experimental results in Table 3 demonstrate that PEACH can transfer the knowledge learned from one language pair to another better than MLM with Reordering model. We believe this stems from our pre-training method in which we ask the model to generate pseudo-translations between each pair of languages. Furthermore, the results confirm Liu et al. (2020)'s experiments and show that whenever a model fine-tuned on a dataset from A to B is evaluated on A to C or C to B or B to A, the results on the evaluation dataset increase more than other combinations. Additionally, because the inputs of PEACH's encoder are human-generated texts while the decoder's expected outputs are the outputs of the denoising models, fine-tuning from A to B increases the performance of C to B more than A to C. Indeed, fine-tuning from A to B helps

Fine-Tuned / Evaluated	PEACH			MLM with Reordering		
	WMT14		WMT19	WMT14		WMT19
	FR↔EN	DE↔EN	DE↔FR	FR↔EN	DE↔EN	DE↔FR
$EN \rightarrow FR$	$- \leftrightarrow 11.38$	$12.35 \leftrightarrow 16.57$	$12.38 \leftrightarrow 21.91$	$- \leftrightarrow 11.25$	$11.52 \leftrightarrow 12.51$	$11.65 \leftrightarrow 11.70$
$FR \rightarrow EN$	$11.30 \leftrightarrow -$	$14.62 \leftrightarrow 21.35$	$15.05 \leftrightarrow 17.28$	$11.27 \leftrightarrow -$	$12.88 \leftrightarrow 12.99$	$12.68 \leftrightarrow 11.28$
$EN \rightarrow DE$	$20.63 \leftrightarrow 11.99$	$- \leftrightarrow 12.70$	$19.88 \leftrightarrow 13.84$	$10.80 \leftrightarrow 11.29$	$- \leftrightarrow 12.64$	$12.89 \leftrightarrow 11.07$
$DE \rightarrow EN$	$18.97 \leftrightarrow 24.54$	$13.39 \leftrightarrow -$	$14.99 \leftrightarrow 18.85$	$10.99 \leftrightarrow 13.85$	$12.71 \leftrightarrow -$	$11.23 \leftrightarrow 11.09$
$FR \rightarrow DE$	$23.64 \leftrightarrow 24.69$	$18.59 \leftrightarrow 22.69$	$- \leftrightarrow 23.35$	$12.07 \leftrightarrow 11.43$	$12.81 \leftrightarrow 11.54$	$- \leftrightarrow 20.65$
$DE \rightarrow FR$	$24.88 \leftrightarrow 24.94$	$20.12 \leftrightarrow 20.74$	$23.03 \leftrightarrow -$	$14.72 \leftrightarrow 11.57$	$12.86 \leftrightarrow 11.92$	$21.56 \leftrightarrow -$

Table 3: The results of experiments on cross-lingual knowledge transfer for translation. We fine-tune the model on one language and evaluate it on other languages. The results are reported using BLEU score.

Model	XNLI		
	EN	FR	DE
MLM	.676	.480	.463
MLM with Reordering	.710	.603	.527
PEACH	**.745**	**.637**	**.636**

Table 4: The accuracy results on the XNLI benchmark.

the decoder of our model learn to generate better outputs by observing human-generated texts in its decoder. This is because our model did not encounter human-generated texts as gold labels in its output during pre-training. On the other hand, observing more human-generated inputs is not as helpful as human-generated outputs since the inputs of the model's encoder were human-generated text in its pre-training.

In support of the previous point, the results in Table 3 show that PEACH fine-tuned on the DE-EN dataset achieves better results than MLM fine-tuned on the FR-EN dataset, when evaluated on the FR-EN dataset. Additionally, PEACH fine-tuned on the EN-FR dataset achieves a comparable result with MLM with Reordering fine-tuned on the DE-FR dataset, when evaluated on the DE-FR dataset (0.54 difference in BLEU). We believe this experiment shows PEACH's ability to transfer the knowledge learned from a language to another effectively.

Cross-Lingual Transfer for natural language inference We focus on translation in this paper. However, we expect that PEACH's ability to transfer knowledge between languages is suitable for other cross-lingual scenarios as well. To test this hypothesis, we evaluate PEACH on the XNLI benchmark (Conneau et al., 2018). We fine-tune our model for 50K steps with a batch size of 256, a learning rate of 10^{-3}, and a maximum output length of 16 on the MultiNLI English dataset (Williams et al., 2018) and apply it to the XNLI benchmark. The results of this experiment are reported in Table 4.

According to Table 4, PEACH outperforms other models in transferring knowledge from English to German and French. Considering our pre-training objective, in which we ask the model to generate pseudo-translations for each pair of pre-training languages, we believe this objective helps PEACH to transfer the knowledge about the English dataset to other languages better than other pre-trained models.

5 Conclusion

We introduced SPDG, a semi-supervised method for pre-training multilingual seq2seq models, to address the lack of parallel data between different languages. In this new method, we use bilingual dictionaries and denoising models trained with reordering, adding, substituting, and removing words to generate a pseudo-translation for each pre-training document. We use this generated data to train our multilingual model, PEACH, for English, French, and German languages. Our results show that PEACH outperforms the common pre-training objectives for training multilingual models. Furthermore, PEACH shows a remarkable ability in zero- and few-shot translation and knowledge transfer between languages.

Limitations

The main limitations of our work can be classified into two types: 1) SPDG's limitations and 2) Computational limitations.

SPDG's Limitations Although our method can address the issue of limited parallel data between different languages, it does not solve the problem completely. First, our method uses bilingual dictionaries to translate each pre-training document from one language to another, which is not always available for low-resource languages. Furthermore, the available dictionaries for low-resource languages do not have a high quality and are not comparable with high-resource languages. Additionally, we use Named Entity Recognition (NER) models to transfer named entities of each pre-training document into its pseudo-translation, which is unavailable for some low-resource languages. Therefore, using unsupervised methods for NER can be a solution for the mentioned problem, which is not investigated in this work.

Computational limitations We did not have access to clusters of GPU or TPU to train our models on a large scale and compare them with the results reported in other papers about multilingual models. However, we tried to provide a realistic setting for our experiments. Further investigation into training models on a larger scale, same as standard multilingual models, can improve this work.

References

Yaser Al-Onaizan, Jan Curin, Michael Jahr, Kevin Knight, John Lafferty, Dan Melamed, Franz-Josef Och, David Purdy, Noah A Smith, and David Yarowsky. 1999. Statistical machine translation. In *Final Report, JHU Summer Workshop*, volume 30.

Dzmitry Bahdanau, Kyunghyun Cho, and Yoshua Bengio. 2015. Neural machine translation by jointly learning to align and translate. *CoRR*, abs/1409.0473.

Loïc Barrault, Ondřej Bojar, Marta R. Costa-jussà, Christian Federmann, Mark Fishel, Yvette Graham, Barry Haddow, Matthias Huck, Philipp Koehn, Shervin Malmasi, Christof Monz, Mathias Müller, Santanu Pal, Matt Post, and Marcos Zampieri. 2019. Findings of the 2019 conference on machine translation (WMT19). In *Proceedings of the Fourth Conference on Machine Translation (Volume 2: Shared Task Papers, Day 1)*, pages 1–61, Florence, Italy. Association for Computational Linguistics.

Ondřej Bojar, Christian Buck, Christian Federmann, Barry Haddow, Philipp Koehn, Johannes Leveling, Christof Monz, Pavel Pecina, Matt Post, Herve Saint-Amand, Radu Soricut, Lucia Specia, and Aleš Tamchyna. 2014. Findings of the 2014 workshop on statistical machine translation. In *Proceedings of the Ninth Workshop on Statistical Machine Translation*, pages 12–58, Baltimore, Maryland, USA. Association for Computational Linguistics.

Jaime G. Carbonell, Richard E. Cullingford, and Anatole Gershman. 1981. Steps toward knowledge-based machine translation. *IEEE Transactions on Pattern Analysis and Machine Intelligence*, PAMI-3:376–392.

Zewen Chi, Li Dong, Shuming Ma, Shaohan Huang, Saksham Singhal, Xian-Ling Mao, Heyan Huang, Xia Song, and Furu Wei. 2021. mT6: Multilingual pretrained text-to-text transformer with translation pairs. In *Proceedings of the 2021 Conference on Empirical Methods in Natural Language Processing*, pages 1671–1683, Online and Punta Cana, Dominican Republic. Association for Computational Linguistics.

Kevin Clark, Minh-Thang Luong, Quoc V. Le, and Christopher D. Manning. 2020. Electra: Pre-training text encoders as discriminators rather than generators.

Alexis Conneau, Kartikay Khandelwal, Naman Goyal, Vishrav Chaudhary, Guillaume Wenzek, Francisco Guzmán, Edouard Grave, Myle Ott, Luke Zettlemoyer, and Veselin Stoyanov. 2020. Unsupervised cross-lingual representation learning at scale. In *Proceedings of the 58th Annual Meeting of the Association for Computational Linguistics*, pages 8440–8451, Online. Association for Computational Linguistics.

Alexis Conneau, Guillaume Lample, Marc'Aurelio Ranzato, Ludovic Denoyer, and Hervé Jégou. 2017. Word translation without parallel data. *arXiv preprint arXiv:1710.04087*.

Alexis Conneau, Ruty Rinott, Guillaume Lample, Adina Williams, Samuel Bowman, Holger Schwenk, and Veselin Stoyanov. 2018. XNLI: Evaluating cross-lingual sentence representations. In *Proceedings of the 2018 Conference on Empirical Methods in Natural Language Processing*, pages 2475–2485, Brussels, Belgium. Association for Computational Linguistics.

Jacob Devlin, Ming-Wei Chang, Kenton Lee, and Kristina Toutanova. 2019. BERT: Pre-training of deep bidirectional transformers for language understanding. In *Proceedings of the 2019 Conference of the North American Chapter of the Association for Computational Linguistics: Human Language Technologies, Volume 1 (Long and Short Papers)*, pages 4171–4186, Minneapolis, Minnesota. Association for Computational Linguistics.

Bill Dolan, Stephen D. Richardson, and Lucy Vanderwende. 1993. Combining dictionary-based and example-based methods for natural language analysis. In *TMI*.

Xiangyu Duan, Baijun Ji, Hao Jia, Min Tan, Min Zhang, Boxing Chen, Weihua Luo, and Yue Zhang. 2020. Bilingual dictionary based neural machine translation without using parallel sentences. In *Proceedings of the 58th Annual Meeting of the Association for Computational Linguistics*, pages 1570–1579, Online. Association for Computational Linguistics.

Philip Gage. 1994. A new algorithm for data compression. *C Users J.*, 12(2):23–38.

Karthikeyan K, Zihan Wang, Stephen Mayhew, and Dan Roth. 2020. Cross-lingual ability of multilingual bert: An empirical study. In *8th International*

Conference on Learning Representations, ICLR 2020, Addis Ababa, Ethiopia, April 26-30, 2020. OpenReview.net.

Hiroyuki Kaji. 1988. An efficient execution method for rule-based machine translation. In *Coling Budapest 1988 Volume 2: International Conference on Computational Linguistics*.

Nal Kalchbrenner and Phil Blunsom. 2013. Recurrent continuous translation models. In *Proceedings of the 2013 conference on empirical methods in natural language processing*, pages 1700–1709.

Yunsu Kim, Jiahui Geng, and Hermann Ney. 2018. Improving unsupervised word-by-word translation with language model and denoising autoencoder. In *Proceedings of the 2018 Conference on Empirical Methods in Natural Language Processing*, pages 862–868, Brussels, Belgium. Association for Computational Linguistics.

Philipp Koehn. 2009. *Statistical machine translation*. Cambridge University Press.

Taku Kudo and John Richardson. 2018. Sentencepiece: A simple and language independent subword tokenizer and detokenizer for neural text processing. In *EMNLP*.

Guillaume Lample and Alexis Conneau. 2019. Cross-lingual language model pretraining. In *NeurIPS*.

Guillaume Lample, Alexis Conneau, Ludovic Denoyer, and Marc'Aurelio Ranzato. 2017. Unsupervised machine translation using monolingual corpora only. *arXiv preprint arXiv:1711.00043*.

Mike Lewis, Yinhan Liu, Naman Goyal, Marjan Ghazvininejad, Abdelrahman Mohamed, Omer Levy, Veselin Stoyanov, and Luke Zettlemoyer. 2020. BART: Denoising sequence-to-sequence pre-training for natural language generation, translation, and comprehension. In *Proceedings of the 58th Annual Meeting of the Association for Computational Linguistics*, pages 7871–7880, Online. Association for Computational Linguistics.

Yinhan Liu, Jiatao Gu, Naman Goyal, Xian Li, Sergey Edunov, Marjan Ghazvininejad, Mike Lewis, and Luke Zettlemoyer. 2020. Multilingual denoising pre-training for neural machine translation. *Transactions of the Association for Computational Linguistics*, 8:726–742.

Yinhan Liu, Myle Ott, Naman Goyal, Jingfei Du, Mandar Joshi, Danqi Chen, Omer Levy, Mike Lewis, Luke Zettlemoyer, and Veselin Stoyanov. 2019. Roberta: A robustly optimized bert pretraining approach.

Adam Meyers, Michiko Kosaka, and Ralph Grishman. 1998. A multilingual procedure for dictionary-based sentence alignment. In *Proceedings of the Third Conference of the Association for Machine Translation in the Americas: Technical Papers*, pages 187–198, Langhorne, PA, USA. Springer.

Teruko Mitamara, Eric H Nyberg 3rd, and Jaime G Carbonell. 1993. Automated corpus analysis and the acquisition of large, multi-lingual knowledge bases for mt. In *Proceedings of the Fifth Conference on Theoretical and Methodological Issues in Machine Translation of Natural Languages*.

Colin Raffel, Noam Shazeer, Adam Roberts, Katherine Lee, Sharan Narang, Michael Matena, Yanqi Zhou, Wei Li, and Peter J. Liu. 2020. Exploring the limits of transfer learning with a unified text-to-text transformer. *Journal of Machine Learning Research*, 21(140):1–67.

Alireza Salemi, Emad Kebriaei, Ghazal Neisi Minaei, and Azadeh Shakery. 2021. ARMAN: Pre-training with Semantically Selecting and Reordering of Sentences for Persian Abstractive Summarization. In *Proceedings of the 2021 Conference on Empirical Methods in Natural Language Processing*, pages 9391–9407, Online and Punta Cana, Dominican Republic. Association for Computational Linguistics.

Noam Shazeer and Mitchell Stern. 2018. Adafactor: Adaptive learning rates with sublinear memory cost. In *Proceedings of the 35th International Conference on Machine Learning*, volume 80 of *Proceedings of Machine Learning Research*, pages 4596–4604. PMLR.

Samuel L. Smith, David H. P. Turban, Steven Hamblin, and Nils Y. Hammerla. 2017. Offline bilingual word vectors, orthogonal transformations and the inverted softmax.

Kaitao Song, Xu Tan, Tao Qin, Jianfeng Lu, and Tie-Yan Liu. 2019. Mass: Masked sequence to sequence pre-training for language generation. In *ICML*.

Ilya Sutskever, Oriol Vinyals, and Quoc V. Le. 2014. Sequence to sequence learning with neural networks. In *Proceedings of the 27th International Conference on Neural Information Processing Systems - Volume 2*, NIPS'14, page 3104–3112, Cambridge, MA, USA. MIT Press.

Chau Tran, Yuqing Tang, Xian Li, and Jiatao Gu. 2020. *Cross-Lingual Retrieval for Iterative Self-Supervised Training*. Curran Associates Inc., Red Hook, NY, USA.

Ashish Vaswani, Noam Shazeer, Niki Parmar, Jakob Uszkoreit, Llion Jones, Aidan N Gomez, Ł ukasz Kaiser, and Illia Polosukhin. 2017. Attention is all you need. In *Advances in Neural Information Processing Systems*, volume 30. Curran Associates, Inc.

Guillaume Wenzek, Marie-Anne Lachaux, Alexis Conneau, Vishrav Chaudhary, Francisco Guzmán, Armand Joulin, and Edouard Grave. 2020. CCNet: Extracting high quality monolingual datasets from web crawl data. In *Proceedings of the 12th Language Resources and Evaluation Conference*, pages 4003–4012, Marseille, France. European Language Resources Association.

Adina Williams, Nikita Nangia, and Samuel Bowman. 2018. A broad-coverage challenge corpus for sentence understanding through inference. In *Proceedings of the 2018 Conference of the North American Chapter of the Association for Computational Linguistics: Human Language Technologies, Volume 1 (Long Papers)*, pages 1112–1122, New Orleans, Louisiana. Association for Computational Linguistics.

Shijie Wu and Mark Dredze. 2019. Beto, bentz, becas: The surprising cross-lingual effectiveness of BERT. In *Proceedings of the 2019 Conference on Empirical Methods in Natural Language Processing and the 9th International Joint Conference on Natural Language Processing (EMNLP-IJCNLP)*, pages 833–844, Hong Kong, China. Association for Computational Linguistics.

Y. Wu, M. Schuster, Z. Chen, Quoc V. Le, Mohammad Norouzi, Wolfgang Macherey, M. Krikun, Yuan Cao, Q. Gao, Klaus Macherey, J. Klingner, Apurva Shah, M. Johnson, X. Liu, Lukasz Kaiser, Stephan Gouws, Y. Kato, Taku Kudo, H. Kazawa, K. Stevens, George Kurian, Nishant Patil, W. Wang, C. Young, J. Smith, Jason Riesa, Alex Rudnick, Oriol Vinyals, G. Corrado, Macduff Hughes, and J. Dean. 2016. Google's neural machine translation system: Bridging the gap between human and machine translation. *ArXiv*, abs/1609.08144.

Linting Xue, Noah Constant, Adam Roberts, Mihir Kale, Rami Al-Rfou, Aditya Siddhant, Aditya Barua, and Colin Raffel. 2021. mT5: A massively multilingual pre-trained text-to-text transformer. In *Proceedings of the 2021 Conference of the North American Chapter of the Association for Computational Linguistics: Human Language Technologies*, pages 483–498, Online. Association for Computational Linguistics.

Jingqing Zhang, Yao Zhao, Mohammad Saleh, and Peter Liu. 2020. PEGASUS: Pre-training with extracted gap-sentences for abstractive summarization. In *Proceedings of the 37th International Conference on Machine Learning*, volume 119 of *Proceedings of Machine Learning Research*, pages 11328–11339. PMLR.

A Pre-Training and Downstream Datasets' Information

We use the CC100 corpus (Wenzek et al., 2020; Conneau et al., 2020) for pre-training all models in this work. More specifically, we used the English (EN), French (FR), and German (DE) parts of the mentioned corpus. Due to the lack of computing power and the massive amount of paragraphs in this corpus, we use around 3GB of the text of each language, approximately 550M words from each language and a total of 1.6B words, to pre-train our models. For more reproducibility, we select 500000×96, the total pre-training steps multiplied by the used batch size, first paragraphs of each mentioned language in the corpus as pre-training samples.

In order to evaluate the models for translation tasks, we use English to French and English to German sections of the WMT14 (Bojar et al., 2014) and the French to German part of the WMT19 dataset (Barrault et al., 2019). The total number of samples in each set of each pre-training dataset is reported in Table 5. We do not use all the samples in all datasets due to the lack of computing power. We use at most 50000×96, the total fine-tuning steps multiplied by the batch size, unique samples of each dataset. We use all the samples for datasets with fewer samples than the mentioned number. To the best of our knowledge, the test set of the WMT19 FR-DE dataset is not publicly available. Therefore, we report the results on the validation set instead of the test set.

For the experiment on transferring knowledge from one language to another, we fine-tune PEACH on the MultiNLI dataset (Williams et al., 2018), consisting of natural language inference samples for the English language. Then, we evaluate the model on English, French, and German samples in test set in the XNLI dataset (Conneau et al., 2018), consisting of natural language inference samples for the mentioned languages. The number of samples for each dataset is reported in Table 6. Both mentioned datasets use three labels; neutral, entailment, and contradiction.

Dataset	Language	Train	Dev	Test
WMT14	EN↔FR	40836715	3000	3003
WMT14	EN↔DE	4508785	3000	3003
WMT19	EN↔FR	9824476	1512	-

Table 5: Number of Samples in supervised stranslation datasets.

Dataset	Language	Train	Test
MultiNLI	EN	392702	-
XNLI	EN	-	5010
XNLI	DE	-	5010
XNLI	FR	-	5010

Table 6: Number of Samples in natural language inference datasets.

B Word-by-Word Translation Implementation Details

The word-by-word translation was performed in batches of 1K documents. The batch size does not affect the algorithm's performance and should be chosen based on the available resources.

After lower casing the documents in a batch, named entities are extracted using the spaCy toolkit. The identified entities should be divided by white space characters since the named entities sometimes consist of multiple words. Since the spaCy toolkit for named entity recognition sometimes chooses definite articles as a part of named entities, we filter out definite articles such as "the," "le," "la," "les," "der," "die," and "das" and translate them using dictionaries in following steps.

In order to perform word-by-word translation, we first tokenize the document. We search for the translation of each token from the source language to the destination language using the appropriate dictionary. If we found more than one possible translation for a token, we uniformly select one of them. Suppose we can not find any translations for a token in the source to the destination language dictionary. In that case, we use source to English and English to destination dictionary to find a translation for the mentioned token. First, we search for a translation from the source language to English using the source to English dictionary. Next, we search for a translation from English to the destination language in the English to the destination dictionary. This technique is just helpful when there is a translation from the source token to English. If we can not find any translations for a token, we mark it as unknown to decide about it later.

For the terms that were marked as unknown, if the token contains numbers or punctuations, we transfer it without any change to the output as a translated word. Otherwise, we check if the word is in the extracted named entities. In this case, we transliterate the word into the destination language using polyglot library [4] and put it in the output as a translated word. For complex words such as "high-end," we break the word into its alphabetical components and search them in the dictionary. If we could find a translation for all components, we would translate each component and concatenate them using the proper separator. In the case that none of the aforementioned scenarios happens, we omit the word and hope the denoising pre-trained model can find a proper translation for it.

[4] https://polyglot.readthedocs.io/en/latest/Transliteration.html

C Denoising Models Pre-Training and Corruption Rate Details

Language	Removing	Addition	Substitution
EN	.066/.061	.01-.03	.05-.07
FR	.152/.087	.01-.03	.05-.07
DE	.137/.085	.01-.03	.05-.07

Table 7: Rates used for pre-training objectives of Denoising models. For removing, we report mean/std.

The procedure for generating pre-training data for training the denoising model is shown in Figure 1. This procedure consists of sentence shuffling, word removing, addition, and substitution.

The first step for generating pre-training data is loading a batch of pre-training documents into the memory as the current batch. We used a batch size of 1K for generating pre-training data for training denoising models. The batch size plays an essential role in this procedure because our algorithm selects candidates for replacing some words in a sample from the words available in other sample in the current batch. We did not investigate the effect of batch size due to the lack of computing power.

After tokenizing the separated sentences using the NLTK toolkit, we shuffle the words in each sentence but keep the relative order of sentences. It helps the denoising model learn the relative order of sentences, which is crucial since the word-by-word translation algorithm might face documents with multiple sentences. Therefore, this will teach the denoising model how to figure out the boundaries of different sentences.

Next, for each sentence, we select $m \times c$ words to be replaced, in which m is the length of the sentence and c is a random number from a uniform distribution between the reported rates in Table 7. The algorithm selects $m \times c$ unique words from other samples in the current batch uniformly to be substituted with the selected words of the current document. The word addition objective works the same way as the substitution, but the algorithm does not replace any words. The word removing objective works the same, but it uses a normal distribution for generating the random number, and it just omits some words from each sentence without replacing them with other words.

The word substitution and addition rates in Table 7 were selected based on observation of the outputs of the word-by-word translation algorithm. On the other hand, we computed the mean and standard deviation for the proportion of words that the word-by-word translation algorithm could not find any translation for them on the pre-training corpus. The main purpose of the word removing objective is to find a translation for the words that the word-by-word translation algorithm could not find any translation for them by considering the context of the sentence. Therefore, computing this number on the pre-training corpus that the final multilingual model will be trained on will improve the denoising model's ability to denoise the word-by-word translation algorithm's outputs. This decreases the number of words that the word-by-word translation algorithm or the denoising model could not find a translation for them.

D Experiment Details and Setup

It takes six days to pre-train PEACH on 500000×96 pre-training documents for 500K steps and a batch size of 96. However, the downstream dataset for English-French translation consists of almost 40M samples, which is only 8M less than our pre-training documents and takes five days to fine-tune for just one epoch. Therefore, choosing 50000×96 samples for fine-tuning is plausible due to the number of total pre-training documents and steps of the model's pre-training. The setup for training denoising models is reported in Table 8. The experiment setups for pre-training multilingual models on English, French, and German are reported in Table 9. The setups for pre-training bilingual models used in different experiments are reported in Table 10. Table 11 reports the details of experiments on fine-tuning models on supervised translation tasks. The experiment setup for the few-shot scenario is reported in Table 12. The experiment setup for the fine-tuning on the XNLI (Conneau et al., 2018) task is reported in Table 13.

E Figures' Details and Information

The reported numbers in Figures 3, 4, and 5 are reported in Tables 14, 15, and 16 for better readability.

Language	Learning rate	Steps	Batch Size	Max Input Length	Max Output Length
English	.01	500K	96	512	512
German	.01	500K	96	512	512
French	.01	500K	96	512	512

Table 8: Pre-training settings for denoising models.

Objective	Learning rate	Steps	Batch Size	Language	Max Input Length	Max Output Length
Multilingual SPDG	.01	500K	96	EN-FR-DE	512	512
MLM with Reordering	.01	500K	96	EN-FR-DE	512	512
MLM	.01	500K	96	EN-FR-DE	512	512

Table 9: Pre-training settings for multilingual models trained on English, German, and French.

Objective	Learning rate	Steps	Batch Size	Language	Max Input Length	Max Output Length
SPDG	.01	200K	96	EN-FR	512	512
SPDG	.01	200K	96	EN-DE	512	512
SPDG	.01	200K	96	DE-FR	512	512

Table 10: Pre-training settings for bilingual models.

Dataset	Learning rate	Steps	Batch Size	Beam Size	Beam alpha	Max Input	Max Output
WMT14 $_{\text{EN-FR}}$	5×10^{-5}	50K	96	1	.6	512	512
WMT14 $_{\text{EN-DE}}$	5×10^{-5}	50K	96	1	.6	512	512
WMT19 $_{\text{DE-FR}}$	5×10^{-5}	50K	96	1	.6	512	512

Table 11: Fine-tuning settings for models used in supervised translation experiments.

Dataset	Learning rate	Sample count	Steps	Batch Size	Beam Size	Beam alpha	Max Input	Max Output
WMT14 $_{\text{EN-FR}}$	5×10^{-5}	50K	1K-50K	96	1	.6	512	512

Table 12: Fine-tuning settings for the few-shot supervised translation experiment.

Dataset	Learning rate	Steps	Batch Size	Beam Size	Beam alpha	Max Input	Max Output	Language
XNLI	1×10^{-3}	50K	256	1	.6	512	16	EN-FR-DE

Table 13: Fine-tuning settings for knowledge transfer experiment on natural language inference.

Dataset // Pre-Training steps	100K steps	200K steps	300K steps	400K steps	500K steps
WMT14 $_{\text{FR} \leftrightarrow \text{EN}}$	$27.40 \leftrightarrow 26.60$	$29.04 \leftrightarrow 28.08$	$30.04 \leftrightarrow 29.01$	$30.86 \leftrightarrow 29.35$	$31.25 \leftrightarrow 29.98$
WMT14 $_{\text{DE} \leftrightarrow \text{EN}}$	$21.21 \leftrightarrow 23.89$	$22.33 \leftrightarrow 25.29$	$22.87 \leftrightarrow 26.07$	$23.25 \leftrightarrow 26.52$	$23.61 \leftrightarrow 26.97$
WMT19 $_{\text{DE} \leftrightarrow \text{FR}}$	$20.49 \leftrightarrow 22.32$	$21.67 \leftrightarrow 23.29$	$22.12 \leftrightarrow 24.07$	$22.65 \leftrightarrow 24.70$	$23.13 \leftrightarrow 25.25$

Table 14: PEACH's performance in different pre-training steps on downstream tasks evaluated with BLEU score. The fine-tuning setup is reported in Table 11. These numbers are reported in Figure 3.

Model	WMT14		WMT19
	FR$\leftrightarrow$EN	DE$\leftrightarrow$EN	DE$\leftrightarrow$FR
MLM	$4.33 \leftrightarrow 5.64$	$6.40 \leftrightarrow 5.69$	$6.39 \leftrightarrow 4.56$
MLM with Reordering	$7.42 \leftrightarrow 6.63$	$7.73 \leftrightarrow 7.96$	$7.17 \leftrightarrow 7.71$
PEACH	$12.89 \leftrightarrow 12.98$	$11.75 \leftrightarrow 14.05$	$11.83 \leftrightarrow 13.11$

Table 15: The zero-shot translation results of the models evaluated with BLEU score. These numbers are reported in Figure 4

Fine-tuning steps	PEACH	MLM	MLM with Reordering	Sample count
0	12.895563	-	7.420614	50K
1K	13.166867	-	8.080425	50K
3K	15.16206	-	14.288106	50K
5K	20.924359	-	17.13509	50K
10K	26.17157	-	21.928285	50K
15K	27.991698	-	24.24655	50K
20K	28.940293	-	25.608678	50K
25K	29.325823	-	26.304938	50K
30K	29.727194	-	26.939679	50K
35K	30.017766	-	27.462619	50K
40K	30.122644	-	27.770637	50K
45K	30.228142	-	28.110951	50K
50K	30.491127	-	28.309444	50K
50K	31.251482	21.384103	29.029701	5M

Table 16: The zero- and few-shot translation results of the models evaluated with BLEU score on EN-FR section of WMT 14. These numbers are reported in Figure 5

A Simplified Training Pipeline for Low-Resource and Unsupervised Machine Translation

Àlex R. Atrio[1,2] and **Alexis Allemann**[1] and
Ljiljana Dolamic[3] and **Andrei Popescu-Belis**[1,2]

[1]HEIG-VD / HES-SO
Yverdon-les-Bains
Switzerland
name.surname@heig-vd.ch

[2]EPFL
Lausanne
Switzerland

[3]Armasuisse, W+T
Thun
Switzerland
ljiljana.dolamic@armasuisse.ch

Abstract

Training neural MT systems for low-resource language pairs or in unsupervised settings (i.e. with no parallel data) often involves a large number of auxiliary systems. These may include parent systems trained on higher-resource pairs and used for initializing the parameters of child systems, multilingual systems for neighboring languages, and several stages of systems trained on pseudo-parallel data obtained through back-translation. We propose here a simplified pipeline, which we compare to the best submissions to the WMT 2021 Shared Task on Unsupervised MT and Very Low Resource Supervised MT. Our pipeline only needs two parents, two children, one round of back-translation for low-resource directions and two for unsupervised ones and obtains better or similar scores when compared to more complex alternatives.

1 Introduction

Several known techniques enable the design of neural MT systems with little or no parallel data for the source and target languages. Among them are the initialization with a parent model trained on parallel data from related languages (Zoph et al., 2016; Kocmi and Bojar, 2018) and repeated cycles of back-translation of monolingual data that create pseudo-parallel corpora used for training (Sennrich et al., 2016a; Hoang et al., 2018). When designing a very low-resource or unsupervised system, many practitioners rightfully consider as a guideline the best-performing systems found in several shared tasks, such as WMT Shared Task on Unsupervised MT and Very Low Resource Supervised MT (Fraser, 2020; Libovický and Fraser, 2021a; Weller-Di Marco and Fraser, 2022), where teams compete in order to obtain the highest scores among them. While these systems typically do obtain very high scores, in this paper we show that the pipelines of the highest-scoring systems in this task may be unnecessarily complex, and they can be substantially simplified while still achieving comparable results.

To solve this shared task, high-resource parent models have been leveraged to initialize child models for low-resource languages, which in turn have been used to warm-start the training for unsupervised directions. However, the submissions to the above-mentioned shared task typically developed several dozen models, with numerous parent/child models in both directions as well as increasingly better models trained on several rounds of back-translated data. These models were finally ensembled for best results.

For the 2021 edition of the task, the unsupervised language pair was Lower Sorbian / German (DSB/DE), with parallel data only available for testing, while the low-resource pair was Upper Sorbian / German (HSB/DE). A large amount of German / Czech (DE/CS) parallel or monolingual data is available to train parent models, due to the similarity of Sorbian dialects to Czech. Moreover, given the similarity of the two Sorbian dialects, child low-resource models can become parents of "grandchild" systems for the unsupervised task. As a result, these systems are quite complex, which raises the question: up to which point can these architectures be simplified with virtually no loss of performance?

Our study answers this question by presenting a simpler pipeline than the ones submitted to the shared task, which reaches superior or comparable scores to the ones from the highest-scoring teams. In our pipeline, we apply the same selection and filtering of data as the best-performing team for comparability. We train high-resource parent models on authentic parallel data in two directions (CS↔DE), and then use them to initialize child low-resource models (HSB↔DE). We improve these systems with one round of back-translated monolingual data, and finally use them to initialize systems and to produce back-translated

Proceedings of the The Sixth Workshop on Technologies for Machine Translation of Low-Resource Languages (LoResMT 2023), pages 47–58
May 6, 2023 ©2023 Association for Computational Linguistics

data for the unsupervised pair (DSB↔DE). More specifically, our simplifications are the following:

1. only training from one initialization per parent-child-grandchild;
2. no multitasking and no multilingual models;
3. length-based filtering of back-translated data instead of language model-based one;
4. no monolingual data and only moderate amount of authentic parallel data for high-resource parent models;
5. a single round of back-translation for low-resource directions and two for unsupervised directions;
6. same subword vocabulary for all translation directions;
7. moderately-sized Transformer-Base instead of Big;
8. unique set of values for hyper-parameters such as learning rate and label smoothing.

We make public the configuration files that create these systems in the OpenNMT-py framework.[1]

2 Related Work

2.1 Techniques for Low-Resource and Unsupervised MT

Transfer learning consists in training a model on a high-resource pair (parent) that initializes a model trained on a lower-resource one (child). Initially, Zoph et al. (2016) kept the same target language between parent and child. Kocmi and Bojar (2018), however, showed that the identity or relatedness of the target languages is not essential, and that all of the weights of the child systems can be initialized with those of the parent model without changing the training routine.

Back-translation consists in automatically translating monolingual data in the target language, in order to create a synthetic parallel corpus which can be used for training (Sennrich et al., 2016a). Edunov et al. (2018) showed that the benefits of back-translated data depend on the decoding algorithms used to generate it, and that beam search is not the best-performing option unless the amount of data to back-translate is small. This, however, can be mitigated by differentiating authentic and synthetic data with tags (Caswell et al., 2019). This process can also be performed iteratively, as shown by Hoang et al. (2018), with either the same model generating initial back-translated data, improving its performance, and re-generating the data, or by training a new model for each round of back-translation, which improves the quality of the synthetic data.

When large monolingual corpora are available, fully unsupervised NMT can be achieved by using masked language modeling, denoising, or translation language modeling (Lample et al., 2017, 2018; Conneau and Lample, 2019). This results in cross-lingual language models (Conneau and Lample, 2019), which can further be trained on back-translated data. Such systems perform best when jointly trained on very large monolingual datasets and when a small amount of parallel data is available (Song et al., 2019; Liu et al., 2020). However, this is not the case for some of the datasets of the WMT shared task considered here.

2.2 Submissions to the WMT21 Shared Task

Six teams competed for the highest scores in the low-resource Upper Sorbian / German and the unsupervised Lower Sorbian / German translation tasks at the WMT 2021 Shared Tasks on Unsupervised MT and Very Low Resource Supervised MT (Libovický and Fraser, 2021a). The datasets used in the tasks are presented in Section 4.1 below. The organizers scored the submissions using automatic metrics over held-out test sets. NRC-CNRC (Knowles and Larkin, 2021) and LMU (Libovický and Fraser, 2021b) achieved some of the highest scores in both tasks. Other competitive scores were achieved by CL_RUG (Edman et al., 2021) and NoahNMT (Zhang et al., 2021), followed at some distance by IICT-Yverdon (Atrio et al., 2021). Since no team participated in both tasks, and NoahNMT used a particularly complex pipeline with very large amounts of training data and a pre-trained BERT encoder, we decided to work towards the simplification of the NRC-CNRC and LMU 2021 pipelines.

The NRC-CNRC submission (Knowles and Larkin, 2021) experimented with various numbers of BPE merges (Sennrich et al., 2016b) for different translation directions and for generating synthetic data for training. Their final vocabularies contain 25k and 20k subwords for the supervised and unsupervised models, respectively. They built the BPE tokenizer from upscaled HSB, CS and DE data, but without DSB. The architecture is

[1]github.com/AlexRAtrio/simplified-pipeline

based on Transformer-Base (Vaswani et al., 2017), with frequent ensembling throughout the pipeline. They use Moore-Lewis filtering (Moore and Lewis, 2010) of back-translated sentences. They train parent CS↔DE models on the entire parallel CS-DE data in Table 1, with BPE-dropout (Provilkov et al., 2020). From them, they initialize child HSB↔DE models, which are further fine-tuned into grandchildren DSB↔DE.

The final HSB→DE system from NRC-CNRC is an ensemble of eight different models. Six of them are children and grandchildren of CS-DE models, and two are multilingual CS-DE and HSB-DE models (with no transfer learning). Among the other six, there are different values for hyperparameters like learning rate or label smoothing. After training with various filtering strategies for back-translated sentences, Moore-Lewis filtering was found to perform best, although differences are generally smaller than 1 BLEU point. Some models are fine-tuned only with back-translations, or only authentic data, or both. For DE→HSB translation, the translation is generated with an ensemble of seven systems. The final NRC-CNRC submission to the DSB→DE unsupervised task is an ensemble of two grandchild systems trained with different back-translated corpora, and for DE→DSB it is an ensemble of four grandchildren, with different rounds of back-translation, different learning rates, and at least one different CS-DE parent model.

The LMU submission (Libovický and Fraser, 2021b) starts with a BPE tokenizer with 16k merges, on the entire HSB, DE, CS and DSB data. Parent Transformer-Base CS↔DE models are trained on the entire CS-DE parallel data, which is filtered by length and language identity. To this authentic data, they add 20M lines of monolingual CS and DE respectively for back-translation, which they use to train another set of parent models with Transformer-Big, sampling and tagged back-translation. Child HSB→DE and DE→HSB models (also Transformer-Big) are trained from CS-DE parents, first on authentic parallel data. Then, they are used to iteratively back-translate 15M lines of DE and the entire HSB monolingual data for four rounds, with a new model initialization for each round. To obtain DSB→DE and DE→DSB grandchildren systems, iterative back-translation is performed for eight rounds, initialized from the respective HSB/DE Transformer-Big child systems.

A similar shared task was again organized at WMT 2022, including HSB↔DE and DSB↔DE translation (Weller-Di Marco and Fraser, 2022). Additional parallel HSB-DE data was provided, increasing the total to about 0.5 million lines, which likely increased scores for the low-resource supervised tasks HSB↔DE. Moreover, an unsupervised HSB↔DE and a low-resource supervised DSB↔HSB translation tasks were introduced.

Four teams participated in the low-resource supervised tasks, and three in the unsupervised ones. In most tasks, HuaweiTSC (Li et al., 2022) achieved by far the highest scores, thanks to a deep 35-layer encoder, 6-layer decoder Transformer (Wei et al., 2021) and a parent multilingual model trained on vast amounts of data (including 55M lines of DE-CS, 66M lines of DE-PL, and 20M of monolingual DE). In addition to the techniques we study in this paper, Li et al. (2022) used regularized dropout (Liang et al., 2021) to improve consistency while training. Their setup thus also consisted of numerous and expensive training steps, just as the NRC-CNRC and LMU systems to which we compare our proposal.

3 Proposed Pipeline

We propose a simplified training pipeline represented in Figure 1, which reaches comparable or better results than the above systems. The pipeline is minimal, in the sense that only eight systems are trained for HSB↔DE and DSB↔DE translation, including parent systems for initialization. We show that one round of back-translation for low-resource directions and two for unsupervised ones are sufficient. In comparison with the numerous rounds and checkpoints of the NRC-CNRC and LMU systems, our pipeline is an order of magnitude smaller.

We start by training from scratch parent models DE→$\text{CS}_{\text{parent}}$ and CS→$\text{DE}_{\text{parent}}$ on authentic parallel data. From their best-performing checkpoint, we respectively initialize DE→$\text{HSB}_{\text{authentic}}$ and HSB→$\text{DE}_{\text{authentic}}$ models, which we train only on authentic parallel data. We then use their best-performing checkpoints to generate synthetic parallel data (back-translations) by translating monolingual target data (resulting in synthetic datasets HSB_{BT}-DE_{mono} and DE_{BT}-HSB_{mono}). We initialize from the best-performing checkpoints of the previous systems new models DE→$\text{HSB}_{\text{authentic+BT}}$ and HSB→$\text{DE}_{\text{authentic+BT}}$ which we train on upscaled authentic parallel data and back-translated

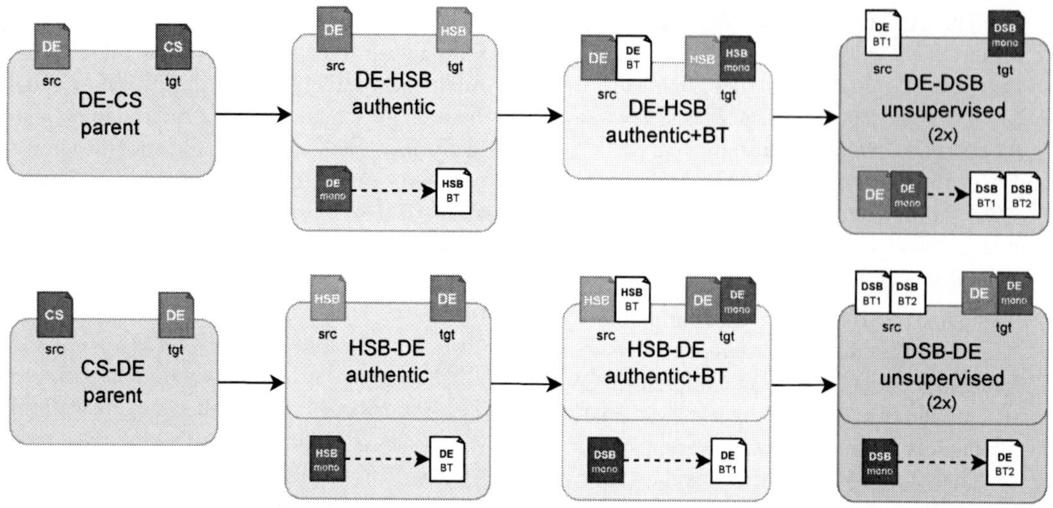

Figure 1: Pipeline of implemented systems. Solid arrows represent the parent systems used, and dashed arrows represent creation of synthetic data through back-translation. The datasets in color are those presented in Table 1. The datasets in white, to the right of dashed lines, are the back-translations (BT) generated by our systems. The unsupervised models are trained with two rounds of back-translation.

data.

Finally, with the best-performing checkpoint of system HSB→$\text{DE}_{\text{authentic+BT}}$, we perform back-translation of monolingual DSB data (resulting in DE_{BT1}-DSB_{mono}), and train with this first round of synthetic parallel data the unsupervised DE→$\text{DSB}_{\text{unsupervised}(a)}$ model. We use this system for the first round of back-translation in the opposite direction, of the DE part of the HSB-DE authentic data and monolingual DE (resulting in DSB_{BT1}-DE and DSB_{BT2}-DE_{mono}) into DSB, on which we train the unsupervised DSB→$\text{DE}_{\text{unsupervised}(a)}$ model. We then use this system for the second round of back-translation of monolingual DSB data and train another unsupervised DE→$\text{DSB}_{\text{unsupervised}(b)}$ model, and with it we perform a second round of back-translation of monolingual DE to train a final unsupervised DSB→$\text{DSB}_{\text{unsupervised}(b)}$ model.

ID - Language	Dataset name	Size (sentences)
DE-CS	DGT v8	4,894
	Europarl v8	569
	JW300	1,039
	News Comm. v16	197
	OpenSubtitles	16,358
	WMT-News	20
DE-HSB	WMT 2020 Train	60
	WMT 2021 Train	88
HSB_{mono}	WMT20 Sorbian Inst.	340
	WMT20 Web	133
	WMT20 Witaj	222
DSB_{mono}	WMT21 Mono.	145
DE_{mono}	WMT21 News Crawl 19	1,500

Table 1: Monolingual and parallel corpora with their languages as presented in Figure 1. We provide the number of lines (sentences) after filtering, in thousands.

4 Data, Preprocessing and Systems

4.1 Corpora

The datasets we use are listed in Table 1, and the identifiers correspond to those in Figure 1. They encode the language and index number for authentic parallel DE-CS, authentic parallel DE-HSB, and monolingual HSB, DSB, and DE. For the CS↔DE parent models we use parallel data from DGT (Tiedemann, 2012; Steinberger et al., 2012), Europarl (Koehn, 2005), JW300 (Agić and Vulić, 2019), OpenSubtitles (Lison and Tiedemann, 2016), News Commentary, and WMT-News.[2] Our HSB↔DE models use datasets from the 2020 edition of the task, with monolingual HSB data from three sources: (a) the Sorbian Institute provided a mix of high- and medium-quality HSB data; (b) the Witaj Sprachzentrum provided high-quality HSB

[2]statmt.org/wmt20/translation-task.html

data; (c) the Web data consists of web-scraped noisier HSB data gathered by the Center for Information and Language Processing at LMU Munich (Fraser, 2020). Our DSB↔DE models use only the monolingual Lower Sorbian (DSB) dataset from the 2021 shared task.

To evaluate our systems, we use the 'Newstest2019-csde' as a test set for our CS↔DE models. For our HSB↔DE and DSB↔DE models we use the 'devel' set from the WMT20 task during development, and 'devel_test' for final evaluations. Since the official scores of the task are calculated on an undisclosed subset of the blind test set, we cannot compare our results with the final official ones. We will thus compare them with the scores on 'devel_test' reported by each team in their articles. Our two evaluation metrics are the same as in the shared task. We use the SacreBLEU library (Post, 2018) to compute BLEU (Papineni et al., 2002).[3] We also use BERTScore[4](Zhang et al., 2019), with the XLM-RoBERTa-Large model (Conneau et al., 2020) for translations into German, as provided with the BERTScore toolkit. We test the statistical significance of differences in scores at the 95% confidence level using paired bootstrap resampling from SacreBLEU.

4.2 Data Filtering

For comparison purposes, we follow closely the data preparation procedure of the NRC-CNRC team (Knowles and Larkin, 2021). We first clean the training data with the `clean_utf8.py` script from `PortageTextProcessing`.[5] Subsequently, parallel training data is filtered with the `clean-corpus-n.perl` script from Moses (Koehn et al., 2007) to remove sentence pairs with a length ratio larger than 15. Punctuation is then normalized using the `normalize-punctuation.perl` script from Moses. Finally, non-breaking spaces (Unicode U+00A0 or '`\xa0`') and empty lines are deleted.

For all DE-CS parallel data and all monolingual DE and CS data, lines that contain characters which have not been observed in DE-HSB training data, WMT-News, or Europarl corpora are deleted. This is done to eliminate encoding issues and text that is clearly in other languages. The DE monolingual dataset consists of a likewise cleaned random sample of the full WMT21 News Crawl 19 corpus. The numbers of lines after filtering are shown in the two rightmost columns of Table 1.

4.3 Tokenization

We start tokenizing sentences into words with the Moses tokenizer: `tokenizer.perl -a -l $LNG`, where `$LNG` is `cs` or `de`, using the `cs` code also for HSB and DSB data. Then, we use Byte Pair Encoding (BPE) (Sennrich et al., 2016b)[6] to build a vocabulary of 20k subwords. For building the BPE models, we used all HSB-DE data, the Sorbian Institute and Witaj monolingual HSB data (but not the Web-crawled HSB data, which is too noisy), both sides of CS-DE data, and News-Commentary (DE) data. The HSB data was upscaled twice. The same datasets were used for extracting the joint vocabulary, which was then used to tokenize the source and target sides with a BPE-Dropout rate of 0.1 (Provilkov et al., 2020).

In post-processing, we detokenize BPE subwords with the BPE toolkit and then with a script from Moses: `detokenizer.perl -a -l $LNG`, where `$LNG` is `cs` or `de`, using the `cs` code also for HSB and DSB data.

4.4 System Architecture

We use Transformer models (Vaswani et al., 2017) from the OpenNMT-py library (Klein et al., 2017) version 2.3.0.[7] We use the following default values of hyper-parameters from Transformer-Base: 6 encoder/decoder layers, 8 attention heads, Adam optimizer (Kingma and Ba, 2014), label smoothing of 0.1, dropout of 0.1, hidden layer of 512 units, and FFN of 2,048 units. We share the vocabulary and use the same embedding matrix for both input and output languages. The batch size is 8,192 tokens, and the maximum sequence length for both source and target is 501 tokens. We keep OpenNMT-py's scaling factor of 2 over the learning rate. We use standard values for hyper-parameters in order to maintain a simplified pipeline, although it is likely that a more regularized system could further improve scores (Atrio and Popescu-Belis, 2022).

We do not use any early stopping measure and train for a sufficiently large amount of steps to ensure convergence. We train the parent CS↔DE

[3] github.com/mjpost/sacrebleu, signature: `nrefs:1|case:mixed|eff:no|tok:13a|smooth:exp|version:2.3.1`.

[4] github.com/Tiiiger/bert_score, signature: `xlm-roberta-large_L17_no-idf_version=0.3.12(hug_trans=4.26.0)_fast-tokenizer`

[5] github.com/nrc-cnrc/PortageTextProcessing

[6] github.com/rsennrich/subword-nmt

[7] github.com/OpenNMT/OpenNMT-py

models for 500,000 steps, and the children and grand-children ones for 100,000 steps. To train our models we use between one and four Nvidia RTX 2080 Ti with 11 GB RAM which amounts to around 80 hours for parent models, 30 hours for children models (systems 3/4 and 5/6), and 15 hours for grandchildren models. As better parent systems lead to better children, we trained the parents for a longer time, given also the larger parallel data available.

We save checkpoints every 4,000 steps during training, and obtain the testing scores from an ensemble of the four best checkpoints in terms of BLEU scores on the validation data. When testing, we use a beam size of 5 for all systems, except when indicated otherwise for back-translation.

5 Results of the Proposed Pipeline

5.1 Parent DE↔CS Systems

We first train the $\text{DE}\rightarrow\text{CS}_{\text{parent}}$ and $\text{CS}\rightarrow\text{DE}_{\text{parent}}$ models (see Figure 1) on the authentic parallel CS-DE data presented in Table 1. The BLEU and BERTScore of these systems, shown in Table 2, are respectively 20.2 and 22.1. These are comparable with the ones reported by NRC-CNRC (22–25 BLEU points) and with those with the same architecture appearing in the Opus-MT leaderboard[8], trained on OPUS parallel data (Tiedemann, 2012) using Opus-MT-Train (Tiedemann and Thottingal, 2020).

Choosing Czech for the parent model is reasonable due to its similarity with Upper and Lower Sorbian, but we have found that this similarity is not crucial (Atrio et al., 2021). Using a similar setup, we observed almost identical results with a Polish↔German parent model, and a loss of only 1.3 BLEU points with a French↔German one.

5.2 Child DE↔HSB Systems

We initialize the child systems $\text{DE}\rightarrow\text{HSB}_{\text{authentic}}$ and $\text{HSB}\rightarrow\text{DE}_{\text{authentic}}$ models from the highest-scoring checkpoint of the respective parent, and trained them on authentic parallel HSB-DE data. The systems reached BLEU scores of 56.7 and 56.1 respectively (see Table 2).

One round of back-translation. We hypothesize that due to the already existing authentic parallel data, one round of back-translation (BT) could be sufficient. We use the above systems to generate synthetic parallel data from monolingual DE and HSB corpora. To generate it, we decode by sampling from the entire model distribution rather than applying beam search, following Edunov et al. (2018). As shown in Figure 1, with the $\text{HSB}\rightarrow\text{DE}_{\text{authentic}}$ and $\text{DE}\rightarrow\text{HSB}_{\text{authentic}}$ systems we translate the DE_{mono} data into HSB_{BT}. Similarly, we translate the HSB_{mono} data into DE_{BT}. Therefore, we obtain two pseudo-parallel datasets with authentic target sides. We apply to them the same filtering process as in Section 4.2, except for a more restrictive cut-off for `clean-corpus-n.perl`, using a maximum ratio of 1.5 between sentences instead of 15. This filtering results in the deletion of respectively 5% and 11% of the HSB-DE and DE-HSB pseudo-parallel datasets.

We continue training the $\text{HSB}\rightarrow\text{DE}_{\text{authentic}}$ and $\text{DE}\rightarrow\text{HSB}_{\text{authentic}}$ systems with authentic parallel HSB-DE data and the back-translated data, with the former being upscaled to match the number of lines of the latter. We obtain respectively the systems noted $\text{HSB}\rightarrow\text{DE}_{\text{authentic+BT}}$ and $\text{DE}\rightarrow\text{HSB}_{\text{authentic+BT}}$. The improvements brought by this round of back-translation are only of about 1 BLEU point (see Table 5). Our scores are similar to those reported by NRC-CNRC without inter-model ensembling (57-58 BLEU). With the highest-scoring checkpoint for each of $\text{HSB}\rightarrow\text{DE}_{\text{authentic+BT}}$ and $\text{DE}\rightarrow\text{HSB}_{\text{authentic+BT}}$ we generate synthetic data for the unsupervised case by translating monolingual DSB and DE.

Iterative back-translation. We found that our pipeline does not benefit from multiple rounds of back-translation thanks to an additional experiment, not included in the final pipeline. Following Libovický and Fraser (2021b), for each round of back-translation i (with i = a, b, c), systems $\text{HSB}\rightarrow\text{DE}_{\text{authentic+BT}(i)}$ and $\text{DE}\rightarrow\text{HSB}_{\text{authentic+BT}(i)}$ are respectively initialized from the parent models $\text{CS}\rightarrow\text{DE}_{\text{parent}}$ and $\text{DE}\rightarrow\text{CS}_{\text{parent}}$ trained on

System	BLEU	BERTScore
$\text{DE}\rightarrow\text{CS}_{\text{parent}}$	20.2	.936
$\text{CS}\rightarrow\text{DE}_{\text{parent}}$	22.1	.938
$\text{DE}\rightarrow\text{HSB}_{\text{authentic}}$	56.7	-
$\text{HSB}\rightarrow\text{DE}_{\text{authentic}}$	56.1	.975

Table 2: BLEU and BERTScore on `newstest2019` for CS-DE parent models and `devel_test` for HSB-DE models trained only on authentic data.

[8]opus.nlpl.eu/leaderboard/DE→CS and CS→DE

CS-DE data, instead of child systems trained on only authentic data HSB→DE$_{\text{authentic}}$ and DE→HSB$_{\text{authentic}}$ as performed above. Decoding and filtering remain as described above as well. Otherwise, the first round of back-translation remains as above, and the second round results in new pseudo-parallel datasets on which we train new systems in both directions (also including upscaled authentic parallel data HSB-DE), resulting in systems HSB→DE$_{\text{authentic+BT}(b)}$ and DE→HSB$_{\text{authentic+BT}(b)}$. We perform a third round to obtain systems HSB→DE$_{\text{authentic+BT}(c)}$ and DE→HSB$_{\text{authentic+BT}(c)}$. Hence, this method differs from our main proposed pipeline in the usage of three rounds versus one, and the initialization of models from CS-DE parents instead of the child HSB-DE systems trained on authentic parallel data.

While several studies have suggested that multiple back-translation rounds are beneficial, our findings are more nuanced. As we observe in Table 3, for the direction DE→HSB, the first round of back-translation improves BLEU by 1.2 points, but afterwards scores decrease. For the direction HSB→DE, on the contrary, BLEU scores continue to improve with more iterations, although with diminishing returns, with a final improvement of 0.7 points. We hypothesize that this is due to the monolingual DE dataset being larger than the HSB one.

Direction	System	BLEU
DE→HSB	DE→HSB$_{\text{authentic}}$	56.7
	DE→HSB$_{\text{authentic+BT}(a)}$	**57.9**⋆
	DE→HSB$_{\text{authentic+BT}(b)}$	**57.6**⋆
	DE→HSB$_{\text{authentic+BT}(c)}$	57.4
HSB→DE	HSB→DE$_{\text{authentic}}$	56.1*
	HSB→DE$_{\text{authentic+BT}(a)}$	56.5*
	HSB→DE$_{\text{authentic+BT}(b)}$	56.5*
	HSB→DE$_{\text{authentic+BT}(c)}$	**56.8**

Table 3: BLEU scores for only authentic parallel data, and three rounds of back-translation: DE→HSB systems are trained with DE$_{\text{BT}(i)}$-HSB$_{\text{mono}}$ and HSB→DE systems are trained with HSB$_{\text{BT}(i)}$-DE$_{\text{mono}}$. We note in bold the highest score in each direction. We denote scores that are *not* significantly different per direction with the same symbol.

In contrast, Libovický and Fraser (2021b) observed more significant improvements over four rounds of iterative back-translation, although also with diminishing returns. For HSB→DE, their improvement was 2.7 (up to 56.1 BLEU), starting however from a lower score than ours (53.4) and getting half of the improvement in the first iteration. For the DE→HSB, they achieve a smaller improvement of 1.6, up to 56.5 overall, starting from 54.9. Their highest scores are obtained after two rounds. We hypothesize that the difference between our results and theirs regarding the HSB→DE direction is explained by their use of ten times more monolingual DE data, coupled with a larger architecture.

Following Edunov et al. (2018) we experimented with various decoding methods for the back-translation stage. As a comparison to the full unrestricted sampling we use in all systems, we studied restricted sampling of the top 10 candidates, as well as the dropout of 10% of the words after standard decoding, and their combination. For DE→HSB$_{\text{authentic+BT}(a)}$ the three methods obtained nearly identical scores (57.54, 57.54, and 57.51), and none of them substantially deviated from our original method. This supports previous observations by Edunov et al. (2018) showing that differences between decoding algorithms for back-translation are only noticeable when the monolingual data size is large (e.g. more than 8M lines).

5.3 Grandchild DE↔DSB Systems

In contrast with the DE↔HSB low-resource case, we hypothesize that more than one round of back-translation may be useful in the unsupervised case. We used system HSB→DE$_{\text{authentic+BT}}$ to create the pseudo-parallel dataset DE$_{\text{BT}}$-DSB$_{\text{mono}}$, with which we trained system DE→DSB$_{\text{unsupervised}(a)}$. With this system, we generated synthetic DSB data from the DE part of the HSB-DE authentic data as well as monolingual DE, resulting in DSB$_{\text{BT1}}$-DE and DSB$_{\text{BT2}}$-DE$_{\text{mono}}$. For rounds b and c we repeated the process as with HSB-DE, initializing system DE→DSB$_{\text{unsupervised}(b)}$, (and then c) and system DSB→DE$_{\text{unsupervised}(b)}$ (and then c), respectively from the highest-scoring checkpoint from systems DE→HSB$_{\text{authentic+BT}}$ and HSB→DE$_{\text{authentic+BT}}$, and generating synthetic data with each other. Filtering removed between 6-9% of the lines. The scores of the resulting systems are shown in Table 4.

For DE→DSB, the second round of back-translation produced a large improvement of 3.3 BLEU points over the first round, but the third round resulted in a minimal improvement of 0.1. The large improvement of system DE→DSB$_{\text{unsupervised}(b)}$ may be explained by the

Direction	System	BLEU
DE→DSB	$\text{DE}\rightarrow\text{DSB}_{\text{unsupervised}(a)}$	26.1
	$\text{DE}\rightarrow\text{DSB}_{\text{unsupervised}(b)}$	**29.4**⋆
	$\text{DE}\rightarrow\text{DSB}_{\text{unsupervised}(c)}$	**29.5**⋆
DSB→DE	$\text{DSB}\rightarrow\text{DE}_{\text{unsupervised}(a)}$	36.5
	$\text{DSB}\rightarrow\text{DE}_{\text{unsupervised}(b)}$	**38.1***
	$\text{DSB}\rightarrow\text{DE}_{\text{unsupervised}(c)}$	**38.4***

Table 4: BLEU scores for three rounds of back-translation: DE→DSB systems are trained with $\text{DE}_{\text{BT}(i)}$-DSB_{mono} and DSB→DE systems are trained with $\text{DSB}_{\text{BT}(i)}$-$\text{DE}_{\text{mono}}$ and $\text{DSB}_{\text{BT}(i)}$-DE (the DE part of the authentic HSB-DE data). The highest score in each direction is in bold. Scores that are *not* significantly different per direction are marked with the same symbol.

fact that the synthetic data used to train it is the first DE set translated by a true DSB system ($\text{DSB}\rightarrow\text{DE}_{\text{unsupervised}(a)}$). For DSB→DE we also observe improvements from several rounds of back-translation, with the second one improving BLEU by 1.6 points and the third round improving only minimally by 0.3 points. We hypothesize that this difference is due to the lower amount of DSB monolingual data versus DE, and the back-translation of the DSB data being generated by a model that had not been trained on DSB. For both directions (DE→DSB and DSB→DE) the difference between systems a and b was significant, but not between b and c. As a result, we excluded extra rounds of back-translation for low-resource HSB-DE from our simplified pipeline, and only performed two rounds for unsupervised DSB-DE.

6 Discussion and Conclusion

We show in Table 5 the final results of our pipeline, compared to the highest scores for each direction obtained in the WMT 2021 shared task (Libovický and Fraser, 2021a). Scores from CFILT (Khatri et al., 2021) are not shown because we do not have access to their 'devel_test' scores. HSB-DE scores from CL_RUG are intermediate scores for their unsupervised DSB-DE systems.

On both low-resource directions (HSB↔DE) our simpler pipeline obtains comparable results to the three highest-scoring teams (NRC-CNRC, LMU and NoahNMT systems). Our scores on one unsupervised direction (DSB→DE) surpass those of the three participants, while on the other (DE→DSB) our scores are comparable to those of the two highest-scoring teams (NRC-CNRC and LMU). To explain the latter result, we hypothesize that our simplified pipeline is more sensitive to weight initialization, and therefore is less robust across all directions than a more complex pipeline.

Compared to the NRC-CNRC submission, our pipeline uses the same data selection and filtering, a single vocabulary for the tokenizer, trains from a single random initialization for each of the translation direction, does not train multitask or multilingual models, uses a much simpler filtering for back-translated sentence pairs, and sets a single set of values for hyper-parameters such as learning rate and label smoothing.

Compared to LMU, our pipeline uses a smaller amount of authentic parallel data for the parent CS↔DE models, does not use monolingual data back-translated for these parent models, and uses an architecture with fewer parameters (Transformer-Base instead of Big). Moreover, we use only one round of back-translation instead of four for the child HSB↔DE systems and two instead of eight for the grandchild DSB↔DE systems submitted by LMU.

NoahNMT also produced high scores on the supervised tasks, although with the use of a pre-trained BERT model (Devlin et al., 2019), vast amounts of monolingual data (100M lines), and dual parent transfer. CL_RUG scored well in the unsupervised tasks, but made use of sequence masking, denoising auto-encoding, cross-lingual back-translation, and vocabulary alignment between HSB and DSB with VecMap (Artetxe et al., 2018). IICT-Yverdon applied a scheduled multi-task training to both the supervised and unsupervised directions, which appeared to be particularly ineffective for the unsupervised task.

We now provide some hypotheses on why our simplified pipeline produces scores that are comparable with those from more complex ones. Firstly, a much better trained parent model does not necessarily result in noticeable better child models. Whatever the cause of the improvement of the parent models (additional parent training data, parent back-translation, or additional parent pairs), when several stages in the training pipeline can be found afterwards (such as training on authentic data, then children back-translation, then grandchildren back-translation, etc.), the initial benefit may be lost later in the pipeline. This is particularly exacerbated when child systems are later trained with data of dubious quality, such as back-translations. Artetxe et al. (2020), for instance, showed that when per-

System	DE→HSB	HSB→DE		DE→DSB	DSB→DE	
	BLEU	BLEU	BERTScore	BLEU	BLEU	BERTScore
NRC-CNRC	**59.9**	**60.0**	-	**31.0**	34.9	-
LMU	56.5	56.2	.938	30.1	33.8	.874
NoahNMT	58.3	58.5	-	-	-	-
CL_RUG	52.1	51.6	-	24.9	32.1	-
IICT-Yverdon	54.6	53.2	-	9.62	-	-
Ours	57.4	57.0	.976	29.4	**38.1**	.958

Table 5: BLEU and BERTScore on the 'devel_test' set of the best-performing system of each team, with our proposals at the bottom. The highest score per direction is in bold. The systems are referenced in Section 2.2 above, and '-' indicates that the score is not available.

forming iterative back-translation, the quality of the initial system has minimal effect on the final performance, as systems tend to converge to scores dictated by the monolingual data.

This first hypothesis feeds into a second hypothesis: large amounts of parent parallel or monolingual data make it reasonable for practitioners to choose larger architectures, which must then be carried over to the lower-resource children, since pruning rarely happens mid-pipeline. Although there is evidence that fitting large models to very small amounts of data is not necessarily detrimental (Belkin et al., 2019) and can even be beneficial (Li et al., 2020), it is unclear if this still holds with a more complex training pipeline. In any case, a smaller architecture in a low-resource setting, while still over-parameterized, can perform as well as a larger one.

As a third hypothesis, and on a more practical note, since it is necessary to carry out the full pipeline to obtain the final results, some practitioners may choose to introduce elements into the pipeline without empirically measuring the extent to which they improve the scores, since that sometimes may require re-training the entire pipeline.

Finally, modern Transformer-based systems are robust, and there seems to be a large area of "acceptable results" which is relatively easy to access, as we have empirically shown with our comparison to five different submissions to the WMT shared task. However, our pipeline is only trained on a group of similar languages (Czech, Upper Sorbian, and Lower Sorbian) to and from German, which may not generalize in the same manner to other languages or domains.

To sum up, although the competition to achieve first place in shared tasks such as the one discussed here leads participants towards increasingly complex pipelines, we have shown that competitive or even better results can be achieved with a much simpler training pipeline. We hope this will encourage practitioners to further participate in shared tasks such as these, while minimizing entry constraints regarding time, training strategy, or computing resources.

Limitations

The simplified pipeline put forward in this paper has demonstrated its merits in one specific context, but should also be tested with different data sizes and differences in language similarity. Although we compared with the main techniques used by the participants, it is possible that other techniques for unsupervised translation based on vector space alignment are also competitive, though this is less likely here given the scarcity of monolingual data for Sorbian.

Ethics Statement

This study does not process personal or sensitive data. While MT in general may facilitate disclosure or cross-referencing of personal information, which may pose threats to minorities, the community appears to consider that the potential benefits far outweigh the risks, judging from the large number of studies for low-resource and unsupervised MT.

Acknowledgments

We thank Armasuisse (UNISUB projet: Unsupervised NMT with Innovative Multilingual Subword Models) and the Swiss National Science Foundation (DOMAT project: On-demand Knowledge for Document-level Machine Translation, n. 175693). We are grateful to the three anonymous LoResMT reviewers for their helpful suggestions.

References

Željko Agić and Ivan Vulić. 2019. JW300: A wide-coverage parallel corpus for low-resource languages. In *Proceedings of the 57th Annual Meeting of the Association for Computational Linguistics*, pages 3204–3210, Florence, Italy. Association for Computational Linguistics.

Mikel Artetxe, Gorka Labaka, and Eneko Agirre. 2018. A robust self-learning method for fully unsupervised cross-lingual mappings of word embeddings. In *Proceedings of the 56th Annual Meeting of the Association for Computational Linguistics (Volume 1: Long Papers)*, pages 789–798, Melbourne, Australia. Association for Computational Linguistics.

Mikel Artetxe, Gorka Labaka, Noe Casas, and Eneko Agirre. 2020. Do all roads lead to Rome? understanding the role of initialization in iterative back-translation. *Knowledge-Based Systems*, 206:106401.

Àlex R. Atrio, Gabriel Luthier, Axel Fahy, Giorgos Vernikos, Andrei Popescu-Belis, and Ljiljana Dolamic. 2021. The IICT-yverdon system for the WMT 2021 unsupervised MT and very low resource supervised MT task. In *Proceedings of the Sixth Conference on Machine Translation*, pages 973–981, Online. Association for Computational Linguistics.

Àlex R. Atrio and Andrei Popescu-Belis. 2022. On the interaction of regularization factors in low-resource neural machine translation. In *Proceedings of the 23rd Annual Conference of the European Association for Machine Translation*, pages 111–120, Ghent, Belgium. European Association for Machine Translation.

Mikhail Belkin, Daniel Hsu, Siyuan Ma, and Soumik Mandal. 2019. Reconciling modern machine-learning practice and the classical bias–variance trade-off. *Proceedings of the National Academy of Sciences*, 116(32):15849–15854.

Isaac Caswell, Ciprian Chelba, and David Grangier. 2019. Tagged back-translation. In *Proceedings of the Fourth Conference on Machine Translation (Volume 1: Research Papers)*, pages 53–63, Florence, Italy. Association for Computational Linguistics.

Alexis Conneau, Kartikay Khandelwal, Naman Goyal, Vishrav Chaudhary, Guillaume Wenzek, Francisco Guzmán, Edouard Grave, Myle Ott, Luke Zettlemoyer, and Veselin Stoyanov. 2020. Unsupervised cross-lingual representation learning at scale. In *Proceedings of the 58th Annual Meeting of the Association for Computational Linguistics*, pages 8440–8451, Online. Association for Computational Linguistics.

Alexis Conneau and Guillaume Lample. 2019. Cross-lingual language model pretraining. In *Advances in Neural Information Processing Systems*, volume 32. Curran Associates, Inc.

Jacob Devlin, Ming-Wei Chang, Kenton Lee, and Kristina Toutanova. 2019. BERT: Pre-training of deep bidirectional transformers for language understanding. In *Proceedings of the 2019 Conference of the North American Chapter of the Association for Computational Linguistics: Human Language Technologies, Volume 1 (Long and Short Papers)*, pages 4171–4186, Minneapolis, Minnesota. Association for Computational Linguistics.

Lukas Edman, Ahmet Üstün, Antonio Toral, and Gertjan van Noord. 2021. Unsupervised translation of German–Lower Sorbian: Exploring training and novel transfer methods on a low-resource language. In *Proceedings of the Sixth Conference on Machine Translation*, pages 982–988, Online. Association for Computational Linguistics.

Sergey Edunov, Myle Ott, Michael Auli, and David Grangier. 2018. Understanding back-translation at scale. In *Proceedings of the 2018 Conference on Empirical Methods in Natural Language Processing*, pages 489–500, Brussels, Belgium. Association for Computational Linguistics.

Alexander Fraser. 2020. Findings of the WMT 2020 shared tasks in unsupervised MT and very low resource supervised MT. In *Proceedings of the Fifth Conference on Machine Translation*, pages 765–771, Online. Association for Computational Linguistics.

Vu Cong Duy Hoang, Philipp Koehn, Gholamreza Haffari, and Trevor Cohn. 2018. Iterative back-translation for neural machine translation. In *Proceedings of the 2nd Workshop on Neural Machine Translation and Generation*, pages 18–24, Melbourne, Australia. Association for Computational Linguistics.

Jyotsana Khatri, Rudra Murthy, and Pushpak Bhattacharyya. 2021. Language model pretraining and transfer learning for very low resource languages. In *Proceedings of the Sixth Conference on Machine Translation*, pages 995–998, Online. Association for Computational Linguistics.

Diederik P. Kingma and Jimmy Ba. 2014. Adam: A method for stochastic optimization. In *arXiv:1412.6980*.

Guillaume Klein, Yoon Kim, Yuntian Deng, Jean Senellart, and Alexander Rush. 2017. OpenNMT: Open-source toolkit for neural machine translation. In *Proceedings of ACL 2017, System Demonstrations*, pages 67–72, Vancouver, Canada. Association for Computational Linguistics.

Rebecca Knowles and Samuel Larkin. 2021. NRC-CNRC systems for Upper Sorbian-German and Lower Sorbian-German machine translation 2021. In *Proceedings of the Sixth Conference on Machine Translation*, pages 999–1008, Online. Association for Computational Linguistics.

Tom Kocmi and Ondřej Bojar. 2018. Trivial transfer learning for low-resource neural machine translation. In *Proceedings of the Third Conference on Machine Translation: Research Papers*, pages 244–252, Brussels, Belgium. Association for Computational Linguistics.

Philipp Koehn. 2005. Europarl: A parallel corpus for statistical machine translation. In *Proceedings of Machine Translation Summit X: Papers*, pages 79–86, Phuket, Thailand.

Philipp Koehn, Hieu Hoang, Alexandra Birch, Chris Callison-Burch, Marcello Federico, Nicola Bertoldi, Brooke Cowan, Wade Shen, Christine Moran, Richard Zens, Chris Dyer, Ondřej Bojar, Alexandra Constantin, and Evan Herbst. 2007. Moses: Open source toolkit for statistical machine translation. In *Proceedings of the 45th Annual Meeting of the Association for Computational Linguistics Companion Volume Proceedings of the Demo and Poster Sessions*, pages 177–180, Prague, Czech Republic. Association for Computational Linguistics.

Guillaume Lample, Alexis Conneau, Ludovic Denoyer, and Marc'Aurelio Ranzato. 2017. Unsupervised machine translation using monolingual corpora only. *arXiv preprint arXiv:1711.00043*.

Guillaume Lample, Myle Ott, Alexis Conneau, Ludovic Denoyer, and Marc'Aurelio Ranzato. 2018. Phrase-based & neural unsupervised machine translation. In *Proceedings of the 2018 Conference on Empirical Methods in Natural Language Processing*, pages 5039–5049, Brussels, Belgium. Association for Computational Linguistics.

Shaojun Li, Yuanchang Luo, Daimeng Wei, Zongyao Li, Hengchao Shang, Xiaoyu Chen, Zhanglin Wu, Jinlong Yang, Zhiqiang Rao, Zhengzhe Yu, Yuhao Xie, Lizhi Lei, Hao Yang, and Ying Qin. 2022. HW-TSC systems for WMT22 very low resource supervised MT task. In *Proceedings of the Seventh Conference on Machine Translation*, pages 1098–1103, Abu Dhabi. Association for Computational Linguistics.

Zhuohan Li, Eric Wallace, Sheng Shen, Kevin Lin, Kurt Keutzer, Dan Klein, and Joey Gonzalez. 2020. Train big, then compress: Rethinking model size for efficient training and inference of transformers. In *International Conference on machine learning*, pages 5958–5968. PMLR.

Xiaobo Liang, Lijun Wu, Juntao Li, Yue Wang, Qi Meng, Tao Qin, Wei Chen, Min Zhang, and Tie-Yan Liu. 2021. R-drop: Regularized dropout for neural networks. In *Advances in Neural Information Processing Systems*, volume 34, pages 10890–10905. Curran Associates, Inc.

Jindřich Libovický and Alexander Fraser. 2021a. Findings of the WMT 2021 shared tasks in unsupervised MT and very low resource supervised MT. In *Proceedings of the Sixth Conference on Machine Translation*, pages 726–732, Online. Association for Computational Linguistics.

Jindřich Libovický and Alexander Fraser. 2021b. The LMU Munich systems for the WMT21 unsupervised and very low-resource translation task. In *Proceedings of the Sixth Conference on Machine Translation*, pages 989–994, Online. Association for Computational Linguistics.

Pierre Lison and Jörg Tiedemann. 2016. OpenSubtitles2016: Extracting large parallel corpora from movie and TV subtitles. In *Proceedings of the Tenth International Conference on Language Resources and Evaluation (LREC'16)*, pages 923–929, Portorož, Slovenia. European Language Resources Association (ELRA).

Yinhan Liu, Jiatao Gu, Naman Goyal, Xian Li, Sergey Edunov, Marjan Ghazvininejad, Mike Lewis, and Luke Zettlemoyer. 2020. Multilingual denoising pre-training for neural machine translation. *Transactions of the Association for Computational Linguistics*, 8:726–742.

Robert C. Moore and William Lewis. 2010. Intelligent selection of language model training data. In *Proceedings of the ACL 2010 Conference Short Papers*, pages 220–224, Uppsala, Sweden. Association for Computational Linguistics.

Kishore Papineni, Salim Roukos, Todd Ward, and Wei-Jing Zhu. 2002. Bleu: a method for automatic evaluation of machine translation. In *Proceedings of the 40th Annual Meeting of the Association for Computational Linguistics*, pages 311–318, Philadelphia, Pennsylvania, USA. Association for Computational Linguistics.

Matt Post. 2018. A call for clarity in reporting BLEU scores. In *Proceedings of the Third Conference on Machine Translation: Research Papers*, pages 186–191, Brussels, Belgium. Association for Computational Linguistics.

Ivan Provilkov, Dmitrii Emelianenko, and Elena Voita. 2020. BPE-dropout: Simple and effective subword regularization. In *Proceedings of the 58th Annual Meeting of the Association for Computational Linguistics*, pages 1882–1892, Online. Association for Computational Linguistics.

Rico Sennrich, Barry Haddow, and Alexandra Birch. 2016a. Improving neural machine translation models with monolingual data. In *Proceedings of the 54th Annual Meeting of the Association for Computational Linguistics (Volume 1: Long Papers)*, pages 86–96, Berlin, Germany. Association for Computational Linguistics.

Rico Sennrich, Barry Haddow, and Alexandra Birch. 2016b. Neural machine translation of rare words with subword units. In *Proceedings of the 54th Annual Meeting of the Association for Computational Linguistics (Volume 1: Long Papers)*, pages 1715–1725, Berlin, Germany. Association for Computational Linguistics.

Kaitao Song, Xu Tan, Tao Qin, Jianfeng Lu, and Tie-Yan Liu. 2019. MASS: masked sequence to sequence pre-training for language generation. In *Proceedings of the International Conference on Machine Learning (ICML)*, pages 5926–5936.

Ralf Steinberger, Andreas Eisele, Szymon Klocek, Spyridon Pilos, and Patrick Schlüter. 2012. DGT-TM: A freely available translation memory in 22 languages. In *Proceedings of the Eighth International Conference on Language Resources and Evaluation (LREC'12)*, pages 454–459, Istanbul, Turkey. European Language Resources Association (ELRA).

Jörg Tiedemann. 2012. Parallel data, tools and interfaces in OPUS. In *Proceedings of the Eighth International Conference on Language Resources and Evaluation (LREC'12)*, pages 2214–2218, Istanbul, Turkey. European Language Resources Association (ELRA).

Jörg Tiedemann and Santhosh Thottingal. 2020. OPUS-MT – building open translation services for the world. In *Proceedings of the 22nd Annual Conference of the European Association for Machine Translation*, pages 479–480, Lisboa, Portugal. European Association for Machine Translation.

Ashish Vaswani, Noam Shazeer, Niki Parmar, Jakob Uszkoreit, Llion Jones, Aidan N Gomez, Łukasz Kaiser, and Illia Polosukhin. 2017. Attention is all you need. In *Advances in Neural Information Processing Systems*, volume 30. Curran Associates, Inc.

Daimeng Wei, Zongyao Li, Zhanglin Wu, Zhengzhe Yu, Xiaoyu Chen, Hengchao Shang, Jiaxin Guo, Minghan Wang, Lizhi Lei, Min Zhang, Hao Yang, and Ying Qin. 2021. HW-TSC's participation in the WMT 2021 news translation shared task. In *Proceedings of the Sixth Conference on Machine Translation*, pages 225–231, Online. Association for Computational Linguistics.

Marion Weller-Di Marco and Alexander Fraser. 2022. Findings of the WMT 2022 shared tasks in unsupervised MT and very low resource supervised MT. In *Proceedings of the Seventh Conference on Machine Translation*, pages 801–805, Abu Dhabi. Association for Computational Linguistics.

Meng Zhang, Minghao Wu, Pengfei Li, Liangyou Li, and Qun Liu. 2021. NoahNMT at WMT 2021: Dual transfer for very low resource supervised machine translation. In *Proceedings of the Sixth Conference on Machine Translation*, pages 1009–1013, Online. Association for Computational Linguistics.

Tianyi Zhang, Varsha Kishore, Felix Wu, Kilian Q. Weinberger, and Yoav Artzi. 2019. BERTScore: evaluating text generation with bert. In *Proceedings of the International Conference on Learning Representations (ICLR 2020)*. arXiv:1904.09675.

Barret Zoph, Deniz Yuret, Jonathan May, and Kevin Knight. 2016. Transfer learning for low-resource neural machine translation. In *Proceedings of the 2016 Conference on Empirical Methods in Natural Language Processing*, pages 1568–1575, Austin, Texas. Association for Computational Linguistics.

Language-Family Adapters for Low-Resource Multilingual Neural Machine Translation

Alexandra Chronopoulou[△] **Dario Stojanovski**[†▽] **Alexander Fraser**[△]
[△]Center for Information and Language Processing, LMU Munich, Germany
[△]Munich Center for Machine Learning, Germany
[▽]Microsoft, Belgrade, Serbia
achron@cis.lmu.de
dstojanovski@microsoft.com, fraser@cis.lmu.de

Abstract

Large multilingual models trained with self-supervision achieve state-of-the-art results in a wide range of natural language processing tasks. Self-supervised pretrained models are often fine-tuned on parallel data from one or multiple language pairs for machine translation. Multilingual fine-tuning improves performance on low-resource languages but requires modifying the entire model and can be prohibitively expensive. Training a new adapter on each language pair or training a single adapter on all language pairs without updating the pretrained model has been proposed as a parameter-efficient alternative. However, the former does not permit any sharing between languages, while the latter shares parameters for all languages and is susceptible to negative interference. In this paper, we propose training *language-family adapters* on top of mBART-50 to facilitate cross-lingual transfer. Our approach outperforms related baselines, yielding higher translation scores on average when translating from English to 17 different low-resource languages. We also show that language-family adapters provide an effective method to translate to languages unseen during pretraining.

1 Introduction

Recent work in multilingual natural language processing (NLP) has created models that reach competitive performance, while incorporating many languages into a single architecture (Devlin et al., 2019; Conneau et al., 2020). Because of its ability to share cross-lingual representations, which largely benefits lower-resource languages, multilingual neural machine translation (NMT) is an attractive research field (Firat et al., 2016; Zoph et al., 2016; Johnson et al., 2017; Ha et al., 2016; Zhang et al., 2020; Fan et al., 2021). Multilingual models are also appealing because they are more efficient in terms of the number of model parameters, enabling simple deployment (Arivazhagan et al., 2019; Aharoni et al., 2019). Massively multilingual pretrained models can be used for multilingual NMT, if they are fine-tuned in a *many-to-one* (to map any of the source languages into a target language, which is usually English) or *one-to-many* (to translate a single source language into multiple target languages) fashion (Aharoni et al., 2019; Tang et al., 2020). Training a *many-to-many* (multiple source to multiple target languages) NMT model (Fan et al., 2021) has also been proposed.

Multilingual pretrained models generally permit improving translation on low-resource language pairs. Specializing the model to a specific language pair further boosts performance, but is computationally expensive. For example, mBART-50 (Tang et al., 2020), a model pretrained on monolingual data of 50 languages using denoising autoencoding with the BART objective (Lewis et al., 2020) still has to be fully fine-tuned for NMT.

To avoid fine-tuning large models, previous work has focused on efficiently building multilingual NMT models. Adapters (Rebuffi et al., 2017; Houlsby et al., 2019), which are lightweight feedforward layers added in each Transformer (Vaswani et al., 2017) layer, have been proposed as a parameter-efficient fine-tuning method. In machine translation, training a different adapter on each language pair on top of a frozen pretrained multilingual NMT model, has shown to improve results for high-resource languages (Bapna and Firat, 2019). Low-resource languages do not benefit from this approach though, as adapters are trained with limited data. In a similar vein, Cooper Stickland et al. (2021) fine-tune a pretrained model for multilingual NMT using a single set of adapters, trained on all languages. Their approach manages to narrow the gap but still does not perform on par with multilingual fine-tuning.

Many-to-one and one-to-many NMT force languages into a joint space (in the encoder or decoder

†Work done prior to joining Microsoft

Proceedings of the The Sixth Workshop on Technologies for Machine Translation of Low-Resource Languages (LoResMT 2023), pages 59–72
May 6, 2023

side) and neglect diversity. One-to-many NMT faces the difficulty of learning a conditional language model and decoding into multiple languages (Arivazhagan et al., 2019; Tang et al., 2020). To better model target languages, recent approaches propose exploiting both the unique and the shared features (Wang et al., 2018), reorganizing parameter-sharing (Sachan and Neubig, 2018), decoupling multilingual word encodings (Wang et al., 2019a), training NMT models from scratch after creating groups of languages (Tan et al., 2019), or inserting language-specific layers (Fan et al., 2021).

In this work, we propose using *language-family* adapters that enable efficient low-resource multilingual NMT. We train adapters for NMT on top of mBART-50 (Tang et al., 2020). The adapters are trained using bi-text from each language family, while the pretrained model is not updated. Groups of languages are formed based on linguistic knowledge bases. Our approach improves positive cross-lingual transfer, compared to *language-pair adapters* (Bapna and Firat, 2019), which do not leverage cross-lingual information between languages, and *language-agnostic adapters* (Cooper Stickland et al., 2021), which are trained on all languages and can suffer from negative interference (Wang et al., 2020). Our approach not only yields better translation scores in the majority of languages examined, but also requires less than 20% of trainable parameters compared to language-pair adapters, i.e., the most competitive baseline.

Our main contributions are:

1. A novel, effective approach for low-resource multilingual translation which trains adapters on top of mBART-50 for each language family. In the English-to-many setting which we examine, language-family adapters achieve a +1 BLEU improvement over language-pair adapters and +2.7 BLEU improvement over language-agnostic adapters on 16 low-resource language pairs from OPUS-100.

2. We propose inserting *embedding-layer adapters* into the Transformer to encode lexical information and conduct an ablation study to assess their utility.

3. We contrast grouping languages based on linguistic knowledge to grouping them based on the representations of a multilingual pretrained language model (PLM) with a Gaussian Mixture Model (GMM).

4. We analyze the effect of our approach when evaluating on languages that are new to mBART-50.

2 Background

Massively Multilingual Models. Multilingual masked language models have pushed the state-of-the-art on cross-lingual language understanding by training a single model for many languages (Devlin et al., 2019; Conneau and Lample, 2019; Conneau et al., 2020). Encoder-decoder Transformer (Vaswani et al., 2017) models that are pretrained using monolingual corpora from multiple languages, such as mBART (Liu et al., 2020), outperform strong baselines in medium- and low-resource NMT. mBART-50 (Tang et al., 2020) is an extension of mBART, pretrained in 50 languages and multilingually fine-tuned for NMT. However, while multilingual NMT models are known to outperform strong baselines and simplify model deployment, they are susceptible to negative interference/transfer (McCann et al., 2018; Arivazhagan et al., 2019; Wang et al., 2019b; Conneau et al., 2020) and catastrophic forgetting (Goodfellow et al., 2014) when the parameters are shared across a large number of languages. Negative transfer affects the translation quality of high-resource (Conneau et al., 2020), but also low-resource languages (Wang et al., 2020). As a remedy, providing extra capacity to a multilingual model using language-specific modules has been proposed (Sachan and Neubig, 2018; Wang et al., 2019a; Fan et al., 2021; Pfeiffer et al., 2022). We take a step forward in this direction and train *language-family adapters* on top of a pretrained model. Our approach introduces modular components which leverage the similarities of languages and can better decode into multiple directions, improving results compared to baselines.

Adapters for NMT. Swietojanski and Renals (2014) and Vilar (2018) initially suggested learning additional weights that rescale the hidden units for domain adaptation. Adapter layers (Rebuffi et al., 2017; Houlsby et al., 2019) are small modules that are typically added to a pretrained Transformer and are fine-tuned on a downstream task, while the pretrained model is frozen. Bapna and Firat (2019) add *language-pair* adapters to a pretrained multilingual NMT model (one set for *each* language pair), to recover performance for high-resource language pairs. Cooper Stickland et al. (2021) start from an unsupervised pretrained model and train *language-agnostic* adapters (one set for *all* language pairs) for multilingual NMT. Philip et al. (2020) train *monolingual* adapters for zero-shot translation, while Üstün et al. (2021) propose *denoising adapters*, i.e., adapters trained using monolingual data, for unsupervised multilingual NMT. Baziotis et al. (2022) inject language-specific parameters in MNMT using adapters, by generating them from a hyper-network, while Lai et al. (2022) adapt a model for both a new domain and a new language pair at the same time by combining domain and language representations using meta-learning with adapters.

We identify some challenges in previous works (Bapna and Firat, 2019; Cooper Stickland et al., 2021). Scaling language-agnostic adapters to a large number of languages is problematic, as when they are updated with data from multiple languages, negative transfer occurs. In contrast, language-pair adapters do not face this problem, but at the same time do not allow any sharing between languages, therefore provide poor translation to low-resource language pairs. Language-family adapters arguably strike a balance, providing a trade-off between the two approaches, and our experiments show that they lead to higher translation quality.

Language Families. Extensive work on cross-lingual transfer has demonstrated that jointly training a model using similar languages can improve low-resource results in several NLP tasks, such as part-of-speech or morphological tagging (Täckström et al., 2013; Straka et al., 2019), entity linking (Tsai and Roth, 2016; Rijhwani et al., 2019), and machine translation (Zoph et al., 2016; Johnson et al., 2017; Neubig and Hu, 2018; Oncevay et al., 2020). Linguistic knowledge bases (Littell et al., 2017; Dryer and Haspelmath, 2013) study language variation and can provide insights to phenomena such as negative interference. Languages can be organized together using linguistic information, forming language families. Tan et al. (2019) and Kong et al. (2021) leverage families for multilingual NMT, the former by training language-family NMT models from scratch, the latter by training a separate shallow decoder for each family. Instead, our approach keeps a pretrained model frozen and only trains language-family adapters, which is parameter-efficient. Compared to fine-tuning the entire model (ML-FT), our approach requires less than 12.5% of the trainable parameters, as is shown in Table 3.

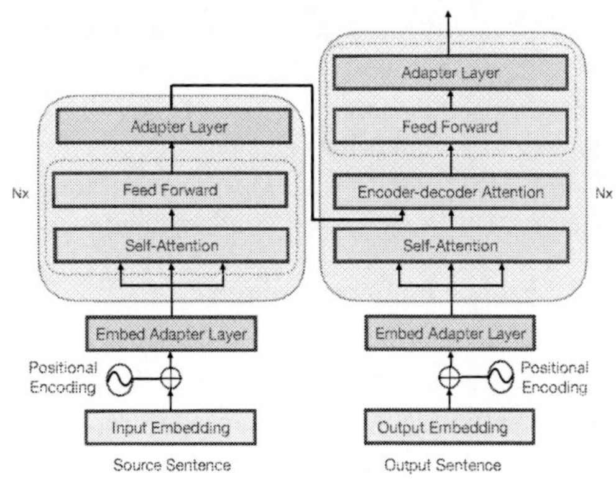

Figure 1: Proposed adapter architecture inside a Transformer model. Adapter layers, shown in green, are trained for NMT. Figure best viewed in color.

3 Language-Family Adapters for Low-Resource NMT

Fine-tuning a pretrained model for multilingual NMT provides a competitive performance, yet is computationally expensive, as all layers of the model need to be updated. A parameter-efficient alternative is to fine-tune a pretrained multilingual model for NMT with data from all languages of interest using adapters while keeping the pretrained model unchanged. However, as multiple language representations are encoded in the same parameters, capacity issues arise. Languages are also grouped together, even though they might be different in terms of geographic location, script, syntax, typology, etc. As a result, linguistic diversity is not modeled adequately and translation quality degrades.

We address the limitations of previous methods by proposing language-family adapters for low-resource multilingual NMT. An illustration of our approach is depicted in Figure 1. We exploit linguistic knowledge to selectively share parameters between related languages and avoid negative interference. Our approach is to train adapters using language pairs of a linguistic family on top of a pretrained model, which is not updated.

3.1 Adapter Architecture

Adapters are usually added to each Transformer layer. An adapter uses as input the output of the previous layer. Formally: Let z_i be the output of the i-th layer, of dimension h. We apply a layer-normalization (Ba et al., 2016), followed by a down-projection $D \in R^{h \times d}$, a ReLU activation and an up-projection $U \in R^{d \times h}$, where d is the bottleneck dimension and the only tunable hyperparameter. The up-projection is combined with a residual connection (He et al., 2016) with z_i according to the following equation: $Adapter_i(z_i) = U\,\mathrm{ReLU}(D\,\mathrm{LN}(z_i)) + z_i$. This follows Bapna and Firat (2019). Adapters are randomly initialized.

3.2 Embedding-layer Adapter

Because we keep the token embeddings of mBART-50 frozen, adding flexibility to the model to encode lexical information of the languages of interest is crucial, especially for unseen languages (not part of its pretraining corpus). Lexical cross-lingual information could be encoded by learning new embeddings for the unseen languages (Artetxe et al., 2020) but this would be computationally expensive. We instead add an adapter after the *embedding* layer, in both the encoder and the decoder, which receives as input the lexical representation of each sequence and aims to capture token-level cross-lingual transformations.

Our approach draws inspiration from Pfeiffer et al. (2020) and simplifies the invertible adapters structure. We use the large vocabulary of mBART-50 to extend the model to unseen languages. We note that adding scripts that do not exist in the vocabulary of mBART-50 is not possible with our approach. We point out that Chronopoulou et al. (2020); Pfeiffer et al. (2021); Vernikos and Popescu-Belis (2021) have proposed approaches to permit fine-tuning to unseen languages/scripts when using PLMs and we leave further exploration to future work.

3.3 Model Architecture

To train a model for multilingual NMT, we leverage mBART-50, a sequence-to-sequence generative model pretrained on monolingual data from 50 languages using a denoising auto-encoding objective. The model has essentially been trained by trying to predict the original text X, given $g(X)$, where g is a noising function that corrupts text.

We want to fine-tune this model on a variety of language pairs, by leveraging similarities between languages. Our model aims to provide a parameter-efficient alternative to traditional fine-tuning of the entire pretrained model. We note that the pretrained mBART-50 model cannot be used as is for MT, as it has never been trained on the task.

To this end, we insert adapters after each *feed-forward* layer both in the encoder and in the decoder and we also add embedding-layer adapters.

Language (code)	**Family**	**Train Set**	
		TED	**OPUS-100**
⋆Bulgarian (bg)	BS	174k	1M
Persian (fa)	I	151k	1M
⋆Serbian (sr)	BS	137k	1M
Croatian (hr)	BS	122k	1M
Ukrainian (uk)	BS	108k	1M
Indonesian (id)	A	87k	1M
⋆Slovak (sk)	BS	61k	1M
Macedonian (mk)	BS	25k	1M
Slovenian (sl)	BS	20k	1M
Hindi (hi)	I	19k	534k
Marathi (mr)	I	10k	27k
⋆Kurdish (ku)	I	10k	45k
⋆Bosnian (bs)	BS	6k	1M
⋆Malay (ms)	A	5k	1M
Bengali (bn)	I	5k	1M
⋆Belarusian (be)	BS	5k	67k
⋆Filipino (fil)	A	3k	-

Table 1: Languages used in the experiments. ⋆ indicates languages that are *unseen* from mBART-50, i.e., they do not belong to the pretraining corpus. *BS* stands for Balto-Slavic, *I* for Indo-Iranian, *A* for Austronesian.

We freeze the pretrained encoder-decoder Transformer and fine-tune *only* the adapters on NMT. We leverage the knowledge of the pretrained model, but encode additional cross-lingual information on each language family using adapters. We fine-tune a new set of adapters multilingually on each *language family* and evaluate the performance on and low-resource language pairs.

4 Experimental Setup

Data. We initially fine-tune the model on TED talks (Qi et al., 2018), using data from 17 languages paired to English. We then scale to a larger parallel dataset, using OPUS-100 (Zhang et al., 2020) for the same languages paired to English (with the only exception being English-Filipino, which does not appear in OPUS-100). For the TED experiments, we choose 17 languages, 9 of which were present during pretraining, while 8 are new to mBART-50. For OPUS-100, we use the same 16 languages (without Filipino), 9 of which were present during pretraining and 7 are new. In both sets of experiments, the languages belong to 3 language families, namely Balto-Slavic, Austronesian and Indo-Iranian. Balto-Slavic and Indo-Iranian are actually distinct branches of the same language family (Indo-European). The parallel data details are reported in Table 1.

Baselines. We compare the proposed language-family adapters with **1)** *language-agnostic*

(LANG-AGNOSTIC) and **2)** *language-pair adapters* (LANG-PAIR). While the adapters are trained using parallel data, mBART-50 (pretrained on monolingual data) is not updated. Moreover, we compare our approach to multilingual fine-tuning (ML-FT), although it requires fine-tuning the entire model and is thus not directly comparable to the parameter-efficient approaches we study. We show this result in the Appendix.

The first baseline, LANG-AGNOSTIC adapters, fine-tunes a set of adapters using data from all languages (similar to Cooper Stickland et al., 2021). The second baseline, LANG-PAIR adapters, follows Bapna and Firat (2019): a new set of adapters is trained for each language pair, so no parameters are shared between different language pairs.

Training details. We start from the mBART-50 checkpoint.* We extend its embedding layer with randomly initialized vectors to account for the new languages. We reuse the 250k sentencepiece (Kudo and Richardson, 2018) model of mBART-50. We use the fairseq (Ott et al., 2019) library for all experiments. We select the final models using validation perplexity. If the model is trained on multiple languages (using mixed mini-batches), we use the overall perplexity. We use beam search with size 5 for decoding and evaluate BLEU scores using SacreBLEU† for OPUS-100 and SacreBLEU without tokenization for TED (Post, 2018). We also compute COMET (Rei et al., 2020) scores using the *wmt-large-da-estimator-1719* pretrained model. Results are reported in the Appendix.

To train the models, we freeze mBART-50. We fine-tune the LANG-FAMILY, LANG-AGNOSTIC adapters in a multilingual, one-to-many setup, using English as the source language. LANG-PAIR adapters are fine-tuned for each language pair. All models have a bottleneck dimension of 512. We otherwise use the same hyperparameters as Tang et al. (2020) and report them in the Appendix.

5 Results and Discussion

5.1 Main results

Table 2 shows translation results for a subset of languages of OPUS-100 and TED in terms of BLEU using parallel data to fine-tune mBART-50 in the $en \rightarrow xx$ direction. We also report COMET scores in the Appendix.

Our approach (LANG-FAMILY) consistently improves results on the OPUS-100 dataset, with an average $+1$ BLEU performance boost across all languages compared to fine-tuning with LANG-PAIR adapters and $+2.7$ improvement compared to LANG-AGNOSTIC adapters. We believe that this shows that representations from similar languages are beneficial to a multilingual model in a low-resource setup. However, training a single adapter over all languages (LANG-AGNOSTIC) is detrimental in terms of translation quality. Moreover, LANG-PAIR trains a different adapter on each language pair and does not permit sharing cross-lingual information. As a result, it obtains worse results compared to our approach; it is also significantly more computationally expensive, requiring $5\times$ parameters of LANG-FAMILY adapters.

Our approach similarly outperforms both baselines on TED. It yields a $+1.5$ improvement compared to LANG-AGNOSTIC and $+0.4$ BLEU compared to LANG-PAIR. These results confirm our main finding, which is that selectively sharing parameters of related languages with adapters is useful for low-resource NMT.

5.2 Computational cost

We show in Table 3 the number of trainable parameters used for each approach. We note that our experiments were conducted using 8 NVIDIA-V100 GPUs. The mBART-50 model has 680M parameters. Our approach trains parameters that add up to just 11.9% of the full model. LANG-AGNOSTIC is the most efficient approach, requiring just 8.4% trainable parameters. However, there is a cost in terms of performance compared to our model. Finally, training LANG-PAIR adapters is relatively expensive (52.2% of the trainable parameters of mBART-50). All in all, our LANG-FAMILY approach provides a trade-off between performance and efficiency in terms of model parameters and is an effective method of adapting pretrained multilingual models to low-resource languages.

5.3 Embedding-layer adapter

Our approach keeps the encoder and decoder embeddings frozen during fine-tuning. Because of that, the lexical representations of the model are not updated to model the languages of interest. To overcome this issue, we introduce an adapter after the *encoder embedding layer*, as well as after the *decoder embedding layer*. We do not tie these

*https://dl.fbaipublicfiles.com/fairseq/models/mbart50/mbart50.pretrained.tar.gz

†Signature "BLEU+c.mixed+#.1+s.exp+tok.13a+v.1.5.1"

Model	Balto-Slavic									Austro-nesian			Indo-Iranian					
	bg*	sr*	hr	uk	sk*	mk	sl	bs*	be*	id	ms*	fil*	fa	hi	mr	ku*	bn	AVG
OPUS-100																		
Lang-pair	**27.8**	17.5	23.7	**17.7**	25.0	**35.0**	**24.1**	**21.0**	10.1	28.0	24.5	-	**10.5**	15.6	17.0	14.1	13.0	20.3
Lang-agnostic	21.6	19.7	21.4	13.8	24.1	28.9	19.6	19.5	11.3	28.6	21.8	-	8.1	16.9	17.8	12.8	11.2	18.6
Lang-family	25.4	**20.9**	23.7	15.1	**27.7**	31.9	22.6	20.3	**15.2**	**31.3**	**25.4**	-	9.8	**18.7**	**25.0**	**15.3**	12.9	**21.3**
TED																		
Lang-pair	**35.7**	21.1	30.5	21.1	**24.2**	27.0	21.4	**28.6**	**12.5**	**35.4**	**23.4**	**12.2**	14.0	14.1	10.0	**4.9**	9.0	20.3
Lang-agnostic	31.7	24.0	29.7	21.9	20.6	26.5	20.2	27.8	7.7	33.8	22.1	11.6	17.0	15.5	7.0	3.3	6.0	19.2
Lang-family	33.8	**25.1**	30.5	22.2	22.8	**28.0**	21.5	27.8	9.5	34.7	22.0	11.5	**17.5**	**19.8**	10.3	4.1	**11.6**	**20.7**

Table 2: Test set BLEU scores when translating out of English ($en \rightarrow xx$) on OPUS-100 and TED. LANG-PAIR stands for language-pair, LANG-AGNOSTIC for language-agnostic, and LANG-FAMILY for language-family adapters. Languages denoted with $\star$ are new to mBART-50. Results in bold are significantly different ($p < 0.01$) from the best adapter baseline.

	Parameters	Runtime	GPUs
LANG-AGNOSTIC	27M	35h	8
LANG-FAMILY	81M	78h	8
LANG-PAIR	432M	192h	8
ML-FT	680M	310h	8

Table 3: Parameters used by our approach and the baselines to train on OPUS-100. We note that the GPUs used are NVIDIA-V100. For completeness, we also include the parameters used for multilingual fine-tuning (ML-FT) of the pre-trained model.

adapter layers, since they only add up a small number of parameters (1M each, i.e., 0.1% of mBART-50 parameters).

As we can see in Table 4, we get consistent gains across almost all language pairs by adding these adapters, for both our model and the LANG-AGNOSTIC baseline. The former yields a +0.5 performance boost, while the latter a +0.7 improvement in terms of BLEU. While the gains are modest, they are consistent and come at a very small computational overhead. For some languages, such as Kurdish (which is an unseen language for mBART-50), results improve by +1.6 when using embedding-layer adapters. Since Kurdish is not part of mBART-50 pretraining corpus, encoding token-level representations is in this case more challenging and embedding-layer adapters allows the model to specialize in this language.

5.4 Automatic clustering of languages

Gaussian Mixture Model. For our main set of experiments, we used language families from WALS. However, it might be that not all languages within a language family share the same linguistic properties (Ahmad et al., 2019). Therefore, we wanted to explore a data-driven approach to induce similarities between languages. To this end, we group languages together using Gaussian Mixture Model (GMM) clustering of text representations obtained from a PLM (Aharoni and Goldberg, 2020). We used released code by the authors of the paper.[‡]

We use XLM-R (Conneau et al., 2020), a multilingual PLM and specifically the *xlmr-roberta-base* HuggingFace (Wolf et al., 2020) checkpoint. We encode 500 sequences of 512 tokens from each language (using OPUS-100) to create sentence representations, by performing average pooling of the last hidden state. We then use PCA projection of dimension 100 and fit the sentence representations to a GMM with 3 components (3 Gaussian distributions, i.e., clusters). As this is a soft assignment, every language belongs with some probability to one or more clusters. For simplicity, we map each language to just one cluster based on where the majority of its samples are assigned to.

Results. Table 5 shows an evaluation of our approach, where we select the language family based on linguistic similarities (*ling. family*, first row), GMM clustering (second row), and random sampling (third row).

The main observation is that training adapters using language groups computed by GMM clustering yields worse translation scores compared to language groups based on linguistic similarities (*ling. family*). We believe that this is the case because some languages were clustered together with linguistically distant languages (e.g., Belarusian is assigned to the same group as Persian, Hindi, Marathi, and Bengali according to GMM clustering). This might be because of a domain mismatch between the English-Belarusian parallel dataset and the datasets of the rest of the languages in the group. Based on our experiments, training adapters on lin-

[‡]`https://github.com/roeeaharoni/unsupervised-domain-clusters`

	BALTO-SLAVIC				AUSTRO-NESIAN		INDO-IRANIAN			
	bg	hr	mk	be	id	ms	fa	ku	bn	AVG-16
LANG-AGNOSTIC w/o emb adapter	21.3	21.5	28.3	10.5	28.7	21.5	7.6	12.4	10.9	18.1
LANG-AGNOSTIC with emb adapter (BASELINE)	21.6	21.4	28.9	11.3	28.6	21.8	8.1	12.8	11.2	**18.6**
LANG-FAMILY w/o emb adapter	24.3	22.6	31.2	13.4	31.4	25.2	9.0	13.7	12.2	20.6
LANG-FAMILY with emb adapter (OURS)	25.4	23.7	31.9	15.2	31.3	25.4	9.8	15.3	12.9	**21.3**

Table 4: Ablation of the proposed architecture for $en \rightarrow xx$ (BLEU scores) on OPUS-100. We present results only for a subset of languages per language family. Full results can be found in the Appendix.

	Language Groups			id	fa	ku	AVG
ling. family (ours)	<be, bg, sr, hr, uk, sk, mk, sl, bs>	<id, ms>	<ku, fa, hi, mr, bn>	31.3	9.8	15.3	21.3
GMM	<bg, sr, hr, uk, sk, mk, sl, bs>	<**ku**, id, ms>	<**be**, fa, hi, mr, bn>	29.7	9.2	14.3	19.4
random	<bg, hr, mk, bs, be, ms, hi, mr, ku>	<sl, id>	<sr, uk, sk, fa, bn>	27.8	7.0	15.0	18.4

Table 5: Evaluation of different methods to form language families for $en \rightarrow xx$ on OPUS-100. We present results only for a subset of languages and the overall average BLEU scores. Full results are shown in the Appendix.

guistic families provides better translation scores and should therefore be preferred, if these exist. As expected, randomly clustering languages together performs worse than all approaches, showing that taking into account similarities between languages is beneficial when training a multilingual model for low-resource NMT.

6 Analysis

6.1 Performance according to language family

To evaluate the contribution of grouping languages based on linguistic information, we present the BLEU scores of the LANG-FAMILY adapters compared to the baselines *per language family*. We show the results in Figure 2.

Compared to the LANG-AGNOSTIC baseline, LANG-FAMILY adapters perform better in all language families. On Balto-Slavic, our approach is on par with LANG-PAIR adapters (<0.5 BLEU difference). On both Austronesian and Indo-Iranian, our approach largely outperforms (more than +2 BLEU) both baselines. This is arguably the case because LANG-AGNOSTIC adapters, trained using parallel data from all languages, group dissimilar languages together and do not take into account language variation. We instead train adapters on languages with common linguistic properties and obtain consistently improved translations.

LANG-AGNOSTIC adapters perform worse than LANG-PAIR adapters on all language families. This is mostly evident for Balto-Slavic. We believe that this happens because Balto-Slavic languages are more similar to English compared to Austronesian or Indo-Iranian. This means that translating between Balto-Slavic and English is relatively easier, especially since mBART-50 has been trained with a large Indo-European bias and it already encodes cross-lingual information for most of the languages in this group. As a result, LANG-PAIR adapters create in this case a very competitive baseline.

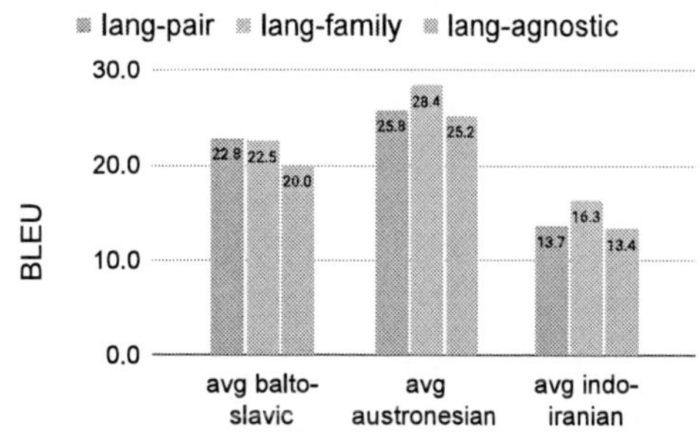

Figure 2: Grouping based on language family using OPUS-100. Translation scores (measured with BLEU) are shown for the our method (LANG-FAMILY), as well as the LANG-PAIR and LANG-AGNOSTIC baselines.

6.2 Performance on seen *vs* unseen languages

We also evaluate the performance of language-family adapters and the baselines on languages that are not included in the mBART-50 pretraining data (*unseen*), compared to languages that belong to its pretraining corpus (*seen*). We present the results in Figure 3.

On unseen languages, LANG-FAMILY adapters improve the translation quality compared to the LANG-PAIR adapter baseline. As the pretrained model has no knowledge of these languages, LANG-FAMILY adapters provide useful cross-

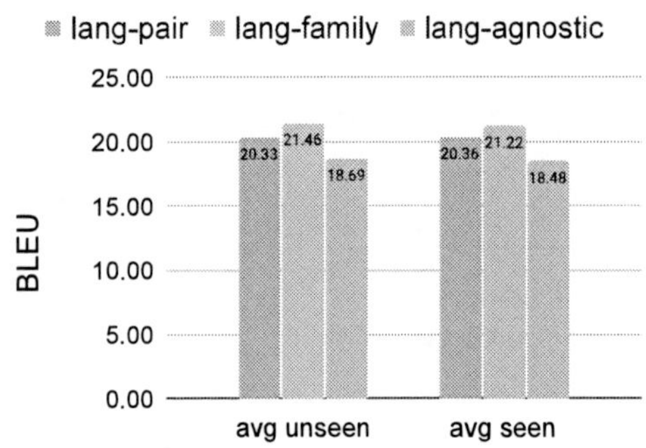

Figure 3: Grouping based on "seen" (existing in the pretraining corpus), or "unseen" language using OPUS-100. BLEU scores are shown for our method (LANG-FAMILY) and the baselines.

lingual signal. This makes our approach suitable for extending an already trained multilingual model to new languages in a scalable way. The improvement is, as expected, smaller for the seen languages.

LANG-AGNOSTIC adapters perform significantly worse than both our approach and the LANG-PAIR baseline. This might be the case because of negative transfer between unrelated languages, that are clustered and trained together using the LANG-AGNOSTIC model. This issue is prevalent for both seen and unseen languages.

7 Conclusion

We presented a novel approach for fine-tuning a pretrained multilingual model for NMT using language-family adapters. Our approach can be used for low-resource multilingual NMT, combining the modularity of adapters with effective cross-lingual transfer between related languages. We showed that language-family adapters perform better than both language-agnostic and language-pair adapters, while being computationally efficient. Finally, for languages new to mBART-50, we showed that our approach provides an effective way of leveraging shared cross-lingual information between similar languages, considerably improving translations compared to the baselines.

In the future, a more elaborate approach to encode lexical-level representations could further boost the performance of language-family adapters. We also hypothesize that the effectiveness of our model could be leveraged for other cross-lingual tasks, such as natural language inference, document classification and question-answering.

Limitations

Our work uses a large seq2seq multilingual pretrained model, mBART-50. This model has been pretrained on large chunks of monolingual data from Common Crawl (Wenzek et al., 2020), but we do not have evaluations of generated text (e.g., on fluency, factuality, or other common metrics used to evaluate generated language). Therefore, this pretrained model can encode biases that could harm marginalized populations (Bender et al., 2021) and could also be used to translate harmful text.

Acknowledgements

This project has received funding from the European Research Council under the European Union's Horizon 2020 research and innovation program (grant agreement #640550) and from DFG (grant FR 2829/4-1).

References

Roee Aharoni and Yoav Goldberg. 2020. Unsupervised domain clusters in pretrained language models. In *Proceedings of the 58th Annual Meeting of the Association for Computational Linguistics*, pages 7747–7763, Online. Association for Computational Linguistics.

Roee Aharoni, Melvin Johnson, and Orhan Firat. 2019. Massively multilingual neural machine translation. In *Proceedings of the 2019 Conference of the North American Chapter of the Association for Computational Linguistics: Human Language Technologies, Volume 1 (Long and Short Papers)*, pages 3874–3884, Minneapolis, Minnesota. Association for Computational Linguistics.

Wasi Ahmad, Zhisong Zhang, Xuezhe Ma, Eduard Hovy, Kai-Wei Chang, and Nanyun Peng. 2019. On difficulties of cross-lingual transfer with order differences: A case study on dependency parsing. In *Proceedings of the 2019 Conference of the North American Chapter of the Association for Computational Linguistics: Human Language Technologies, Volume 1 (Long and Short Papers)*, pages 2440–2452, Minneapolis, Minnesota. Association for Computational Linguistics.

Naveen Arivazhagan, Ankur Bapna, Orhan Firat, Dmitry Lepikhin, Melvin Johnson, Maxim Krikun, Mia Xu Chen, Yuan Cao, George Foster, Colin Cherry, Wolfgang Macherey, Zhifeng Chen, and Yonghui Wu. 2019. Massively multilingual neural machine translation in the wild: Findings and challenges.

Mikel Artetxe, Sebastian Ruder, and Dani Yogatama. 2020. On the cross-lingual transferability of monolingual representations. In *Proceedings of the 58th Annual Meeting of the Association for Computational Linguistics*, pages 4623–4637, Online. Association for Computational Linguistics.

Jimmy Lei Ba, Jamie Ryan Kiros, and Geoffrey E. Hinton. 2016. Layer normalization.

Ankur Bapna and Orhan Firat. 2019. Simple, scalable adaptation for neural machine translation. In *Proceedings of the 2019 Conference on Empirical Methods in Natural Language Processing and the 9th International Joint Conference on Natural Language Processing (EMNLP-IJCNLP)*, pages 1538–1548, Hong Kong, China. Association for Computational Linguistics.

Christos Baziotis, Mikel Artetxe, James Cross, and Shruti Bhosale. 2022. Multilingual machine translation with hyper-adapters. In *Proceedings of the Conference on Empirical Methods in Natural Language Processing (EMNLP)*.

Emily M. Bender, Timnit Gebru, Angelina McMillan-Major, and Shmargaret Shmitchell. 2021. On the dangers of stochastic parrots: Can language models be too big? In *Proceedings of the 2021 ACM Conference on Fairness, Accountability, and Transparency*, FAccT '21, page 610–623, New York, NY, USA. Association for Computing Machinery.

Alexandra Chronopoulou, Dario Stojanovski, and Alexander Fraser. 2020. Reusing a Pretrained Language Model on Languages with Limited Corpora for Unsupervised NMT. In *Proceedings of the 2020 Conference on Empirical Methods in Natural Language Processing (EMNLP)*, pages 2703–2711, Online. Association for Computational Linguistics.

Alexis Conneau, Kartikay Khandelwal, Naman Goyal, Vishrav Chaudhary, Guillaume Wenzek, Francisco Guzmán, Edouard Grave, Myle Ott, Luke Zettlemoyer, and Veselin Stoyanov. 2020. Unsupervised cross-lingual representation learning at scale. In *Proceedings of the 58th Annual Meeting of the Association for Computational Linguistics*, pages 8440–8451, Online. Association for Computational Linguistics.

Alexis Conneau and Guillaume Lample. 2019. Cross-lingual language model pretraining. In *Advances in Neural Information Processing Systems*.

Asa Cooper Stickland, Xian Li, and Marjan Ghazvininejad. 2021. Recipes for adapting pre-trained monolingual and multilingual models to machine translation. In *Proceedings of the 16th Conference of the European Chapter of the Association for Computational Linguistics: Main Volume*, pages 3440–3453, Online. Association for Computational Linguistics.

Jacob Devlin, Ming-Wei Chang, Kenton Lee, and Kristina Toutanova. 2019. BERT: Pre-training of deep bidirectional transformers for language understanding. In *Proceedings of the 2019 Conference of the North American Chapter of the Association for Computational Linguistics: Human Language Technologies, Volume 1 (Long and Short Papers)*, pages 4171–4186, Minneapolis, Minnesota. Association for Computational Linguistics.

Matthew S. Dryer and Martin Haspelmath, editors. 2013. *WALS Online*. Max Planck Institute for Evolutionary Anthropology.

Angela Fan, Shruti Bhosale, Holger Schwenk, Zhiyi Ma, Ahmed El-Kishky, Siddharth Goyal, Mandeep Baines, Onur Celebi, Guillaume Wenzek, Vishrav Chaudhary, Naman Goyal, Tom Birch, Vitaliy Liptchinsky, Sergey Edunov, Edouard Grave, Michael Auli, and Armand Joulin. 2021. Beyond english-centric multilingual machine translation. *J. Mach. Learn. Res.*, 22(1).

Orhan Firat, Kyunghyun Cho, and Yoshua Bengio. 2016. Multi-way, multilingual neural machine translation with a shared attention mechanism. In *Proceedings of the 2016 Conference of the North American Chapter of the Association for Computational Linguistics: Human Language Technologies*, pages 866–875, San Diego, California. Association for Computational Linguistics.

Ian J. Goodfellow, Mehdi Mirza, Da Xiao, Aaron Courville, and Yoshua Bengio. 2014. An empirical investigation of catastrophic forgeting in gradient based neural networks. In *Proceedings of International Conference on Learning Representations (ICLR)*.

Thanh-Le Ha, Jan Niehues, and Alexander H. Waibel. 2016. Toward multilingual neural machine translation with universal encoder and decoder. *CoRR*.

Kaiming He, Xiangyu Zhang, Shaoqing Ren, and Jian Sun. 2016. Deep residual learning for image recognition. In *2016 IEEE Conference on Computer Vision and Pattern Recognition (CVPR)*, pages 770–778.

Neil Houlsby, Andrei Giurgiu, Stanislaw Jastrzebski, Bruna Morrone, Quentin De Laroussilhe, Andrea Gesmundo, Mona Attariyan, and Sylvain Gelly. 2019. Parameter-efficient transfer learning for NLP. In *Proceedings of the International Conference on Machine Learning*, Proceedings of Machine Learning Research, pages 2790–2799.

Melvin Johnson, Mike Schuster, Quoc V. Le, Maxim Krikun, Yonghui Wu, Zhifeng Chen, Nikhil Thorat, Fernanda Viégas, Martin Wattenberg, Greg Corrado, Macduff Hughes, and Jeffrey Dean. 2017. Google's multilingual neural machine translation system: Enabling zero-shot translation. *Transactions of the Association for Computational Linguistics*, 5:339–351.

Xiang Kong, Adithya Renduchintala, James Cross, Yuqing Tang, Jiatao Gu, and Xian Li. 2021. Multilingual neural machine translation with deep encoder and multiple shallow decoders. In *Proceedings of the 16th Conference of the European Chapter of the Association for Computational Linguistics: Main Volume*, pages 1613–1624, Online. Association for Computational Linguistics.

Taku Kudo and John Richardson. 2018. SentencePiece: A simple and language independent subword tokenizer and detokenizer for neural text processing. In *Proceedings of the 2018 Conference on Empirical Methods in Natural Language Processing: System Demonstrations*, pages 66–71, Brussels, Belgium. Association for Computational Linguistics.

Wen Lai, Alexandra Chronopoulou, and Alexander Fraser. 2022. m^4 adapter: Multilingual multi-domain adaptation for machine translation with a meta-adapter. In *Findings of the Association for Computational Linguistics: EMNLP 2022*, pages 4282–4296, Abu Dhabi, United Arab Emirates. Association for Computational Linguistics.

Mike Lewis, Yinhan Liu, Naman Goyal, Marjan Ghazvininejad, Abdelrahman Mohamed, Omer Levy, Veselin Stoyanov, and Luke Zettlemoyer. 2020. BART: Denoising sequence-to-sequence pre-training for natural language generation, translation, and comprehension. In *Proceedings of the 58th Annual Meeting of the Association for Computational Linguistics*, pages 7871–7880, Online. Association for Computational Linguistics.

Patrick Littell, David R. Mortensen, Ke Lin, Katherine Kairis, Carlisle Turner, and Lori Levin. 2017. URIEL and lang2vec: Representing languages as typological, geographical, and phylogenetic vectors. In *Proceedings of the 15th Conference of the European Chapter of the Association for Computational Linguistics: Volume 2, Short Papers*, pages 8–14, Valencia, Spain. Association for Computational Linguistics.

Yinhan Liu, Jiatao Gu, Naman Goyal, Xian Li, Sergey Edunov, Marjan Ghazvininejad, Mike Lewis, and Luke Zettlemoyer. 2020. Multilingual Denoising Pre-training for Neural Machine Translation. *Transactions of the Association for Computational Linguistics*, 8:726–742.

Bryan McCann, Nitish Shirish Keskar, Caiming Xiong, and Richard Socher. 2018. The natural language decathlon: Multitask learning as question answering. *CoRR*.

Graham Neubig and Junjie Hu. 2018. Rapid adaptation of neural machine translation to new languages. In *Proceedings of the 2018 Conference on Empirical Methods in Natural Language Processing*, pages 875–880, Brussels, Belgium. Association for Computational Linguistics.

Arturo Oncevay, Barry Haddow, and Alexandra Birch. 2020. Bridging linguistic typology and multilingual machine translation with multi-view language representations. In *Proceedings of the 2020 Conference on Empirical Methods in Natural Language Processing (EMNLP)*, pages 2391–2406, Online. Association for Computational Linguistics.

Myle Ott, Sergey Edunov, Alexei Baevski, Angela Fan, Sam Gross, Nathan Ng, David Grangier, and Michael Auli. 2019. fairseq: A fast, extensible toolkit for sequence modeling. In *Proceedings of the 2019 Conference of the North American Chapter of the Association for Computational Linguistics (Demonstrations)*, pages 48–53, Minneapolis, Minnesota. Association for Computational Linguistics.

Jonas Pfeiffer, Naman Goyal, Xi Lin, Xian Li, James Cross, Sebastian Riedel, and Mikel Artetxe. 2022. Lifting the curse of multilinguality by pre-training modular transformers. In *Proceedings of the 2022 Conference of the North American Chapter of the Association for Computational Linguistics: Human Language Technologies*, pages 3479–3495, Seattle, United States. Association for Computational Linguistics.

Jonas Pfeiffer, Ivan Vulić, Iryna Gurevych, and Sebastian Ruder. 2020. MAD-X: An Adapter-Based Framework for Multi-Task Cross-Lingual Transfer. In *Proceedings of the 2020 Conference on Empirical Methods in Natural Language Processing (EMNLP)*, pages 7654–7673, Online. Association for Computational Linguistics.

Jonas Pfeiffer, Ivan Vulić, Iryna Gurevych, and Sebastian Ruder. 2021. UNKs everywhere: Adapting multilingual language models to new scripts. In *Proceedings of the 2021 Conference on Empirical Methods in Natural Language Processing*, pages 10186–10203, Online and Punta Cana, Dominican Republic. Association for Computational Linguistics.

Jerin Philip, Alexandre Berard, Matthias Gallé, and Laurent Besacier. 2020. Monolingual adapters for zero-shot neural machine translation. In *Proceedings of the 2020 Conference on Empirical Methods in Natural Language Processing (EMNLP)*, pages 4465–4470, Online. Association for Computational Linguistics.

Matt Post. 2018. A call for clarity in reporting BLEU scores. In *Proceedings of the Third Conference on Machine Translation: Research Papers*, pages 186–191, Brussels, Belgium. Association for Computational Linguistics.

Ye Qi, Devendra Sachan, Matthieu Felix, Sarguna Padmanabhan, and Graham Neubig. 2018. When and why are pre-trained word embeddings useful for neural machine translation? In *Proceedings of the 2018 Conference of the North American Chapter of the Association for Computational Linguistics: Human Language Technologies, Volume 2 (Short Papers)*, pages 529–535, New Orleans, Louisiana. Association for Computational Linguistics.

Sylvestre-Alvise Rebuffi, Hakan Bilen, and Andrea Vedaldi. 2017. Learning multiple visual domains with residual adapters. In *Advances in Neural Information Processing Systems*.

Ricardo Rei, Craig Stewart, Ana C Farinha, and Alon Lavie. 2020. COMET: A neural framework for MT evaluation. In *Proceedings of the 2020 Conference on Empirical Methods in Natural Language Processing (EMNLP)*, pages 2685–2702, Online. Association for Computational Linguistics.

Nils Reimers and Iryna Gurevych. 2020. Making monolingual sentence embeddings multilingual using knowledge distillation. In *Proceedings of the Conference on Empirical Methods in Natural Language Processing (EMNLP)*, pages 4512–4525.

Shruti Rijhwani, Jiateng Xie, Graham Neubig, and Jaime Carbonell. 2019. Zero-shot neural transfer for cross-lingual entity linking. In *The AAAI Conference on Artificial Intelligence*.

Devendra Sachan and Graham Neubig. 2018. Parameter sharing methods for multilingual self-attentional translation models. In *Proceedings of the Third Conference on Machine Translation: Research Papers*, pages 261–271, Brussels, Belgium. Association for Computational Linguistics.

Milan Straka, Jana Straková, and Jan Hajic. 2019. UDPipe at SIGMORPHON 2019: Contextualized embeddings, regularization with morphological categories, corpora merging. In *Proceedings of the 16th Workshop on Computational Research in Phonetics, Phonology, and Morphology*, pages 95–103, Florence, Italy. Association for Computational Linguistics.

Pawel Swietojanski and Steve Renals. 2014. Learning hidden unit contributions for unsupervised speaker adaptation of neural network acoustic models. In *2014 IEEE Spoken Language Technology Workshop (SLT)*, pages 171–176.

Oscar Täckström, Dipanjan Das, Slav Petrov, Ryan McDonald, and Joakim Nivre. 2013. Token and type constraints for cross-lingual part-of-speech tagging. *Transactions of the Association for Computational Linguistics*, 1:1–12.

Xu Tan, Jiale Chen, Di He, Yingce Xia, Tao Qin, and Tie-Yan Liu. 2019. Multilingual neural machine translation with language clustering. In *Proceedings of the 2019 Conference on Empirical Methods in Natural Language Processing and the 9th International Joint Conference on Natural Language Processing (EMNLP-IJCNLP)*, pages 963–973, Hong Kong, China. Association for Computational Linguistics.

Y. Tang, C. Tran, Xian Li, Peng-Jen Chen, Naman Goyal, Vishrav Chaudhary, Jiatao Gu, and Angela Fan. 2020. Multilingual translation with extensible multilingual pretraining and finetuning. *ArXiv*, abs/2008.00401.

Chen-Tse Tsai and Dan Roth. 2016. Cross-lingual wikification using multilingual embeddings. In *Proceedings of the 2016 Conference of the North American Chapter of the Association for Computational Linguistics: Human Language Technologies*, pages 589–598, San Diego, California. Association for Computational Linguistics.

Ahmet Üstün, Alexandre Berard, Laurent Besacier, and Matthias Gallé. 2021. Multilingual unsupervised neural machine translation with denoising adapters. In *Proceedings of the Conference on Empirical Methods in Natural Language Processing*, pages 6650–6662.

Ashish Vaswani, Noam Shazeer, Niki Parmar, Jakob Uszkoreit, Llion Jones, Aidan N Gomez, Łukasz Kaiser, and Illia Polosukhin. 2017. Attention is all you need. In *Advances in Neural Information Processing Systems*.

Giorgos Vernikos and Andrei Popescu-Belis. 2021. Subword mapping and anchoring across languages. In *Findings of the Association for Computational Linguistics: EMNLP 2021*, pages 2633–2647, Punta Cana, Dominican Republic. Association for Computational Linguistics.

David Vilar. 2018. Learning hidden unit contribution for adapting neural machine translation models. In *Proceedings of the 2018 Conference of the North American Chapter of the Association for Computational Linguistics: Human Language Technologies, Volume 2 (Short Papers)*, pages 500–505, New Orleans, Louisiana. Association for Computational Linguistics.

Xinyi Wang, Hieu Pham, Philip Arthur, and Graham Neubig. 2019a. Multilingual neural machine translation with soft decoupled encoding. In *International Conference on Learning Representations*.

Yining Wang, Jiajun Zhang, Feifei Zhai, Jingfang Xu, and Chengqing Zong. 2018. Three strategies to improve one-to-many multilingual translation. In *Proceedings of the 2018 Conference on Empirical Methods in Natural Language Processing*, pages 2955–2960, Brussels, Belgium. Association for Computational Linguistics.

Zirui Wang, Zihang Dai, Barnabas Poczos, and Jaime Carbonell. 2019b. Characterizing and avoiding negative transfer. In *Proceedings of the IEEE/CVF Conference on Computer Vision and Pattern Recognition (CVPR)*.

Zirui Wang, Zachary C. Lipton, and Yulia Tsvetkov. 2020. On negative interference in multilingual models: Findings and a meta-learning treatment. In *Proceedings of the 2020 Conference on Empirical Methods in Natural Language Processing (EMNLP)*, pages 4438–4450, Online. Association for Computational Linguistics.

Guillaume Wenzek, Marie-Anne Lachaux, Alexis Conneau, Vishrav Chaudhary, Francisco Guzmán, Armand Joulin, and Edouard Grave. 2020. CCNet: Extracting high quality monolingual datasets from web crawl data. In *Proceedings of the 12th Language Resources and Evaluation Conference*, pages 4003–4012, Marseille, France. European Language Resources Association.

Thomas Wolf, Lysandre Debut, Victor Sanh, Julien Chaumond, Clement Delangue, Anthony Moi, Pierric Cistac, Tim Rault, Remi Louf, Morgan Funtowicz, Joe Davison, Sam Shleifer, Patrick von Platen, Clara Ma, Yacine Jernite, Julien Plu, Canwen Xu, Teven Le Scao, Sylvain Gugger, Mariama Drame, Quentin Lhoest, and Alexander Rush. 2020. Transformers: State-of-the-art natural language processing. In *Proceedings of the 2020 Conference on Empirical Methods in Natural Language Processing: System Demonstrations*, pages 38–45, Online. Association for Computational Linguistics.

Biao Zhang, Philip Williams, Ivan Titov, and Rico Sennrich. 2020. Improving massively multilingual neural machine translation and zero-shot translation. In *Proceedings of the 58th Annual Meeting of the Association for Computational Linguistics*, pages 1628–1639, Online. Association for Computational Linguistics.

Barret Zoph, Deniz Yuret, Jonathan May, and Kevin Knight. 2016. Transfer learning for low-resource neural machine translation. In *Proceedings of the 2016 Conference on Empirical Methods in Natural Language Processing*, pages 1568–1575, Austin, Texas. Association for Computational Linguistics.

A Appendix

A.1 Dataset statistics

First, we show the script and language family (according to linguistic information) of each language used in our set of experiments in Table 6. We also present in detail the statistics of all parallel data used in our set of experiments in Table 8. We note that the number of train, validation and test set presented refers to sentences.

The TED dataset can be downloaded from phontron.com/data/ted_talks.tar.gz while OPUS-100 can be downloaded from object.pouta.csc.fi/OPUS-100/v1.0/opus-100-corpus-v1.0.tar.gz.

A.2 Training details

We train each model for 130k updates with a batch size of 900 tokens per GPU for OPUS-100 and 1024 tokens per GPU for TED. We use 8 NVIDIA-V100 GPUs for OPUS-100 and 2 GPUs for TED (much smaller dataset). We evaluate models after 5k training steps. We use early stopping with a patience of 5. To balance high and low-resource language pairs, we use temperature-based sampling (Arivazhagan et al., 2019) with $T = 1.5$.

A.3 Evaluation of main results using 2 metrics

We evaluate the translations of our model (LANG-FAMILY adapters) and all the baselines trained on OPUS-100 using COMET (Rei et al., 2020). COMET leverages progress in cross-lingual language modeling, creating a multilingual machine translation evaluation model that takes into account both the source input and a reference translation in the target language. We rely on `wmt-large-da-estimator-1719`. COMET scores are not bounded between 0 and 1; higher scores signify better translations. Our results are summarized in Table 10. We see that COMET correlates with BLEU in our experiments.

Language (code)	Family	Script
⋆Bulgarian (bg)	Balto-Slavic	Cyrillic
Persian (fa)	Indo-Iranian	Arabic
⋆Serbian (sr)	Balto-Slavic	Cyrillic
Croatian (hr)	Balto-Slavic	Latin
Ukrainian (uk)	Balto-Slavic	Cyrillic
Indonesian (id)	Austronesian	Latin
⋆Slovak (sk)	Balto-Slavic	Latin
Macedonian (mk)	Balto-Slavic	Cyrillic
Slovenian (sl)	Balto-Slavic	Latin
Hindi (hi)	Indo-Iranian	Devanagari
Marathi (mr)	Indo-Iranian	Devanagari
⋆Kurdish (ku)	Indo-Iranian	Arabic
⋆Bosnian (bs)	Balto-Slavic	Cyrillic
⋆Malay (ms)	Austronesian	Latin
Bengali (bn)	Indo-Iranian	Bengali
⋆Belarusian (be)	Balto-Slavic	Cyrillic
⋆Filipino (fil)	Austronesian	Latin

Table 6: Languages that are used in the experiments. ⋆ indicates languages that are *unseen* from mBART-50, i.e., they do not belong to the pretraining corpus. Filipino is only used in the TED experiments.

Adapter size	Dropout	Lang-Family	Lang-Agnostic
128	0.1	16.8	10.1
128	0.3	16.4	9.5
256	0.1	19.0	14.9
256	0.3	18.6	14.0
512	0.1	20.7	19.2
512	0.3	19.9	18.5

Table 7: Hyperparameter tuning for dropout, adapter bottleneck size on TED. Average performance (on all language pairs using TED) per model. We chose the best-performing combination of dropout and bottleneck size for our experiments.

A.4 Hyperparameters

We tune the dropout and the adapter bottleneck size on TED. We use values 0.1, 0.3 for the dropout and 128, 256, 512 for the bottleneck size. We list the hyperparameters we used to train both our proposed model and the baselines in Table 9.

Language	Source	Train	Valid	Test	Source	Train	Valid	Test
Bulgarian (bg)	TED	174k	4082	5060	OPUS-100	1M	2k	2k
Persian (fa)	TED	151k	3930	4490	OPUS-100	1M	2k	2k
Serbian (sr)	TED	137k	3798	4634	OPUS-100	1M	2k	2k
Croatian (hr)	TED	122k	3333	4881	OPUS-100	1M	2k	2k
Ukrainian (uk)	TED	108k	3060	3751	OPUS-100	1M	2k	2k
Indonesian (id)	TED	87k	2677	3179	OPUS-100	1M	2k	2k
Slovak (sk)	TED	61k	2271	2445	OPUS-100	1M	2k	2k
Macedonian (mk)	TED	25k	640	438	OPUS-100	1M	2k	2k
Slovenian (sl)	TED	20k	1068	1251	OPUS-100	1M	2k	2k
Hindi (hi)	TED	19k	854	1243	OPUS-100	534k	2k	2k
Marathi (mr)	TED	10k	767	1090	OPUS-100	27k	2k	2k
Kurdish (ku)	TED	10k	265	766	OPUS-100	45k	2k	2k
Bosnian (bs)	TED	6k	474	463	OPUS-100	1M	2k	2k
Malay (ms)	TED	5k	539	260	OPUS-100	1M	2k	2k
Bengali (bn)	TED	5k	896	216	OPUS-100	1M	2k	2k
Belarusian (be)	TED	5k	248	664	OPUS-100	67k	2k	2k
Filipino (fil)	TED2020	3k	338	338	OPUS-100	-	-	-

Table 8: Dataset details for TED (Qi et al., 2018; Reimers and Gurevych, 2020) and OPUS-100 (Zhang et al., 2020).

Hyperparameter	Value
Checkpoint	mbart50.pretrained
Architecture	mbart_large
Optimizer	Adam
β_1, β_2	0.9, 0.98
Weight decay	0.0
Label smoothing	0.2
Dropout	0.1
Attention dropout	0.1
Batch size	1024 tokens
Update frequency	2
Warmup updates	4k
Total number of updates	130k
Max learning rate	1e-04
Temperature sampling	5
Adapter dim.	512

Table 9: Fairseq hyperparameters used for our set of experiments.

A.5 Embedding-layer results

We report in Table 11 the results of the ablation study concerning the use of *embedding-layer* adapters on all languages.

A.6 Results using GMM, random clustering and language families

Full results of Table 5 can be seen in Table 12.

Lang	LANG-FAMILY BLEU	LANG-FAMILY COMET	LANG-PAIR BLEU	LANG-PAIR COMET	LANG-AGNOSTIC BLEU	LANG-AGNOSTIC COMET	ML-FT BLEU	ML-FT COMET
bg	25.4	67.2	27.8	72.1	21.6	44.6	28.0	76.5
sr	20.9	44.3	17.5	38.2	19.7	41.1	21.1	48.4
hr	23.7	55.0	23.7	53.1	21.4	43.4	24.5	55.1
uk	15.1	-17.0	17.7	14.4	13.8	-18.5	17.1	35.9
sk	27.7	54.3	25.0	50.1	24.1	57.0	30.5	64.9
mk	31.9	62.9	35.0	64.1	28.9	65.2	35.6	62.1
sl	22.6	48.9	24.1	65.8	19.6	42.3	24.5	64.3
bs	20.3	44.1	21.0	37.1	19.5	43.9	22.1	50.8
be	15.2	-10.2	10.1	-21.6	11.3	-13.9	17.9	36.6
id	31.3	60.1	28.0	64.0	28.6	77.0	31.5	60.1
ms	25.4	53.5	24.5	66.1	21.8	49.8	25.5	68.0
fa	9.8	-23.5	10.5	-22.1	8.1	-24.4	9.5	-15.0
hi	18.7	39.1	15.6	-19.1	16.9	10.1	18.4	36.4
mr	25.0	67.0	17.0	9.0	17.8	19.5	24.7	58.1
ku	15.3	-18.5	14.1	-12.9	12.8	-11.5	15.6	-9.1
bn	12.9	-16.0	13.0	-24.1	11.2	-18.1	14.1	-8.5
avg	21.3	32.0	20.3	27.1	18.6	25.5	22.5	42.8

Table 10: Test set BLEU and COMET scores when translating out of English using OPUS-100. Languages are presented by decreasing amount of parallel data per language family. LANG-PAIR stands for language-pair adapters, LANG-AGNOSTIC for language-agnostic, while LANG-FAMILY for language-family adapters. ML-FT stands for multilingual fine-tuning of the entire mBART-50 model.

	bg*	sr*	hr	uk	sk*	mk	sl	bs*	be*	id	ms*	fa	hi	mr	ku*	bn	AVG
Lang-agnostic w/o emb	21.3	19.0	21.5	13.9	23.6	28.3	19.1	18.9	10.5	28.7	21.5	7.6	16.1	16.9	12.4	10.9	18.1
Lang-agnostic with emb	21.6	19.7	21.4	13.8	24.1	28.9	19.6	19.5	11.3	28.6	21.8	8.1	16.9	17.8	12.8	11.2	18.6
Lang-family w/o emb	24.3	20.4	22.6	14.8	26.3	31.2	21.9	20.6	13.4	31.4	25.2	9.0	18.3	23.7	13.7	12.2	20.6
Lang-family with emb	25.4	20.9	23.7	15.1	27.7	31.9	22.6	20.3	15.2	31.3	25.4	9.8	18.7	25.0	15.3	12.9	**21.3**

Table 11: Full results of the ablation of the proposed architecture for $en \rightarrow xx$ (BLEU scores) on OPUS-100. Bold results indicate best performance on average.

	bg	sr	hr	uk	sk	mk	sl	bs	be	id	ms	fil	fa	hi	mr	ku	bn	AVG
GMM	23.9	17.7	24.4	11.0	19.3	22.9	19.0	23.6	14.9	29.7	23.4	-	9.2	18.8	25.5	14.3	13.2	19.4
random	22.9	18.8	23.5	10.0	22.5	31.9	21.1	20.1	12.1	25.8	24.9	-	5.0	18.6	22.9	15.0	8.1	18.4

Table 12: Evaluation of different methods to form language families for $en \rightarrow xx$ (BLEU) on OPUS-100.

Improving Neural Machine Translation of Indigenous Languages with Multilingual Transfer Learning

Wei-Rui Chen[1] **Muhammad Abdul-Mageed**[1,2]
[1]Deep Learning & Natural Language Processing Group, The University of British Columbia
[2]Department of Natural Language Processing & Department of Machine Learning, MBZUAI
{weirui.chen,muhammad.mageed}@ubc.ca

Abstract

Machine translation (MT) involving Indigenous languages, including endangered ones, is challenging primarily due to lack of sufficient parallel data. We describe an approach exploiting bilingual and multilingual pretrained MT models in a transfer learning setting to translate from Spanish into ten South American Indigenous languages. Our models set new SOTA on five out of the ten language pairs we consider, even doubling performance on one of these five pairs. Unlike previous SOTA that perform data augmentation to enlarge the train sets, we retain the low-resource setting to test the effectiveness of our models under such a constraint. In spite of the rarity of linguistic information available about the Indigenous languages, we offer a number of quantitative and qualitative analyses (e.g., as to morphology, tokenization, and orthography) to contextualize our results.

1 Introduction

Artificial intelligence (AI) is being widely integrated into many natural language processing (NLP) applications in our daily lives. However, these language technologies have focused almost exclusively on widely-spoken languages (Choudhury and Deshpande, 2021). Under-represented languages such as endangered languages are thus left out. For example, the Google machine translation (MT) system does not support any of the languages included in our current study.[1] Our objective in this work is hence to build machine translation (MT) models for Indigenous languages, which are by definition low-resource and possibly endangered. More specifically, we focus on South American Indigenous languages. In a MT scenario, a language pair is considered 'low-resource' if the parallel corpora consists of less than 0.5 million of parallel sentences and 'extremely low-resource' if less than 0.1 million of parallel sentences (Ranathunga et al., 2021). In this work, nine out of ten languages pairs we consider have under 0.1 million pairs of sentences (with only one language pair having roughly 0.1 million pairs of sentences). Developing MT systems for endangered languages can help preserve these languages.

Neural Machine Translation (NMT) is a branch of MT that leverages neural networks to build translation systems. Despite that NMT is able to produce powerful MT systems, it is data-hungry. That is, it requires large amounts of data to train a quality NMT model (Koehn and Knowles, 2017). Contemporary machine translation systems are oftentimes trained on over a million of parallel sentences (Fan et al., 2021; Tang et al., 2020) for high-resource language pairs. In contrast, the size of the dataset we have is limited. Transfer learning has been shown to help mitigate this issue by porting knowledge e.g. from a parent model to a child model (Zoph et al., 2016a). We leverage two types of pretrained MT models: *bilingual* models and a *multilingual* model. The overall training approach is illustrated in Figure 1. Our datasets are provided by AmericasNLP2021 (Mager et al., 2021) shared task. We compare our performance to the winner of the shared task (Vázquez et al., 2021).

The rest of this study is organized as follows: Section 2 is a literature review on Indigenous MT, transfer learning, the application of transfer learning to NMT, and the challenge of cross-lingual transfer. In Section 3, we describe our experimental settings. We present our results in Section 4, and provide discussions in Section 5. We conclude in Section 6.

2 Background

2.1 MT on Indigenous Languages

Languages are diverse. For example, in South America, there are 108 language families, 55 of which are in a language family with one single

[1]https://translate.google.com/about/languages/

Proceedings of the The Sixth Workshop on Technologies for Machine Translation of Low-Resource Languages (LoResMT 2023), pages 73–85
May 6, 2023 ©2023 Association for Computational Linguistics

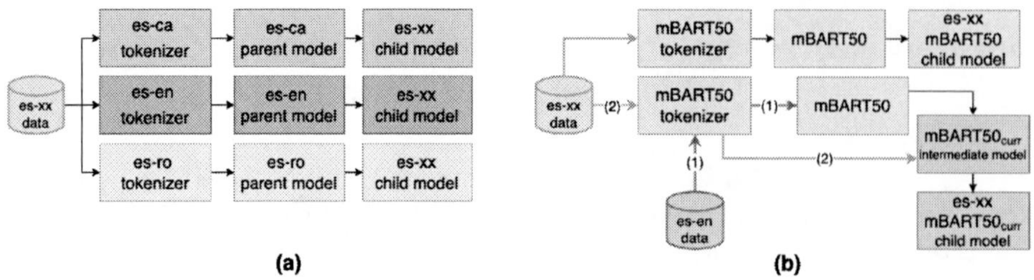

Figure 1: Model Training in **(a)** bilingual setting and **(b)** multilingual setting for one `es-xx` language pair. For both **(a)** and **(b)**, child models are those being used for prediction. xx represents arbitrary one of the ten South American Indigenous languages. For **(b)**, the blue es-xx mBART50 child model represents the model directly fine-tuned with `es-xx` data. The purple es-xx mBART50$_{\text{curr}}$ child model represents the model that is first being fine-tuned with `es-en` data to produce an intermediate model, indicated as (1). Afterwards, it is fine-tuned with `es-xx` data, indicated as (2).

member (i.e., language isolates) (Campbell et al., 2012). Due to this linguistic diversity, to the best of our knowledge, there is no single MT method that fits all Indigenous languages. However, since many Indigenous languages suffer the low-resource issue (Mager et al., 2018a), many researchers borrow ideas from low-resource MT to tackle the task of MT of Indigenous languages. We survey some approaches here.

Nagoudi et al. (2021) create models based on the T5 architecture (Raffel et al., 2019) and train it with monolingual Indigenous data before fine-tuning on parallel data, thus attempting to acquire knowledge of the Indigenous languages to benefit MT. Ngoc Le and Sadat (2020) focus on data preprocessing, and build a morphological segmenter for the source language Inuktitut to achieve better performance in Inuktitut-English translation. These aforementioned works all adopt methods invented to tackle the task of MT on low-resource languages.

2.2 Transfer Learning and NMT

It can sometimes be very expensive to collect data for MT. This is true especially for endangered languages when the number of speakers is decreasing. Therefore, many endangered languages suffer from the the low-resource issue. This motivates methods that can help port knowledge from existing resources to a down-stream task of interest with low-resources employing transfer learning methods. An additional motivation for studying and applying transfer learning is that human beings are able to apply knowledge/skills they acquired earlier from some jobs to better perform new related jobs with less efforts. An analogy is this: a person who has learned a music instrument may be able to pick up another instrument easier and quicker (Zhuang et al., 2020). When applying transfer learning in the context of NMT, a scenario can be as follows: a model previously trained on parent language pair(s) (called *parent model*) is further fine-tuned on child language pair(s) to form a *child model*. Under such a scenario, a parent language pair is one of the language pairs whose bilingual data is used to train a model from scratch and produce a parent model. A child language pair is one of the language pairs whose bilingual data is used to fine-tune a parent model and produce a child model. Again, the intuition here is that an experienced translator (pre-trained MT model) on one language pair may be able to translate into another language pair with shorter time and less effort compared to a unexperienced person (new randomly-initialized model). The core idea is to retain the parameters of parent model as the starting point for the child model, instead of training from scratch where the parameters are randomly initialized (Zoph et al., 2016a; Kocmi and Bojar, 2018; Nguyen and Chiang, 2017).

2.3 Cross-lingual Transfer

One of the challenges of transfer learning in MT is the mismatch in parent and child vocabularies. Only when the parent language pair and child language pair are identical can there be no such issue. Otherwise, when at least one of the languages in child language pair is distinct from parent languages, such an issue would arise. This is the case since vocabulary is language-specific and discrete (Kim et al., 2019). For example, if a parent model has its vocabulary built upon Spanish-English text, the vocabulary will contain only Spanish and English tokens. It can be unpredictable

Figure 2: A map of the ten South American Indigenous languages in our data. The color for each country and each language is arbitrarily assigned.

when tokenizing French text with such a vocabulary.

Zoph et al. (2016b) tackle this challenge by retaining the token embeddings for their target language since the parent target language and child target language are the same in their work. For parent and child source languages, they randomly map tokens of parent source language to tokens of child source language. Kocmi and Bojar (2018) take another approach of vocabulary building: the vocabulary is built upon 50% of parallel sentences of the parent language pair and 50% of those of the child language pair, so the vocabulary will contain tokens of both parent and child language pairs. Kocmi and Bojar (2020) introduce yet another simpler idea named 'Direct Transfer' where the parent vocabulary is used to train a child model. Although the parent vocabulary is not optimized for child language pair and can oversegment words in child language pair to smaller pieces than necessary, such a method still shows significant improvement in many language pairs. Kocmi and Bojar (2020) suspect that this could be due to good generalization of the transformer architecture to short subwords.

3 Experiments

3.1 Dataset

Our dataset is from AmericasNLP 2021 Shared Task on Open Machine Translation, which was co-located with the 2021 Annual Conference of the North American Chapter of the Association for Computational Linguistics (NAACL-HLT 2021) (Mager et al., 2021). The dataset contains

Language	ISO	Major location	Speakers
Aymara	aym	Bolivia	1,677,100
Bribri	bzd	Costa Rica	7,000
Asháninka	cni	Peru	35,200
Guarani	gn	Paraguay	6,652,790
Wixarika	hch	Mexico	52,500
Nahuatl	nah	Mexico	410,000
Hñähñu	oto	Mexico	88,500
Quechua	quy	Peru	7,384,920
Shipibo-Konibo	shp	Peru	22,500
Rarámuri	tar	Mexico	9,230

Table 1: Overview of the ten Indigenous languages (Eberhard et al., 2021).

Language Pair	Train	Dev	Test
es-aym	6,531	996	1,003
es-bzd	7,506	996	1,003
es-cni	3,883	883	1,003
es-gn	26,032	995	1,003
es-hch	8,966	994	1,003
es-nah	16,145	672	996
es-oto	4,889	599	1,001
es-quy	125,008	996	1,003
es-shp	14,592	996	1,003
es-tar	14,720	995	1,003

Table 2: Number of parallel sentences

parallel data of 10 language pairs: from Spanish to Aymara, Asháninka, Bribri, Guarani, Hñähñu, Nahuatl, Quechua, Rarámuri, Shipibo-Konibo, and Wixarika. An overview of these 10 Indigenous languages is shown in Table 1. The geographical distribution of the languages is depicted in Figure 2. We offer information about the dataset splits as distributed by the shared task organizers in Table 2. The shared task has two tracks: **Track One**, where the training split (Train) involves an arbitrary portion of development set, and **Track Two**, where Train involves *no* development data. In this work, we take *Track One* as our main focus and concatenate 90% of Dev split to Train to acquire a bigger training set. We also conduct experiments for *Track Two*, and we put the results in Appendix.

3.2 Baselines

We compare our results with the winner of the shared task Vázquez et al. (2021) who achieve highest performance in evaluation metrics for all language pairs in Track One (and winning 9 out of 10 language pairs in Track Two). They augment the training data by (1) gathering external parallel data, e.g. Bibles and Constitutions (2) collecting monolingual data of Indigenous languages and adopt back-translation method to generate syn-

Pair	Source	Target
es-aym	Los artistas de IRT ayudan a los niños en las escuelas.	IRT artistanakax jisk'a yatiqañ utankir wawanakaruw yanapapxi.
	Los artistas de I RT ayudan a los niños en las escuelas .	I RT artist ana ka x ji sk ' a y ati qa ñ u tank ir wa wan aka ru w ya nap ap xi .
es-bzd	Fui a un seminario que se hizo vía satélite.	Ye' dë'rö seminario ã wéx yö' satélite kĩ.
	Fui a un seminario que se hizo vía satélite .	Ye ' d ë ' r ö seminar io ã w é x y ö ' sat éli te k ĩ .
es-cni	Pensé que habías ido al campamento.	Nokenkeshireashitaka pijaiti imabeyetinta.
	Pensé que había s ido al campamento.	No ken ke shire ashi t aka p ija iti im ab eye tin ta .
es-gn	Veía a su hermana todos los días.	Ko'êko'êre ohecha heindýpe.
	Ve ía a su hermana todos los días .	Ko ' ê ko ' ê re oh e cha he in d ý pe .
es-hch	Era una selva tropical.	pe h+k+t+kai metsi+ra+ ye tsie nieka ti+x+kat+.
	Era una selva tropical .	pe h + k + t + ka i met si + ra + ye t s ie nie ka ti + x + ka t + .
es-nah	Santo trabajó para Disney y operó las tazas de té.	zanto quitequitilih Disney huan quinpexontih in cafen caxitl
	Santo trabajó para Disney y o per ó las taza s de té .	zan to quite qui til ih Disney h uan quin pex on t ih in cafe n ca xi t l
es-oto	Otros continúan reconociendo nuestro éxito.	ymana ditantho anumahditho goma npâgu
	Otros continúan reconociendo nuestro éxito .	y man a di tant ho an um ah di th o go ma n p â gu
es-quy	De vez en cuando me gusta comer ensalada.	Yananpiqa ensaladatam mikuytam munani
	De vez en cuando me gusta comer ensalada .	Yan an pi qa en s ala data m m iku y tam mun ani
es-shp	El Museo se ve afectado por las inversiones.	Ja Museora en oinai inversionesbaon afectana.
	El Museo se ve afectado por las inversiones .	Ja Museo ra en o ina i in version es ba on a fect ana .
es-tar	Es un hombre griego.	Bilé rejói Griego ju
	Es un hombre griego .	Bil é re j ó i Gri ego ju

Table 3: Example sentences tokenized by `es-en` tokenizer. **Light blue** : Original sentences (source or target). **Light green** : tokenized sentenses with tokens separated by whitespace.

thetic parallel data. They build a 6-layered transformer (Vaswani et al., 2017) with 8 heads by first pretrain it with `es-en` parallel data and then finetune it with both internal dataset provided by the organizer and external augmented datasets of all 10 language pairs to produce a multilingual MT model. In this work, we leverage solely the dataset provided by the shared task organizer to test if our method works with scarce data.

3.3 Data Preprocessing

As mentioned in section 2.3, the cross-lingual challenge exists when one or both sides of child language pair is distinct from the parent languages which is the case to all of the our 10 language pairs. To tackle this, we opt for 'direct transfer' method, due to its simplicity, to exploit parent vocabulary for child model. As Kocmi and Bojar (2020) find that the words of child language are oversegmented with direct transfer, similar to their finding, we observe that the words of Indigenous language words can be oversegmented. As shown in Table 3, it can be seen that the source sentences are tokenized reasonably well with mostly one token per word. By contrast, the words of child target language are generally oversegmented into short subwords. The statistics of the tokenization is shown in Table 8. An analysis of oversegmentation phenomenon is given in section 5.3.

3.4 Parent Models

We offer two types of parent models, bilingual models and multilingual models.

Bilingual Models. For bilingual models, we leverage publicly accessible pretrained models from Huggingface (Wolf et al., 2020) as provided by Helsinki-NLP (Tiedemann and Thottingal, 2020). The pretrained MT models released by Helsinki-NLP are trained on OPUS, an open source parallel corpus (Tiedemann, 2012). Underlying these models is the Transformer architecture of Marian-NMT framework implementation (Junczys-Dowmunt et al., 2018). Each model has six self-attention layers in encoder and decoder parts, and each layer has eight attention heads. The three bilingual models we specifically use are each pretrained with OPUS Spanish-Catalan, Spanish-English, and Spanish-Romanian data.[2]

We choose these models because their source language is Spanish so they may have good Spanish subword embeddings. In this regard, as Adelaar (2012) point out, during the colonial period, Spanish grammatical concepts were introduced to some

[2]Tiedemann and Thottingal (2020) do not provide information about the size of OPUS data exploited in each of these models.

South American Indigenous languages. In addition, we pick Spanish-Catalan and Spanish-Romanian MT models because Catalan and Romanian are two languages in the same Romance language family as Spanish, and we suspect our ten Indigenous languages of South America may have some affinity to Spanish. We also choose Spanish-English as a contrastive model because English is in the Germanic language family rather than Romance and that the MT models built around English usually are well-performing due to its rich resource of parallel data.

Multilingual Models. For our multilingual models, we exploit mBART50 (Tang et al., 2020). mBART50 can be seen as an extension of mBART (Liu et al., 2020). mBART (or more specifically mBART25) is a multilingual sequence-to-sequence generative model pretrained on 25 monolingual datasets and fine-tuned on 24 bilingual datasets which cover all 25 languages used in pretraining. mBART50 takes mBART as a starting point and enlarges its embedding layers to accommodate tokens of 25 new languages to support 50 languages. mBART50 adopts multilingual fine-tuning under three scenarios: one-to-many, many-to-one, and many-to-many where 'one' represents English. We choose the one that is trained under many-to-many scenario to ensure (1) Spanish is fine-tuned as a source language so it may maintain a good representation for Spanish tokens (2) `es-en` language pair is covered so we can produce an intermediate model with `es-en` fine-tuning to test the effectiveness of curriculum learning.

Model	Target	Our BLEU	Our chrF	SOTA BLEU	SOTA chrF
es-ca		1.445	0.2344		
es-en		2.432	0.277		
es-ro	aym	2.009	0.2705	**2.8**	**0.31**
mBart50		2.017	0.2672		
mBART50$_{curr}$		2.23	0.2725		
es-ca		7.242	0.2378		
es-en		9.952	0.2753		
es-ro	bzd	10.278	0.2867	5.18	0.213
mBart50		**12.898**	**0.3082**		
mBART50$_{curr}$		12.495	0.3036		
es-ca		4.742	0.2984		
es-en		5.973	0.3367		
es-ro	cni	5.21	0.3229	6.09	0.332
mBart50		5.632	0.3183		
mBART50$_{curr}$		**6.255**	**0.3432**		
es-ca		4.395	0.2909		
es-en		5.918	0.3341		
es-ro	gn	5.853	0.3279	**8.92**	**0.376**
mBart50		6.329	0.3367		
mBART50$_{curr}$		6.449	0.3387		
es-ca		13.375	0.3061		
es-en		15.922	0.3461		
es-ro	hch	15.298	0.3444	15.67	**0.36**
mBart50		**16.731**	0.3397		
mBART50$_{curr}$		16.659	0.3391		
es-ca		1.95	0.2763		
es-en		2.045	0.2913		
es-ro	nah	1.734	0.2929	**3.25**	0.301
mBart50		2.422	0.2969		
mBART50$_{curr}$		2.947	**0.3015**		
es-ca		4.344	0.2268		
es-en	oto	6.414	0.2522		
es-ro		4.14	0.2315	5.59	0.228
mBart50		**7.504**	**0.265**		
mBART50$_{curr}$		7.489	0.2617		
es-ca		2.817	0.3449		
es-en		4.149	0.3788		
es-ro	quy	3.192	0.3718	**5.38**	**0.394**
mBart50		4.689	0.3928		
mBART50$_{curr}$		4.95	0.3881		
es-ca		5.184	0.2627		
es-en		7.664	0.3326		
es-ro	shp	6.663	0.32	**10.49**	**0.399**
mBart50		10.022	0.3556		
mBART50$_{curr}$		9.702	0.349		
es-ca		1.724	0.217		
es-en		2.432	0.248		
es-ro	tar	2.034	0.2358	**3.56**	**0.258**
mBart50		2.433	0.2396		
mBART50$_{curr}$		2.261	0.2362		

Table 4: Modeling results (of Track One). The boldfaced numeric values are the best performances. Source language is always Spanish so it is ignored. SOTA values represent the state-of-the-art performance which are all from Vázquez et al. (2021)

3.5 Training Approach

Bilingual Model Training. We fine-tune each of our three bilingual models for $60,000$ steps with Spanish-Indigenous data, acquiring performance on Dev every $1,000$ steps. The final model is the checkpoint that has the lowest validation/Dev loss, and it is what we use for predicting on Test. Our beam size (for beam search) (Reddy et al., 1977; Graves, 2012) is 6. We use a batch size [3] of 15 for our bilingual models. It takes $\sim$ 6 hours to train on four Nvidia V100-SXM2-16GB GPUs for each model per language pair.

Multilingual Model Training. For our multilingual setting, we train a model for each of the Spanish→Indigenous language pairs and it takes $\sim$ 12 hours to train on four NVIDIA Tesla V100 32GB NVLink GPUs for each model per language pair. We have two scenarios: mBART50 and mBART50$_{curr}$. Both of them have batch size [3] to be 5, and the beam size to be 6.

mBART50. For our first multilingual scenario, we fine-tune mBART50 on Spanish-Indigenous data immediately after tokenization. Similar to our bilingual models, we fine-tune the mBART50 model for $60,000$ steps, measuring performance on Dev every $1,000$ steps, and taking the checkpoint with the best validation loss as our final model used for prediction on Test.

mBART50$_{curr}$. For the second scenario, mBART50$_{curr}$ is first fine-tuned on `es-en` data for 300 steps. The validation is done every 20

[3]The batch sizes are small so the data can be loaded in the GPU memory.

Pair	Sentence
es-aym	nanakan utaxax khaysa Concord uksanx kimsatunka waranqa acres ukhamarac walja uywanakarakiw utjaraki.
	Concord markan nanakan utanx 30000 acre ukhamarak walja uywanaka utji.
es-bzd	Sa' ù Concord wã 30000 acres tã' nã tãîx íyiwak.
	Sa' ù ã Concord e' kĩ káx dör 20.000 acres tãîx íyiwak tãîx.
es-cni	Abanko Concordki otimi 30000 acres jeri osheki birantsipee.
	Ashi pankotsi Concordi timatsi 30000 acres aisati osheki piratsipee.
es-gn	Ore róga Concord-pe otroko 30000 acres ha hetaiterei orerymba.
	Ñane óga Concord-pe oreko 30000 acre ha hetaiterei mymba.
es-hch	ta kí wana Concord pe xeiya 30000 acres tsiere y+ wa+kawa yeuta meteu uwa.
	ta ki wana Concord pexeiya xeiya xeitewiyari acre meta wa+kawa te+teri.
es-nah	tochan Concord quipiya miyac tlalli nohiya miyac tlapiyalli.
	Tehuancalco Concord quipiah macualli tlatqui ihuan miyac yolcameh.
es-oto	mangû game ane Concord phodi 30000 yñi xi nā hmudi on yzuî
	Goma na madoongû ane Concord phodi 30000 yqhēya xi na ngû on ybaoni
es-quy	Corcord nisqapi wasiykum kimsa chunka waranqa acres nisqan kan hinataq achkallaña uywa.
	Concordpi wasiykuqa 30000 acres hinaspa achka uywakunam
es-shp	Non xobo Concordainra 30000 acresya iki itan kikin icha yoinabo.
	Concordainra non xoboa riki 30000 acres itan kikin icha yoinabo.
es-tar	Tamó e'perélachi Concord anelíachi besá makói acres nirú a'lí weká namúti jákami shi.
	Concord anelíachi benéalachi, bilé mili akí weká nirú, wekabé namuti nirú.

Table 5: Example of ground truth and prediction of the Spanish sentence "Nuestra casa en Concord tiene 30000 acres y un montón de animales." (**Eng.** *Our home in Concord has 30,000 acres and lots of animals.*) by mBART50. The 'z' in 'yzuî' of es-oto is actually a Unicode character of code point U+0225 which is a 'z' with hook. **Light blue**: Ground Truth . **Light green**: Prediction .

steps where the checkpoint with lowest loss will be fine-tuned on Spanish-Indigenous language pair for $60,000$ steps, validated every $1,000$ steps to pick the best checkpoint with lowest validation loss. Our mBART50$_{\text{curr}}$ is inspired by the concept of *curriculum learning* (Soviany et al., 2021) where a model can possibly be improved when first trained on an easier task and followed by training on a harder task. In our case here, translating Spanish to English is considered an easier task because mBART50 is pretrained with `es-en` language pair; whereas Spanish to South American Indigenous languages is considered a more difficult job since mBART50 has not seen any of the 10 Indigenous languages before.

4 Results

We evaluate the translation performance with two automatic MT evaluation metrics: BLEU (Papineni et al., 2002) and chrF (Popović, 2015). chrF is an automatic evaluation metric for MT task which can be seen as a F-score for text and has value between 0 and 1. BLEU and chrF are the two metrics adopted by AmericasNLP 2021 Shared Task. We surpassed the winner of AmericasNLP2021 (Vázquez et al., 2021), in either or both metrics, for 5 language pairs with the following languages as target: Bribri (bzd), Asháninka (cni), Wixarika (hch), Nahuatl (nah), and Hñähñu (oto). Notably, we double the performance in BLEU score for `es-bzd`, increasing by about 7.7 BLEU scores and 0.1 chrF. We increase $\sim$ 2 BLEU points in `es-oto` and $\sim$ 1 BLEU points in es-hch. For both `es-cni` and `es-nah`, we slightly surpass their performance in both metrics. The performance of experiments are shown in Table 4. We also offer example predictions in Table 5.

All surpassing results are achieved by mBART50 or mBART50$_{\text{curr}}$. Surprisingly, mBART50$_{\text{curr}}$ does not consistently improve the performance if compared to mBART50; some of the best performances are achieved by mBART50 (`es-bzd`, `es-hch`, `es-oto`). Nevertheless, mBART50$_{\text{curr}}$ performs slightly better than mBART50 on average by 0.076 BLEU and 0.0034 chrF. Averagely, mBART50$_{\text{curr}}$ achieves 7.143 BLEU score and 0.3134 chrF while mBART50 achieves 7.068 BLEU score and 0.31 chrF. Generally, multilingual models perform better than bilingual model despite that in some language pairs, `es-en` model performs nearly as good as multilingual models and outperform multilingual models in `es-aym` and `es-tar`. For 3 bilingual models, `es-en` model generally outperforms the other two `es-ca` and `es-ro` models.

5 Discussion

5.1 Comparisons to SOTA

We are able to surpass previous SOTA in five language pairs and $\text{mBART50}_{\text{curr}}$ achieves 7.143 BLEU and 0.3134 chrF on average, comparing to previous SOTA having 6.693 BLEU and 0.3171 chrF on average. It can be hypothesized that the reason why we are able to improve average BLEU score by 0.45, accomplish comparable average chrF, and surpass in five language pairs is because we use an MT model pretrained on 50 languages, while Vázquez et al. (2021) pretrain their model only on `es-en`. We suspect that there could be some languages, other than Spanish and English, which contribute to positive transfer to Indigenous languages. Unlike Vázquez et al. (2021), we do not leverage external data to build a larger train set. Nor do we build a single multilingual model for all 10 language pairs, but we rather train one model for each language pair (where every single language pair is independent from the other pairs). The approach of Vázquez et al. (2021) may be able to afford some positive transfer between different Indigenous languages, and hence can be one of our future directions.

5.2 Fusional to Polysynthetic Translation

There is literature showing that when translating between a polynthetic[4] and a fusional language, some morphological information of the polysynthetic language is 'lost'. This is especially relevant to our work since Spanish is a fusional language and many Indigenous languages in our work are polysynthetic (Mager et al., 2021). Mager et al. (2018b) carry out a morpheme-to-morpheme alignment between Spanish and polynthetic Indigenous languages, including Nahuatl (nah) and Wixarika (hch) which are both in our data and show that the meanings carried by some polysynthetic morphemes have no Spanish counterpart. This makes it difficult to translate from polysynthetic languages to fusional Spanish without losing some morphological information. This is also a challenge to translate from fusional Spanish to polysynthetic languages, as there may be no contexts provided to infer the missing parts. This is particularly the case for sentence-level (vs. document level) translation.

We hypothesize that if there is loss in morphological information when translating from a fusional to polysynthetic languages, either or both the sentence length and word length of prediction will be shorter than the gold standard because some parts in the prediction are left out while the ground truth may contain them. We therefore compare average sentence length and average word length between our gold standard and prediction as shown in Table 6. However, we find that this hypothesis does not hold for most language pairs as most of them are having similar average sentence and word lengths in gold standard and predictions. We suspect that this is because the test sets are translated from Spanish to Indigenous languages by human translators in a sentence-level fashion, the translators may leave out the missing morphological information when translating Spanish into Indigenous languages due to inability to infer the missing information. As Mager et al. (2018b) state:

> The important Wixarika independent asserters "p+" and "p" are the most frequent morphemes in this language. However, as they have no direct equivalent in Spanish, their translation is mostly ignored. ...This is particularly problematic for the translation in the other direction, i.e., from Spanish into Wixarika, as a translator has no information about how the target language should realize such constructions. Human translators can, in some cases, infer the missing information. However, without context it is generally complicated to get the right translation.

As this is a sentence-level translation task where contexts can be hard to infer, the gold standard may not contain these parts at the first place. However, a further qualitative linguistic investigation is required to spot the cause of this phenomenon.

[4]Polysynthetic languages generally have a more complex morphological system, possibly each word consisting of several morphemes (Haspelmath and Sims, 2013; Campbell et al., 2012).

Target	Sent (Gold)	Sent (Pred)	Word (Gold)	Word (Pred)
aym	6.71	7.97	7.83	5.88
bzd	11.66	10.83	3.79	3.86
cni	6.41	6.1	8.57	8.17
gn	6.46	6.66	6.5	6.46
hch	9.97	8.55	5.35	5.61
nah	6.7	6.9	7.11	7.16
oto	10.38	9.69	4.47	4.01
quy	6.73	6.04	7.71	8.19
shp	8.82	7.77	5.95	5.98
tar	9.36	8.75	5.15	4.86

Table 6: The averages of sentence and word length of test set. The predictions are produced by mBART50. Sent (Gold) and Sent (Pred) are the average sentence length of gold standard and prediction, respectively. Word (Gold) and Word (Pred) are the average word length of gold standard and prediction, respectively. Sentence length is calculated as number of words in each sentence (by splitting sentence with whitespace). Word length is calculated as number of characters in each word.

5.3 Tokenization with Parent Vocabulary

As discussed in Section 3.3, we re-use the tokenizer of parent models without building new ones for child language pairs. We observe that the tokens in target sentences tend to be very short. That is, tokens in these target sentences often consist of one or two characters as can be seen in Table 3. Hence, target sentences do seem to be encountering oversegmentation. This could be causing loss of meaning as these smaller segments differ from what would be suited for a given Indigenous language.

We further offer statistics related to tokenization with the calculation details provided in Appendix A.2, and results shown in Table 8 (in Appendix). The difference between the average length of tokens in source and target languages is quite large. For example, for the language pair `es-bzd`, when tokenized with the `es-en` tokenizer, average token length for the source language is 3.43 while that for the target language is 1.21. This indicates that tokens in source data consist averagely of $\sim$ 3.5 characters while tokens in target data consist averagely of $\sim$ 1.2 characters. For this particular `es-bzd` language pair whose words in target sentences are on average oversegmented into nearly one character per token, the performance is surprisingly better than the previous SOTA. For the other nine language pairs whose words in target sentences are segmented into tokens consisting of $\sim$ 1 to $\sim$ 2 characters, the models are still capable of reasonably carrying out the translation task. As Kocmi and Bojar (2020) conjecture, this may be a case in point where a model is able to simply generalize well to short subwords.

5.4 Non-Standard Orthography

Based on a pilot investigation, we find the lack of orthographic standardization to be potentially problematic. We place relevant sample predictions in Table 5. For example, for the prediction of `es-aym` pair, we find that a word is predicted nearly correctly with just a difference in one character: ground truth 'ukhamarac' is predicted to be 'ukhamarak'. As Coler (2014) point out, this may be an issue of non-standard orthography since some Aymara speakers do not consistently differentiate between 'c' and 'k'. It can be hypothesized that the model generalizes to the 'ukhamarak' as a translation of a phrase/word because of potentially relatively higher number of occurrences of 'ukhamarak' than 'ukhamarac' in training data. In fact, 'ukhamarak' (including its variants with characters following such as in 'ukhamaraki' and 'ukhamarakiw') appears 489 times in the training set while 'ukhamarac' appears zero time (it only exist in test set). Although 'ukhamarac' and 'ukhamarak' can be viewed as the same word, these are still not counted as a match by some automatic evaluation metrics (including metrics based on BLEU, which we adopt in this work). Interestingly, cases such as the current one illustrates a challenge for automatic MT metrics when evaluating on languages without standard orthography.

6 Conclusion

In this paper, we describe how we apply transfer learning to MT from Spanish to ten low-resource South American Indigenous languages. We finetune pretrained bilingual and multilingual MT models on downstream Spanish to Indigenous language pairs and show the utility of these models. We are able to surpass SOTA in five language pairs using multilingual pretrained MT models without leveraging any external data. Empirically, our results show that this method performs robustly even with an oversegmentation issue on the target side. We also discuss multiple issues that interact with our task, including translating between languages of different morphological structures, effect of tokenization, and non-standard orthography.

Limitations

One challenge for working on a wide host of Indigenous languages is insufficient knowledge of these languages, which also applies to us: We report models on ten different Indigenous languages none of which is the native tongue of us. In spite of this limitation, we strive to acquire linguistic knowledge about the languages we work on so that our arguments are informed. Regardless, we believe that lack of native knowledge of the languages remains a limitation at our side.

In section 5.3, our claim of potential oversegmentation is based on an assumption that human languages tend to not have morphemes with just a single character. That is, we assume that these languages should have longer morphemes in general. However, again, a more definitive approach to the problem would perhaps require expert linguistic knowledge of the languages under study. In absence of (detailed) linguistic analyses of the Indigenous language we treat, this again remains a constraint.

Ethics Statement

We develop methods for low-resource machine translation. Because our models are trained on limited amounts of data, and hence make frequent errors, they may not be immediately useful for the general public. However, our hope is that our work will propel MT progress on the ten Indigenous languages we tackle.

There are also some biases in the models and the textual data we use to train them. The datasets we use to train our models (Mager et al., 2021) is a translations of XNLI (Conneau et al., 2018), which itself is derived from MultiNLI (Williams et al., 2018). Our bilingual model for each pair is trained on OPUS corpus that is derived from different sources. The multilingual model mBART50 is also trained on multiple datasets, including IWSLT, WMT, and TED. Due to the complexity of neural models, it is hard to explicitly state how these biases can contribute to the failure modes. However, we explicitly state the existence of sources of potential biases to raise the awareness of the readers.

References

Willem FH Adelaar. 2012. Chapter historical overview: Descriptive and comparative research on south american indian languages. In *The indigenous languages of South America: A comprehensive guide*. De Gruyter.

Lyle Campbell, Verónica Grondona, and HH Hock. 2012. *The indigenous languages of South America*. de Gruyter.

Monojit Choudhury and Amit Deshpande. 2021. How linguistically fair are multilingual pre-trained language models? In *Proceedings of the AAAI Conference on Artificial Intelligence*, volume 35, pages 12710–12718.

Matt Coler. 2014. *A grammar of Muylaq'Aymara: Aymara as spoken in Southern Peru*. Brill.

Alexis Conneau, Ruty Rinott, Guillaume Lample, Adina Williams, Samuel Bowman, Holger Schwenk, and Veselin Stoyanov. 2018. XNLI: Evaluating cross-lingual sentence representations. In *Proceedings of the 2018 Conference on Empirical Methods in Natural Language Processing*, pages 2475–2485, Brussels, Belgium. Association for Computational Linguistics.

David M. Eberhard, Gary F. Simons, and Charles D. Fennig. 2021. Ethnologue: Languages of the world. twenty-fourth edition. Dallas, Texas. SIL International.

Angela Fan, Shruti Bhosale, Holger Schwenk, Zhiyi Ma, Ahmed El-Kishky, Siddharth Goyal, Mandeep Baines, Onur Celebi, Guillaume Wenzek, Vishrav Chaudhary, et al. 2021. Beyond english-centric multilingual machine translation. *Journal of Machine Learning Research*, 22(107):1–48.

Alex Graves. 2012. Sequence transduction with recurrent neural networks. *CoRR*, abs/1211.3711.

Martin Haspelmath and Andrea Sims. 2013. *Understanding morphology*. Routledge.

Marcin Junczys-Dowmunt, Roman Grundkiewicz, Tomasz Dwojak, Hieu Hoang, Kenneth Heafield, Tom Neckermann, Frank Seide, Ulrich Germann, Alham Fikri Aji, Nikolay Bogoychev, André F. T. Martins, and Alexandra Birch. 2018. Marian: Fast neural machine translation in C++. In *Proceedings of ACL 2018, System Demonstrations*, pages 116–121, Melbourne, Australia. Association for Computational Linguistics.

Yunsu Kim, Yingbo Gao, and Hermann Ney. 2019. Effective cross-lingual transfer of neural machine translation models without shared vocabularies. In *Proceedings of the 57th Annual Meeting of the Association for Computational Linguistics*, pages 1246–1257, Florence, Italy. Association for Computational Linguistics.

Tom Kocmi and Ondrej Bojar. 2018. Trivial transfer learning for low-resource neural machine translation. *CoRR*, abs/1809.00357.

Tom Kocmi and Ondřej Bojar. 2020. Efficiently reusing old models across languages via transfer learning. In *Proceedings of the 22nd Annual Conference of the European Association for Machine Translation*, pages 19–28, Lisboa, Portugal. European Association for Machine Translation.

Philipp Koehn and Rebecca Knowles. 2017. Six challenges for neural machine translation. In *Proceedings of the First Workshop on Neural Machine Translation*, pages 28–39, Vancouver. Association for Computational Linguistics.

Taku Kudo and John Richardson. 2018. SentencePiece: A simple and language independent subword tokenizer and detokenizer for neural text processing. In *Proceedings of the 2018 Conference on Empirical Methods in Natural Language Processing: System Demonstrations*, pages 66–71, Brussels, Belgium. Association for Computational Linguistics.

Yinhan Liu, Jiatao Gu, Naman Goyal, Xian Li, Sergey Edunov, Marjan Ghazvininejad, Mike Lewis, and Luke Zettlemoyer. 2020. Multilingual denoising pretraining for neural machine translation. *Transactions of the Association for Computational Linguistics*, 8:726–742.

Manuel Mager, Ximena Gutierrez-Vasques, Gerardo Sierra, and Ivan Meza-Ruiz. 2018a. Challenges of language technologies for the indigenous languages of the Americas. In *Proceedings of the 27th International Conference on Computational Linguistics*, pages 55–69, Santa Fe, New Mexico, USA. Association for Computational Linguistics.

Manuel Mager, Elisabeth Mager, Alfonso Medina Urrea, Iván Meza, and Katharina Kann. 2018b. Lost in translation: Analysis of information loss during machine translation between polysynthetic and fusional languages. *CoRR*, abs/1807.00286.

Manuel Mager, Arturo Oncevay, Abteen Ebrahimi, John Ortega, Annette Rios, Angela Fan, Ximena Gutierrez-Vasques, Luis Chiruzzo, Gustavo Giménez-Lugo, Ricardo Ramos, Ivan Vladimir Meza Ruiz, Rolando Coto-Solano, Alexis Palmer, Elisabeth Mager-Hois, Vishrav Chaudhary, Graham Neubig, Ngoc Thang Vu, and Katharina Kann. 2021. Findings of the AmericasNLP 2021 shared task on open machine translation for indigenous languages of the Americas. In *Proceedings of the First Workshop on Natural Language Processing for Indigenous Languages of the Americas*, pages 202–217, Online. Association for Computational Linguistics.

Oscar Moreno. 2021. The REPU CS' Spanish–Quechua submission to the AmericasNLP 2021 shared task on open machine translation. In *Proceedings of the First Workshop on Natural Language Processing for Indigenous Languages of the Americas*, pages 241–247, Online. Association for Computational Linguistics.

El Moatez Billah Nagoudi, Wei-Rui Chen, Muhammad Abdul-Mageed, and Hasan Cavusoglu. 2021. Indt5: A text-to-text transformer for 10 indigenous languages. *CoRR*, abs/2104.07483.

Tan Ngoc Le and Fatiha Sadat. 2020. Revitalization of indigenous languages through pre-processing and neural machine translation: The case of Inuktitut. In *Proceedings of the 28th International Conference on Computational Linguistics*, pages 4661–4666, Barcelona, Spain (Online). International Committee on Computational Linguistics.

Toan Q. Nguyen and David Chiang. 2017. Transfer learning across low-resource, related languages for neural machine translation. *CoRR*, abs/1708.09803.

Kishore Papineni, Salim Roukos, Todd Ward, and Wei-Jing Zhu. 2002. Bleu: a method for automatic evaluation of machine translation. In *Proceedings of the 40th Annual Meeting of the Association for Computational Linguistics*, pages 311–318, Philadelphia, Pennsylvania, USA. Association for Computational Linguistics.

Maja Popović. 2015. chrF: character n-gram F-score for automatic MT evaluation. In *Proceedings of the Tenth Workshop on Statistical Machine Translation*, pages 392–395, Lisbon, Portugal. Association for Computational Linguistics.

Colin Raffel, Noam Shazeer, Adam Roberts, Katherine Lee, Sharan Narang, Michael Matena, Yanqi Zhou, Wei Li, and Peter J. Liu. 2019. Exploring the limits of transfer learning with a unified text-to-text transformer. *CoRR*, abs/1910.10683.

Surangika Ranathunga, En-Shiun Annie Lee, Marjana Prifti Skenduli, Ravi Shekhar, Mehreen Alam, and Rishemjit Kaur. 2021. Neural machine translation for low-resource languages: A survey.

D Raj Reddy et al. 1977. Speech understanding systems: A summary of results of the five-year research effort. *Department of Computer Science. Camegie-Mell University, Pittsburgh, PA*, 17:138.

Petru Soviany, Radu Tudor Ionescu, Paolo Rota, and Nicu Sebe. 2021. Curriculum learning: A survey. *arXiv preprint arXiv:2101.10382*.

Yuqing Tang, Chau Tran, Xian Li, Peng-Jen Chen, Naman Goyal, Vishrav Chaudhary, Jiatao Gu, and Angela Fan. 2020. Multilingual translation with extensible multilingual pretraining and finetuning. *arXiv preprint arXiv:2008.00401*.

Jörg Tiedemann. 2012. Parallel data, tools and interfaces in OPUS. In *Proceedings of the Eighth International Conference on Language Resources and Evaluation (LREC'12)*, pages 2214–2218, Istanbul, Turkey. European Language Resources Association (ELRA).

Jörg Tiedemann and Santhosh Thottingal. 2020. OPUS-MT — Building open translation services for the World. In *Proceedings of the 22nd Annual Conferenec of the European Association for Machine Translation (EAMT)*, Lisbon, Portugal.

Ashish Vaswani, Noam Shazeer, Niki Parmar, Jakob Uszkoreit, Llion Jones, Aidan N. Gomez, Lukasz Kaiser, and Illia Polosukhin. 2017. Attention is all you need.

Raúl Vázquez, Yves Scherrer, Sami Virpioja, and Jörg Tiedemann. 2021. The Helsinki submission to the AmericasNLP shared task. In *Proceedings of the First Workshop on Natural Language Processing for Indigenous Languages of the Americas*, pages 255–264, Online. Association for Computational Linguistics.

Adina Williams, Nikita Nangia, and Samuel Bowman. 2018. A broad-coverage challenge corpus for sentence understanding through inference. In *Proceedings of the 2018 Conference of the North American Chapter of the Association for Computational Linguistics: Human Language Technologies, Volume 1 (Long Papers)*, pages 1112–1122. Association for Computational Linguistics.

Thomas Wolf, Lysandre Debut, Victor Sanh, Julien Chaumond, Clement Delangue, Anthony Moi, Pierric Cistac, Tim Rault, Remi Louf, Morgan Funtowicz, Joe Davison, Sam Shleifer, Patrick von Platen, Clara Ma, Yacine Jernite, Julien Plu, Canwen Xu, Teven Le Scao, Sylvain Gugger, Mariama Drame, Quentin Lhoest, and Alexander Rush. 2020. Transformers: State-of-the-art natural language processing. In *Proceedings of the 2020 Conference on Empirical Methods in Natural Language Processing: System Demonstrations*, pages 38–45, Online. Association for Computational Linguistics.

Fuzhen Zhuang, Zhiyuan Qi, Keyu Duan, Dongbo Xi, Yongchun Zhu, Hengshu Zhu, Hui Xiong, and Qing He. 2020. A comprehensive survey on transfer learning. *Proceedings of the IEEE*, 109(1):43–76.

Barret Zoph, Deniz Yuret, Jonathan May, and Kevin Knight. 2016a. Transfer learning for low-resource neural machine translation. In *Proceedings of the 2016 Conference on Empirical Methods in Natural Language Processing*, pages 1568–1575, Austin, Texas. Association for Computational Linguistics.

Barret Zoph, Deniz Yuret, Jonathan May, and Kevin Knight. 2016b. Transfer learning for low-resource neural machine translation. In *Proceedings of the 2016 Conference on Empirical Methods in Natural Language Processing*, pages 1568–1575.

A Appendix

A.1 Additional Experiments

We conduct additional experiments for Track Two as mentioned in Section 3.1. This additional experiment have identical settings as Track One except that the train set does not involve sentences in development set. We surpass the state-of-the-art performance in 4 out of 10 language pairs in either or both BLEU and chrF. Similar to the results in Track One, multilingual MT models perform better than bilingual ones while there are no consistent winner between mBART50 and mBART50$_{\text{curr}}$.

A.2 Tokenization Output

As mentioned in Section 5.3, we calculate statistics related to tokenization on training data as shown in Table 8. To calculate these statistics, padding tokens, end of sentence tokens and the underscore (or more precisely, U+2581) prepended due to sentencePiece technique (Kudo and Richardson, 2018) are removed from the tokenized sentences. Sentence length is calculated as number of tokens in a sentence. Token length is calculated as the number of characters in a token. Average sentence length is calculated by averaging the sentence lengths of all sentences. Average token length is calculated as

$$\frac{\sum_{i=1}^{N}\sum_{j=1}^{n_i}|s_{ij}|}{\sum_{i=1}^{N}n_i}$$

where n_i denotes the number of tokens in i^{th} sentence and N denotes the number of sentences in training data. $|s_{ij}|$ denotes the length (number of characters) of jth token in i^{th} sentence.

Model	Target	Dev BLEU	Dev chrF	Test BLEU	Test chrF	SOTA BLEU	SOTA chrF
es-ca		2.415	0.227	1.0	0.197		
es-en		2.503	0.261	1.253	0.22		
es-ro	aym	2.642	0.2666	1.369	0.2273	**2.29**	**0.283**
mBART50		3.105	0.275	1.38	0.236		
$\text{mBART50}_{\text{curr}}$		3.034	0.2679	1.37	0.2291		
es-ca		2.033	0.15	2.217	0.153		
es-en		2.987	0.168	3.437	0.178		
es-ro	bzd	2.803	0.1709	3.308	0.1816	2.39	0.165
mBART50		4.205	0.188	4.272	**0.197**		
$\text{mBART50}_{\text{curr}}$		4.072	0.1871	**4.438**	0.1911		
es-ca		2.628	0.212	2.429	0.201		
es-en		1.671	0.212	1.623	0.208		
es-ro	cni	1.639	0.2225	1.829	0.209	3.05	**0.258**
mBART50		3.074	0.26	**3.539**	0.25		
$\text{mBART50}_{\text{curr}}$		3.404	0.2573	3.537	0.2491		
es-ca		3.637	0.245	3.523	0.254		
es-en		4.206	0.282	4.217	0.297		
es-ro	gn	3.784	0.2771	4.699	0.291	**6.13**	**0.336**
mBART50		4.911	0.287	4.801	0.304		
$\text{mBART50}_{\text{curr}}$		4.496	0.2795	4.702	0.2918		
es-ca		5.618	0.191	7.595	0.197		
es-en		6.578	0.234	8.995	0.245		
es-ro	hch	7.536	0.2594	10.123	0.2732	9.63	**0.304**
mBART50		8.617	0.254	11.526	0.272		
$\text{mBART50}_{\text{curr}}$		9.067	0.2582	**11.539**	0.2731		
es-ca		0.753	0.239	0.705	0.222		
es-en		0.73	0.25	0.772	0.22		
es-ro	nah	1.06	0.2619	0.6983	0.2363	**2.38**	**0.266**
mBART50		1.69	0.281	1.497	0.255		
$\text{mBART50}_{\text{curr}}$		1.704	0.2731	1.78	0.2412		
es-ca		0.536	0.122	0.86	0.12		
es-en		0.745	0.124	1.039	0.121		
es-ro	oto	0.5125	0.1198	0.8811	0.1226	**1.69**	**0.147**
mBART50		0.816	0.133	1.354	0.132		
$\text{mBART50}_{\text{curr}}$		0.8851	0.1348	1.338	0.1331		
es-ca		2.199	0.322	2.191	0.328		
es-en		2.217	0.337	2.892	0.347		
es-ro	quy	2.081	0.3416	2.094	0.3539	2.91	0.346
mBART50		2.242	0.356	**3.167**	**0.366**		
$\text{mBART50}_{\text{curr}}$		2.516	0.355	3.038	0.3659		
es-ca		1.511	0.178	1.234	0.168		
es-en		2.134	0.21	2.017	0.196		
es-ro	shp	1.964	0.2205	1.43	0.2048	**5.43**	**0.329**
mBART50		2.131	0.194	2.013	0.185		
$\text{mBART50}_{\text{curr}}$		2.067	0.1947	1.809	0.1856		
es-ca		0.256	0.095	0.047	0.084		
es-en		0.034	0.057	0.023	0.05		
es-ro	tar	0.1583	0.094,38	0.2985	0.089,32	**1.07**	**0.184**
mBART50		0.09	0.093	0.073	0.101		
$\text{mBART50}_{\text{curr}}$		0.1212	0.094,63	0.090,13	0.1007		

Table 7: Modeling results of Track Two. The boldfaced numeric values are the best performances. SOTA values represent the state-of-the-art performance which are all from Vázquez et al. (2021) except that the es-quy SOTA chrF value is from (Moreno, 2021). Source language is always Spanish so it is ignored.

model	Target Lang	source avg sentence length	target avg sentence length	source avg token length	target avg token length
es-ca	aym	26.37	49.1	3.61	1.81
es-en		24.55	45.07	3.88	1.99
es-ro		25.74	47.9	3.71	1.91
mBART50		27.4	37.85	3.66	2.53
es-ca	bzd	9.42	22.42	3.24	1.28
es-en		8.9	21.43	3.43	1.21
es-ro		9.13	21.52	3.34	1.23
mBART50		10.75	19.67	3.3	1.54
es-ca	cni	17.6	30.56	3.33	1.92
es-en		16.72	27.78	3.51	2.12
es-ro		17.31	29.17	3.44	2.04
mBART50		19.38	23.9	3.27	2.69
es-ca	gn	31.89	50.6	3.69	2.01
es-en		30.15	50.77	3.9	2.0
es-ro		31.92	52.45	3.73	1.97
mBART50		33.79	41.34	3.63	2.6
es-ca	hch	11.15	23.01	3.24	1.68
es-en		10.49	21.56	3.44	1.79
es-ro		10.76	22.27	3.35	1.73
mBART50		13.34	20.14	3.08	2.17
es-ca	nah	33.7	51.39	3.03	1.83
es-en		34.36	49.58	2.96	1.94
es-ro		34.44	51.52	2.95	1.83
mBART50		36.78	45.54	2.87	2.32
es-ca	oto	18.0	37.72	3.14	1.64
es-en		18.2	36.06	3.1	1.51
es-ro		18.49	37.58	3.07	1.7
mBART50		20.62	32.91	2.98	1.82
es-ca	quy	20.16	42.8	3.65	1.83
es-en		19.26	37.68	3.82	2.08
es-ro		20.16	41.45	3.73	1.92
mBART50		22.96	31.47	3.42	2.65
es-ca	shp	9.71	16.53	3.19	1.75
es-en		9.06	15.56	3.41	1.85
es-ro		9.42	15.84	3.28	1.82
mBART50		11.12	13.54	3.23	2.5
es-ca	tar	12.48	19.4	2.97	1.48
es-en		12.83	18.32	2.89	1.57
es-ro		13.08	19.33	2.84	1.5
mBART50		14.15	15.64	2.98	2.16

Table 8: Token statistics for our Train set. The way of calculating these figures is presented in Appendix A.2. Since mBART50 and mBART50$_{\text{curr}}$ are having exactly same statistics as they use same tokenizer, the statistics of mBART50$_{\text{curr}}$ are ignored.

Investigating Lexical Replacements for Arabic-English Code-Switched Data Augmentation

Injy Hamed,[1,2] Nizar Habash,[1] Slim Abdennadher,[3] Ngoc Thang Vu[2]

[1]Computational Approaches to Modeling Language Lab, New York University Abu Dhabi

[2]Institute for Natural Language Processing, University of Stuttgart

[3]Informatics and Computer Science, The German International University in Cairo

injy.hamed@nyu.edu

Abstract

Data sparsity is a main problem hindering the development of code-switching (CS) NLP systems. In this paper, we investigate data augmentation techniques for synthesizing dialectal Arabic-English CS text. We perform lexical replacements using word-aligned parallel corpora where CS points are either randomly chosen or learnt using a sequence-to-sequence model. We compare these approaches against dictionary-based replacements. We assess the quality of the generated sentences through human evaluation and evaluate the effectiveness of data augmentation on machine translation (MT), automatic speech recognition (ASR), and speech translation (ST) tasks. Results show that using a predictive model results in more natural CS sentences compared to the random approach, as reported in human judgements. In the downstream tasks, despite the random approach generating more data, both approaches perform equally (outperforming dictionary-based replacements). Overall, data augmentation achieves 34% improvement in perplexity, 5.2% relative improvement on WER for ASR task, +4.0-5.1 BLEU points on MT task, and +2.1-2.2 BLEU points on ST over a baseline trained on available data without augmentation.

1 Introduction

Code-switching (CS) is the alternation of language in text or speech. CS can occur at the levels of sentences (inter-sentential CS), words (intra-sentential CS/code-mixing), and morphemes (intra-word CS/morphological CS). Given that CS data is scarce and that collecting such data is expensive and time-consuming, data augmentation serves as a successful solution for alleviating data sparsity.

In this paper, we investigate lexical replacements for augmenting CS dialectal Arabic-English data. Researchers have investigated approaches that do not require parallel data, including translating source words into target language with the use of dictionaries (Tarunesh et al., 2021), machine translation (Li and Vu, 2020), and word embeddings (Sabty et al., 2021), as well as relying on parallel data and performing substitutions of words/phrases using alignments (Menacer et al., 2019; Appicharla et al., 2021; Gupta et al., 2021). As will be discussed in Section 2, most of the previous studies on this front have focused on one augmentation technique without exploring others, or reported results using only one type of word alignments configuration, or evaluated effectiveness of augmentation on only one downstream task.

We attempt to provide a comprehensive study where we systematically explore the use of neural-based models to decide on CS points for performing replacements using word-aligned parallel corpora versus randomly-chosen CS points, along with the interaction of different alignment configurations. We compare these approaches against dictionary-based replacements. We provide a rigorous evaluation of the different settings, where we assess the quality of the generated CS sentences through human evaluation as well as the impact on language modeling (LM), automatic speech recognition (ASR), machine translation (MT), and speech translation (ST) tasks.

Our human evaluation study shows that for the purpose of generating high-quality CS sentences, learning to predict CS points and integrating this information in the augmentation process improves the quality of generated sentences. On the downstream tasks, we report that performing alignment-based replacement outperforms dictionary-based replacement. For alignment-based replacement, utilizing a predictive model to decide on where CS points should occur as opposed to replacing at random positions both lead to similar results for ASR, MT, and ST tasks. For both approaches, we investigate different word alignment configurations, and we report that performing segment replacements using symmetrized alignments outperforms

Proceedings of the The Sixth Workshop on Technologies for Machine Translation of Low-Resource Languages (LoResMT 2023), pages 86–100
May 6, 2023 ©2023 Association for Computational Linguistics

word-replacements using intersection alignments on both human evaluation and extrinsic evaluation. We also investigate controlling the amount of generated data, to eliminate the effect of random producing more data over the predictive model. Under the constrained condition, using a predictive model outperforms the random approach on the MT task.

In this work, we tackle the following research questions (RQs):

- **RQ1:** Can a model learn to predict CS points using limited amount of CS data?
- **RQ2:** Can this information be used to generate more natural synthetic CS data?
- **RQ3:** Would higher quality of synthesized CS data necessarily reflect in performance improvements in downstream tasks?

2 Related Work

Most of the work done for CS data augmentation has been focused on LM, mostly for ASR. Several techniques have been proposed based on linguistic theories (Pratapa et al., 2018; Lee et al., 2019; Hussein et al., 2023), heuristics (Shen et al., 2011; Vu et al., 2012; Kuwanto et al., 2021a), neural networks (Chang et al., 2018; Winata et al., 2018, 2019; Li and Vu, 2020), and MT (Tarunesh et al., 2021). CS data augmentation has been less investigated for MT. Previous work has mainly involved lexical replacements (Menacer et al., 2019; Song et al., 2019; Appicharla et al., 2021; Gupta et al., 2021; Xu and Yvon, 2021) and back translation (Kuwanto et al., 2021b). In this section, we discuss previous work that we find closest to ours.

Hussein et al. (2023) generated synthetic CS Arabic-English text based on the equivalence constraint (EC) theory (Poplack, 1980) using the GCM tool (Rizvi et al., 2021), as well as random lexical replacements. It was shown that while relying on the EC theory generates more natural CS sentences, as shown in human evaluation, using lexical replacements outperforms the linguistic-based approach on LM and ASR tasks.

In the direction of lexical replacements, Appicharla et al. (2021) generated synthetic CS Hindi-English sentences by replacing all source words (except for stopwords) by the corresponding target words using 1-1 alignments, achieving improvements on MT task. Gupta et al. (2021) trained a neural-based model to predict CS points on monolingual source text. Using 1-n alignments, the

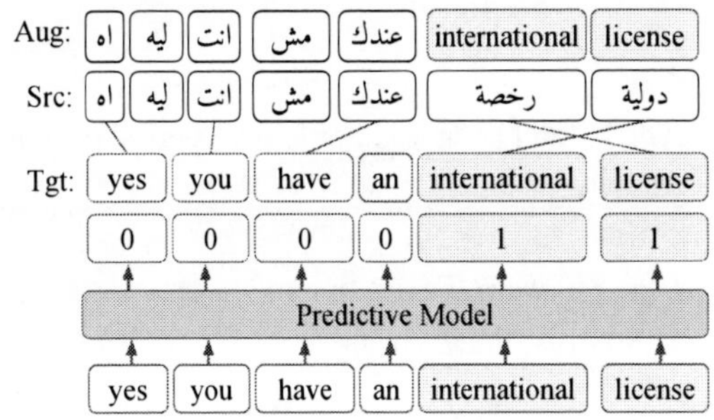

Figure 1: Data augmentation process.

source word is replaced by the aligned word(s). They evaluate their approach against unigram and bigram random replacements, and test its effectiveness on MT task for CS Hindi-English. Xu and Yvon (2021) use data augmentation for MT task for CS Spanish-English and French-English. Symmetrized alignments are used to identify small aligned phrases (minimal alignment units) and phrase replacements are performed randomly. We also notice that in literature, human evaluation of generated CS data is mainly used to evaluate the synthetic data produced by the best model, rather than comparing different techniques. Such a comparison was provided by Pratapa and Choudhury (2021), where a large-scale human evaluation was presented comparing different linguistic-driven and lexical replacement techniques. However, the study was focused on human evaluation without exploring the effectiveness of those techniques on downstream tasks.

3 Data Augmentation

For generating synthetic CS data, we investigate the use of word-aligned parallel sentences as well as dictionary-based replacements. In the latter approach, monolingual Arabic sentences are augmented by replacing words at random locations with their English glossary entry. In the former approach, utilizing monolingual Arabic-English parallel corpora, we inject words from the target side to the source side, where replacements are performed at random locations or using a CS point predictive model. As shown in Figure 1, the augmentation process consists of two main steps: (1) CS point prediction: identifying the target words to be borrowed, and (2) CS generation: performing the replacements. In Sections 3.1 and 3.2, we will elaborate on the methodology for both steps.

	Examples
Src	← و i was a junior ta في فترة جربت الموضوع ف i love ال academic life شوية .
Tgt	and i was a junior ta for a period of time so i have tried this and i love the academic life a bit .
Output	0 1 1 1 1 1 0 0 0 0 0 00 0 0 0 0 1 1 0 1 1 0 0 0
Src	← ماكنتش م expect اني اشوف city زي دي اساسا
Tgt	i wasn 't expecting to see such a city in the first place .
Output	0 0 0 1 0 0 0 0 1 0 0 0 0 0

Table 1: Example showing the matching algorithm output for given source and target sentences. The matched words on the target side are underlined. The arrows show the sentence starting direction, as Arabic is read right to left.

3.1 CS Point Prediction

Similar to Gupta et al. (2021), we model the task of CS point prediction as a sequence-to-sequence classification task. The neural network takes as input the word sequence $x = \{x_1, x_2, .., x_N\}$, where N is the length of the input sentence. The network outputs a sequence $y = \{y_1, y_2, .., y_N\}$, where $y_n \in \{1,0\}$ represents whether the word x_n is to be code-switched or not. We learn CS points using ArzEn-ST corpus (Hamed et al., 2022b), which contains CS Egyptian Arabic-English sentences and their English translations. We then utilize the learnt CS model to augment a large number of monolingual Arabic-English parallel sentences by inserting the tagged words on the (English) target side into the (Egyptian Arabic) source side.

In order to learn CS points, the neural network needs to take as input monolingual sentences from either the source or target sides, along with tags representing whether this word should be code-switched or not. In Gupta et al. (2021), the authors generated synthetic monolingual sentences from CS sentences by translating CS segments to the source language, and then learning CS points on the source side. While this approach seems more intuitive, CS segments abide by the grammatical rules of the embedded language, thus direct translation of embedded words would result in sentences having incorrect structures in the matrix language in case of syntactic divergence, which is present between Arabic and English. Instead, we opt to learn CS points on the target side. This approach provides another advantage, as English is commonly used in CS, having the predictive model trained on English as opposed to the primary language (which could be low-resourced) allows for the use of available resources such as pretrained LMs.

The challenge in this approach is identifying the words on the target side which correspond to the CS words on the source side. Relying on the translators to perform this annotation task is costly, time consuming, and error-prone.[1] Relying on word alignments is also not optimal, where only 83% of CS words in ArzEn-ST train set were matched using intersection alignment. Recall could increase using a less strict alignment approach, but would be at the risk of less accurate matches. Therefore, we develop a matching algorithm that is based on the following idea: if a CS segment occurs x times in the source and target sentences, then we identify these segments as matching segments. We match segments starting with the longest segments (and sub-segments) first. When matching words, we check their categorial variation (Habash and Dorr, 2003) as well as stems to match words having slight modifications in translation.[2] This matching algorithm provides a language-agnostic approach to identify words on the target side that are code-switched segments on the source side.[3] Examples of algorithm output are shown in Table 1, where it is seen that *expect* and *expecting* are matched as a result of the categorial variation check.

3.2 CS Generation

After identifying the target words to be embedded into the source side, we rely on alignments using GIZA++ (Casacuberta and Vidal, 2007) to perform the replacements. While direct replacements can be performed in the case of single word switches, in the case of replacing multiple consecutive words, direct word replacements would produce incorrect CS structures in the case of syntactic divergence.

[1] We have tried this annotation task for ArzEn-ST and only 72% of the CS words got annotated.

[2] In case $|matches_{tgt}| > |matches_{src}|$, we first rely on alignments to make the decision, achieving 99.6% matches on ArzEn-ST train set, then we randomly pick matched target segments to cover the number of matches on the source side in order to increase recall.

[3] Code available: http://arzen.camel-lab.com/

In the case of Arabic-English, this is particularly evident for adjectival phrases. Accordingly, when performing word replacements, we maintain the same order of consecutive English words, which we refer to as the "Continuity Constraint". In Figure 2, the importance of applying this constraint is illustrated. Without such a constraint, the generated sentence outlined in Figure 2 would follow the Arabic syntactic structure resulting in "ده topic important very" (*this [is a] topic important very*).

When performing replacements, we investigate the use of intersection alignments as well as grow-diag-final alignments.[4] While intersection alignment provides high precision, relying on 1-1 alignments is not always correct, as an Arabic word can map to multiple English words and vice versa. Therefore, we investigate the use of grow-diag-final (symmetrized) alignments to identify aligned segments. The aligned segments consist of pairs of the minimal number of consecutive words (S,T) where all words in source segment (S) are aligned to one or more words in target segment (T) and are not aligned to any other words outside (T), with the same constraints applying in the opposite (target-source) direction. Afterwards, for each English word receiving a positive CS tag, the whole target segment containing this word replaces the aligned source segment. Throughout the paper, we will refer to the two approaches as using 1-1 and n-n alignments. In Figure 3, we present an example showing the results of augmentation using predictive CS models versus random CS point prediction along with using 1-1 or n-n alignments.

3.3 Augmentation Approaches

We investigate the following approaches:

DICTIONARY: We randomly pick x source words and replace them with an English glossary entry using MADAMIRA (Pasha et al., 2014). We set x to 19% of the source words, where this number is chosen based on the percentage of English words in CS sentences in ArzEn-ST train set, given that we would like to mimic natural CS behaviour.

[4]We experiment with relying on alignments trained on word space only, stem space only, and the merge of both alignments, where for intersection alignments, we first rely on the alignments obtained in stem space, and add remaining alignments obtained from word space, such that 1-1 alignments are retained, and for grow-diag-final alignments, we take the union of alignments in both spaces. We find that merging alignments in both spaces achieves higher alignment coverage as well as better results in extrinsic tasks. Therefore, we will only be presenting the results using the merged alignments.

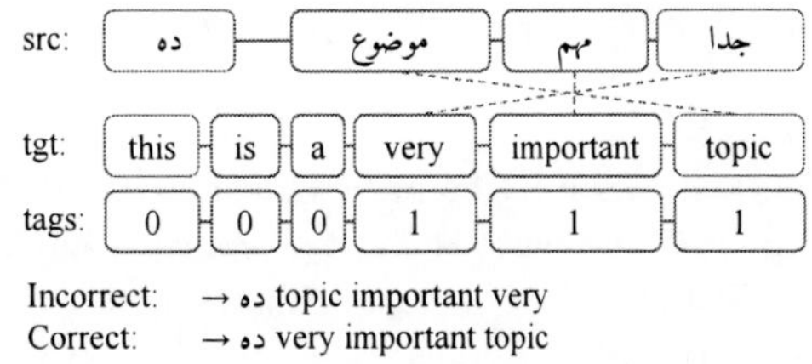

Figure 2: Data augmentation under the Continuity Constraint.

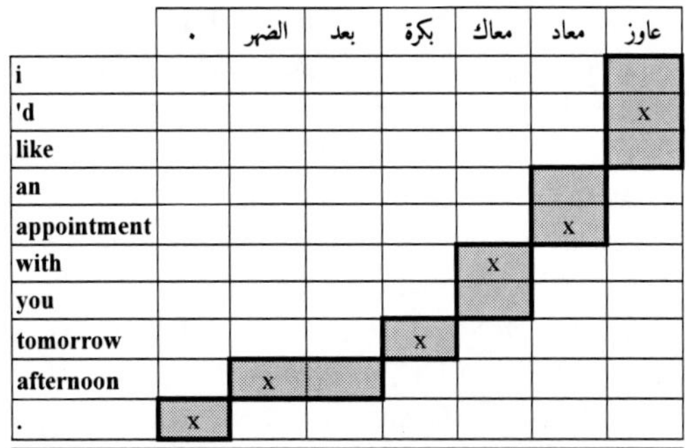

Rand (1-1)	← عاوز معاد معاك بكرة بعد afternoon . *I'd like an appointment with you tomorrow after afternoon*
Rand (n-n)	← عاوز معاد معاك بكرة afternoon . *I'd like an appointment with you tomorrow afternoon*
Pred (1-1)	→ i 'd appointment معاك بكرة بعد الضهر . *I'd appointment with you tomorrow afternoon*
Pred (n-n)	→ i 'd like an appointment معاك بكرة بعد الضهر . *I'd like an appointment with you tomorrow afternoon*

Figure 3: Example showing 1-1 and n-n alignments. The intersection alignments are marked with 'x' and the grow-diag-final alignments are highlighted. We show the generated sentences with translations for each setup.

MAPRAND: We randomly pick x target words having source-target intersection alignments. We set x to 19% of the source words. We use word and segment replacements, where the models are referred to as MAPRAND$_{1-1}$ and MAPRAND$_{n-n}$.

MAPPRED: We fine-tune pretrained mBERT model using NERDA framework (Kjeldgaard and Nielsen, 2021) to predict the target words to be injected into the source side.[5] We use 1-1 and n-n alignments to perform replacements, where the models are referred to as MAPPRED$_{1-1}$ and MAPPRED$_{n-n}$.[6] For finetuning mBERT, we set the epochs to 5, drop-out rate to 0.1, warmup steps to 500, batch size to 13, and learning rate to 0.0001.

[5]We maintain the original tokenization of the input text, where we project further tokenization performed on the output into the original tokenization.

[6]For training the predictive models, we also tried using BERT models, which gave slightly lower results.

4 Experiments

4.1 Data

We use ArzEn-ST corpus (Hamed et al., 2022b) as our CS corpus. The corpus contains English translations of an Egyptian Arabic-English code-switched speech corpus (Hamed et al., 2020) that is gathered through informal interviews with bilingual speakers. The corpus is divided into train, dev, and test sets having $3.3k$, $1.4k$, and $1.4k$ sentences (containing $2.2k$, $0.9k$, and $0.9k$ CS sentences), respectively. We follow the same data splits. In Appendix A, we provide an overview of ArzEn-ST corpus.

We also utilize the following Egyptian Arabic-English parallel corpora: Callhome Egyptian Arabic-English Speech Translation Corpus (Gadalla et al., 1997; LDC, 2002b,a; Kumar et al., 2014), LDC2012T09 (Zbib et al., 2012), LDC2017T07 (Chen et al., 2017), LDC2019T01 (Chen et al., 2019), LDC2021T15 (Tracey et al., 2021), and MADAR (Bouamor et al., 2018). The corpora contain $308k$ monolingual parallel sentences as well as $15k$ CS parallel sentences. We use the same data splits as defined for each corpus. For corpora with no defined data splits, we use the guidelines provided in (Diab et al., 2013). Data preprocessing for ArzEn-ST and the parallel corpora is discussed in Appendix C.

Data Augmentation: For data augmentation, we use the monolingual parallel sentences and augment them into CS parallel sentences. For the CS point predictive model, we use the CS sentences in ArzEn-ST train and dev sets for training and development, respectively.

MT: The MT baseline system is trained on ArzEn-ST train set, in addition to the $308k$ monolingual parallel sentences. In the augmentation experiments, we add the augmented sentences to the baseline training data. For development and testing, we use ArzEn-ST dev and test sets.

ASR: The ASR baseline system is trained on the following Egyptian Arabic data: ArzEn speech corpus (Hamed et al., 2020), Callhome (Gadalla et al., 1997), and MGB-3 (Ali et al., 2017). A subset of 5-hours was used from each of Librispeech (Panayotov et al., 2015) (English) and MGB-2 (Ali et al., 2016) (MSA), where adding more data from these corpora deteriorated the ASR performance (Hamed et al., 2022a). The LM baseline model is trained on corpora transcriptions. For the LM models using augmented data, we append the augmented data to those transcriptions. For development and testing, we use ArzEn-ST dev and test sets.

As an extra experiment, we compare the performance of the systems relying on synthetic CS data versus using available real CS data. For MT, we use the $15k$ CS parallel sentences in addition to the baseline data. For ASR rescoring, we train the LM on the baseline data in addition to 117,844 code-switched sentences collected from social media platforms (Hamed et al., 2019). We denote these experiments as *ExtraCS* in the results.

4.2 Machine Translation System

We train a Transformer model using Fairseq (Ott et al., 2019) on a single GeForce RTX 3090 GPU. We use the hyperparameters from the FLORES benchmark for low-resource machine translation (Guzmán et al., 2019).[7] The hyperparameters are given in Appendix D. We use a BPE model trained jointly on source and target sides with a vocabulary size of $16k$ (which outperforms $1, 3, 5, 8, 32, 64k$).[8] The BPE model is trained using Fairseq with character_coverage set to 1.0.

4.3 Automatic Speech Recognition System

We train a joint CTC/attention based E2E ASR system using ESPnet (Watanabe et al., 2018). The encoder and decoder consist of 12 and 6 Transformer blocks with 4 heads, feed-forward inner dimension 2048 and attention dimension 256. The CTC/attention weight (λ_1) is set to 0.3. SpecAugment (Park et al., 2019) is applied for data augmentation. For LM, the RNNLM consists of 1 LSTM layer with 1000 hidden units and is trained for 20 epochs. For decoding, the beam size is 20 and the CTC weight is 0.2.

4.4 Speech Translation System

We build a cascaded ST system using the ASR and MT models. We opt for a cascaded system over an end-to-end system due to the limitation of available resources to build an end-to-end system, in addition to the fact that cascaded systems have shown to outperform end-to-end systems in low-resource settings (Denisov et al., 2021).

[7]We follow (Gaser et al., 2022), where it was shown that FLORES hyperparameters outperform Vaswani et al. (2017) using the same datasets.

[8]For the *ExtraCS* experiment, we use a vocabulary size of $8k$, which outperforms $16k$ and $32k$.

5 Results

In order to evaluate our augmentation techniques, we provide intrinsic evaluation, extrinsic evaluation, as well as human evaluation.[9] According to human evaluation, the synthetic data generated using a CS predictive model is perceived as more natural. However, our extrinsic evaluation shows that both aligned-based approaches (random replacements and relying on a predictive model) perform equally on downstream tasks. We observe that using a predictive model generates less data than the random approach. When controlling for size, we observe that using a predictive model brings improvements on the MT task. Both aligned-based approaches outperform dictionary-based replacements on human evaluation and extrinsic evaluation. Regarding the effect of word alignment configurations, the improvements of using n-n alignments versus 1-1 alignments is confirmed in both human evaluation and extrinsic evaluation.

5.1 Intrinsic Evaluation

Predictive Model Evaluation We compare the CS point predictions provided by the predictive model against the actual CS points in the CS sentences in ArzEn-ST dev set. We present accuracy, precision, recall, and F1 scores in Table 2. While these figures give us an intuition on the performance of the predictive models, it is to be noted that false positives are not necessarily incorrect. It is also to be noted that the high accuracy values are due to the high rate of true negative predictions.

As another evaluation, we check the POS distribution of the words predicted as CS by both the random and predictive models, against that of CS words in ArzEn-ST dev set. The predictive model shows a higher correlation (0.984) versus random approach (0.938). The POS distribution of the top frequent tags is shown in Appendix B. The predictions of the learnt model are dominated by nouns, followed by verbs and adjectives, where other POS tags have lower frequencies than in ArzEn-ST. The random approach gives better coverage for POS tags, however, introduces higher frequencies for low-frequent POS tags of CS words in ArzEn-ST.

CS Synthetic Data Analysis We look into how similar the synthetic data is to naturally occurring CS sentences. In Table 3, we evaluate the synthetic data in terms of the percentage of English words, the Code-Mixing Index (CMI) (Das and Gambäck, 2014), the average length of CS segments, as well as the percentage of monolingual English sentences generated. We observe that using 1-1 alignments, the generated CS sentences are close to natural occurring CS sentences in ArzEn-ST in terms of CS metrics. Using n-n alignments, the amount of CS in the synthetic data increases considerably.

Model	Accuracy	Precision	Recall	F1
Random	77.1	18.8	21.0	0.198
Predictive	**91.9**	**76.6**	**57.4**	**0.656**

Table 2: Evaluating the performance of the predictive model on the code-switched sentences in ArzEn-ST dev set.

Model	%En (words)	CMI	av.|CS|	%En (sent.)
DICTIONARY	21.1	0.23	1.2	0.0
MAPRAND$_{1-1}$	19.9	0.22	1.14	0.0
MAPPRED$_{1-1}$	16.7	0.22	1.23	6.3
MAPRAND$_{n-n}$	27.7	0.25	2.26	6.8
MAPPRED$_{n-n}$	28.9	0.26	2.84	18.3
ArzEn-ST	18.6	0.19	1.88	3.7

Table 3: Evaluating augmented sentences in terms of CS metrics against ArzEn-ST train set.

5.2 Extrinsic Evaluation

We evaluate the improvements achieved through data augmentation on LM, ASR, MT, and ST tasks. Results are shown in Table 4. We present perplexity (PPL) for LM and Word Error Rate (WER) and Character Error Rate (CER) for ASR. For MT and ST, we use BLEU (Papineni et al., 2002), chrF, chrF++ (Popović, 2017), and BERTScore (F1) (Zhang et al., 2019). BLEU, chrF and chrF++ are calculated using SacrebleuBLEU (Post, 2018). In Table 4, we present the chrF++ scores. We present the results for all metrics in Appendix E.

Language Modeling PPL reductions are observed when using n-n over 1-1 alignments for random-based replacements. While MAPRAND$_{n-n}$ generates more data than MAPPRED$_{n-n}$, both approaches achieve similar PPL, outperforming DICTIONARY. Overall, we achieve a 34% reduction in PPL over baseline.

[9]The MT models require around 4 hours for training. The ASR system required around 48 hours for training, as well as 6 hours for ASR rescoring. The CS predictive model using mBERT required around 10 hours for inference.

		LM	ASR		MT		ST	
Model	**|Train|**	**PPL$_{All}$**	**WER$_{All}$**	**CER$_{All}$**	**chrF++$_{All}$**	**chrF++$_{CS}$**	**chrF++$_{All}$**	**chrF++$_{CS}$**
Baseline		415.1	34.7	20.0	53.0	54.0	39.4	40.4
+DICTIONARY	+240,678	313.3	33.2	19.1	52.6	53.5	40.1	41.0
+MAPRAND$_{1-1}$	+240,869	306.1	32.9	19.0	55.2*	57.0*	41.0*	42.1*
+MAPPRED$_{1-1}$	+177,633	273.4	33.2	19.1	55.5†	57.4†	40.9†	42.2†
+MAPRAND$_{n-n}$	+207,026	273.8	**32.9**	**18.9**	**56.0***	**57.9***	41.4*	42.7*
+MAPPRED$_{n-n}$	+138,544	274.5	33.0	**18.9**	**56.0**†	57.8†	**41.5**†	**42.8**†
+ExtraCS		228.1	33.3	19.0	55.7	57.6	41.6	42.9
Constrained Experiments								
+c[DICTIONARY]	+99,725	324.2	33.5	19.3	52.3	53.3	39.4	40.1
+c[MAPRAND$_{n-n}$]	+99,725	293.4	33.1	19.0	55.6*	57.3*	<u>41.2</u>	<u>42.6</u>
+c[MAPPRED$_{n-n}$]	+99,725	<u>270.4</u>	<u>33.0</u>	<u>18.9</u>	<u>56.0</u>*	<u>57.9</u>*	<u>41.2</u>	<u>42.6</u>

Table 4: We report the results of the extrinsic tasks on ArzEn-ST test set. For language modeling, we report PPL on all sentences. For ASR, we report WER and CER on all sentences. For MT and ST, we report chrF++ on all and CS sentences. We report the results of using all augmentations (non-constrained), followed by the constrained experiments. The best performing approach in the non-constrained setting is bolded. The best performing approach in the constrained setting is underlined. We run statistical significance tests between MAPRAND and MAPPRED as well as 1-1 and n-n experiments, and mark models that are statistically significant (*p-values*< 0.05) with superscript symbols ($*, \dagger, \star$).

ASR All models utilizing augmented data outperform the baseline. The best results are achieved using MAPPRED$_{n-n}$ and MAPRAND$_{n-n}$, which perform equally well, achieving 5.2% absolute WER reduction over baseline. We observe that these models slightly outperform those trained on extra real CS data.[10]

Machine Translation Evaluation Results show that using n-n alignments outperforms 1-1 alignments on all settings. However, using a predictive model does not outperform random replacements. We observe that dictionary-based replacement negatively affects the MT systems. We also observe that our top two models perform equally well as the model utilizing real CS data, confirming the effectiveness of data augmentation, achieving 3-3.9 chrF++ points over the baseline.

MT Qualitative Analysis When looking into the translations provided by the baseline model, we observe that many CS words get dropped in translation or get mistranslated. When checking the translations provided by the MT systems trained using augmentations, we observe that the majority of the CS words are retained through translation. We also observe that these MT systems are able to retain CS OOV words, where the words are not available in the baseline training data, nor introduced in the synthetic data. This shows that by adding CS synthetic sentences to the training set, the models learn to retain English words in translation. Examples are shown in Appendix F.

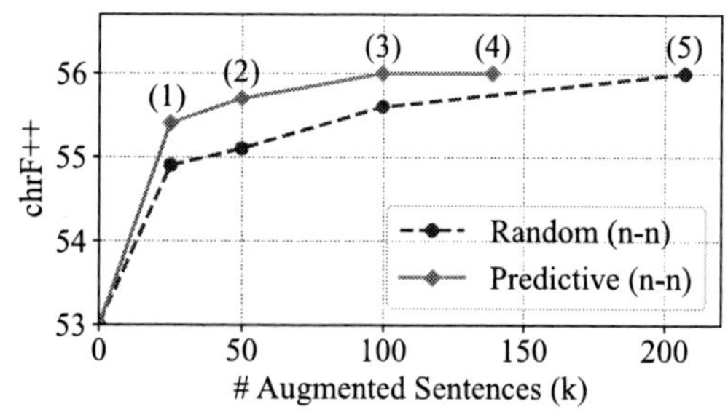

Figure 4: The chrF++ scores reported on ArzEn-ST test set when adding: (1) 25% of the sentences in the constrained experiment (=24.9k), (2) 50% of the sentences in the constrained experiment (=49.8k), (3) 100% of the sentences in the constrained experiment (=99.7k), (4) all sentences generated by MAPPRED$_{n-n}$ (=138.5k), and (5) all sentences generated by MAPRAND$_{n-n}$ (=207k).

Speech Translation Evaluation Similar to previous results, both MAPPRED and MAPRAND outperform DICTIONARY. We observe improvements for using n-n alignments over using 1-1 alignments. However, no improvements are achieved by using predictive model over random predictions.

[10]It is to be noted that the data collected from social media platforms is noisy, however, it still brings improvements in LM and ASR tasks.

	Understandability
1	No, this sentence doesn't make sense.
2	Not sure, but I can guess the meaning of this sentence.
3	Certainly, I get the meaning of this sentence.
	Naturalness
1	Unnatural, and I can't imagine people using this style of code-mixed Arabic-English.
2	Weird, but who knows, it could be some style of code-mixed Arabic-English.
3	Quite natural, but I think this style of code-mixed Arabic-English is rare.
4	Natural, and I think this style of code-mixed Arabic-English is used in real life.
5	Perfectly natural, and I think this style of code-mixed Arabic-English is very frequently used.

Table 5: The evaluation dimensions for human evaluation, following (Pratapa and Choudhury, 2021).

Constrained Experiments In order to control existing variables, such as the number of generated sentences, and how similar they are to the test set, we conduct further experiments where we restrict the augmented sentences in each approach to the CS sentences that are generated across the three techniques: DICTIONARY, MAPRAND$_{n-n}$, and MAPPRED$_{n-n}$. We report results by training our models using these restricted augmentations ($99.7k$ sentences) in addition to the baseline training data in Table 4. We find that, under this condition, for the MT task, the predictive model outperforms random, where the improvements are statistically significant on BLEU, chrF, and chrF++, as shown in Table 10. For the ASR task, while MAPPRED$_{n-n}$ achieves lower PPL over MAPRAND$_{n-n}$, both models perform equally. In Figure 4, we show the learning curves for MAPRAND$_{n-n}$ and MAPPRED$_{n-n}$ MT scores when including 25%, 50%, and 100% of the generated sentences in the constrained setting, in addition to the scores of the non-constrained setting. We see that MAPPRED$_{n-n}$ achieves overall the same performance as MAPRAND$_{n-n}$ with half the amount of generated sentences.

5.3 Human Evaluation

We perform a human evaluation study to assess the quality of sentences generated by the five models: MAPRAND$_{1-1}$, MAPPRED$_{1-1}$, MAPRAND$_{n-n}$, MAPPRED$_{n-n}$, and DICTIONARY. Out of the sentences that get augmented in all five techniques, we randomly sample 150 sentences, and ask human annotators to judge the synthetic sentences generated by each model, giving a total of 750 sentences to be evaluated.[11] We also include 150 random CS sentences from ArzEn-ST to act as control sentences. These 900 sentences were judged by three bilingual Egyptian Arabic-English speakers. Following (Pratapa and Choudhury, 2021), the sentences are evaluated against understandability and naturalness, where the rubrics are outlined in Table 5.

MOS	ArzEn	DICT	RAND (1-1)	PRED (1-1)	RAND (n-n)	PRED (n-n)
Understandability						
$1\leq * < 2$	2.7	62.0	32.7	32.0	21.3	16.7
$2\leq * < 3$	97.3	38.0	67.3	68.0	78.7	83.3
Naturalness						
$1\leq * < 2$	0.7	82.7	70.7	50.0	46.7	30.0
$2\leq * < 3$	6.0	8.7	12.7	18.0	26.0	25.3
$3\leq * < 4$	11.3	6.0	8.0	20.0	14.0	26.0
$4\leq * \leq 5$	82.0	2.7	8.7	12.0	13.3	18.7

Table 6: The mean opinion score (MOS) distribution for synthetic sentences, showing the percentage of sentences falling in each evaluation range.

For each synthetic/real sentence, we calculate the mean opinion score (MOS), which is the average of the three annotators' scores for that sentence. In Table 6, we present the MOS distribution for each augmentation approach, presenting the percentage of sentences falling in each evaluation range. We observe that the annotators prefer the synthetic data generated using segment replacements (n-n alignments) over those using word replacements (1-1 alignments). The annotators also prefer the synthetic data generated using trained predictive models over those using random CS point prediction. The highest scores are achieved by MAPRAND$_{n-n}$, where 44% of the synthetic sentences are perceived as natural.

[11]The sentences are sampled uniformly across the 6 corpora used in data augmentation to have equal representation of the different data sources (web/chat/conversational).

6 Discussion

In this section, we revisit our RQs:

RQ1 - Can a model learn to predict CS points using limited amount of CS data? As shown in the intrinsic evaluation, the model learns to predict CS points to some extent, as shown in the improvements in accuracy, precision, and F1 scores over random predictions. This is also observed where the POS distribution of the CS predictions using a predictive model has higher correlation to the distribution found in natural CS sentences compared to random predictions.

RQ2 - Can this information be used to generate more natural synthetic CS data? Yes, this was confirmed though human evaluation, where annotators reported higher scores for understandability and naturalness using the predictive model over using random replacements.

RQ3 - Would higher quality of synthesized CS data necessarily reflect in performance improvements in downstream tasks? In the scope of our experiments, such an entailment does not necessarily hold. We believe two limitations are affecting the performance of the predictive model. First of all, the MAPPRED approach is based on the assumption that the data provided to the predictive model is representative enough of the CS phenomenon and includes all CS patterns. Due to the scarcity of CS corpora and the dynamic behaviour of CS (El Bolock et al., 2020), this point presents a challenge and could be restricting the potential power of this model, and it could be the case that MAPRAND is able to cover more CS patterns. This is supported by the POS distribution analysis in Section 5.1. Secondly, random has the power of generating more data as opposed to using a predictive model. When we control for size, we observe improvements in MT using the predictive model. In the future, we plan to work on improving the predictive approach to generate more CS sentences. For ASR, both approaches perform equally. It was also shown in (Hussein et al., 2023) that random lexical replacement outperforms the use of Equivalence Constraint linguistic theorem for ASR. Therefore, we believe further research is needed to draw strong conclusions about the relation between the quality of generated CS data and the improvements on different downstream tasks.

7 Conclusion and Future Work

In this paper, we investigate data augmentation for CS Egyptian Arabic-English. We utilize parallel corpora to perform lexical replacements, where CS points are either selected randomly or based on predictions of a neural-based model that is trained on a limited amount of CS data. We investigate word replacements using intersection alignments as well as segment replacements using symmetrized alignments. We compare both aligned-based replacements with dictionary-based replacements. We evaluate the effectiveness of data augmentation on LM, MT, ASR, and ST tasks, as well as assess the quality through human evaluation. Across all evaluations, we report that segment replacements outperform word replacements, and aligned-based replacements outperform dictionary-based replacements. The human evaluation study shows that utilizing predictive models produces augmented data of highest quality. For the downstream tasks, random and predictive techniques achieve similar results, both outperforming dictionary-based replacements. We observe that random has the advantage of generating more data. When controlling for the amount of generated data, the predictive technique outperforms random on the MT task. Our best models achieve 34% improvement in perplexity, 5.2% relative improvement on WER for ASR task, +4.0-5.1 BLEU points on MT task, and +2.1-2.2 BLEU points on ST task.

Acknowledgements

We would like to thank Bashar Alhafni for the helpful discussions and the reviewers for their insightful comments. This project has benefited from financial support by DAAD (German Academic Exchange Service).

References

Ahmed Ali, Peter Bell, James Glass, Yacine Messaoui, Hamdy Mubarak, Steve Renals, and Yifan Zhang. 2016. The MGB-2 challenge: Arabic multi-dialect broadcast media recognition. In *SLT*, pages 279–284.

Ahmed Ali, Stephan Vogel, and Steve Renals. 2017. Speech recognition challenge in the wild: Arabic MGB-3. In *Proceedings of ASRU*, pages 316–322.

Ramakrishna Appicharla, Kamal Kumar Gupta, Asif Ekbal, and Pushpak Bhattacharyya. 2021. IITP-MT at CALCS2021: English to Hinglish neural machine translation using unsupervised synthetic code-mixed parallel corpus. In *Proceedings of CALCS*, pages 31–35.

Mohamed Balabel, Injy Hamed, Slim Abdennadher, Ngoc Thang Vu, and Özlem Çetinoğlu. 2020. Cairo student code-switch (CSCS) corpus: An annotated Egyptian Arabic-English corpus. In *Proceedings of LREC*, pages 3973–3977.

Houda Bouamor, Nizar Habash, Mohammad Salameh, Wajdi Zaghouani, Owen Rambow, Dana Abdulrahim, Ossama Obeid, Salam Khalifa, Fadhl Eryani, Alexander Erdmann, and Kemal Oflazer. 2018. The MADAR Arabic Dialect Corpus and Lexicon. In *Proceedings of LREC*.

Francisco Casacuberta and Enrique Vidal. 2007. Giza++: Training of statistical translation models. *Polytechnic University of Valencia, Valencia, Spain*.

Ching-Ting Chang, Shun-Po Chuang, and Hung-Yi Lee. 2018. Code-switching sentence generation by generative adversarial networks and its application to data augmentation. In *Proceedings of Interspeech*, pages 554–558.

Song Chen, Dana Fore, Stephanie Strassel, Haejoong Lee, and Jonathan Wright. 2017. BOLT Egyptian Arabic SMS/Chat and Transliteration LDC2017T07. Philadelphia: Linguistic Data Consortium.

Song Chen, Jennifer Tracey, Christopher Walker, and Stephanie Strassel. 2019. BOLT Arabic discussion forum parallel training data. Linguistic Data Consortium (LDC) catalog number LDC2019T01, ISBN 1-58563-871-4.

Amitava Das and Björn Gambäck. 2014. Identifying languages at the word level in code-mixed Indian social media text. In *Proceedings of the 11th International Conference on Natural Language Processing*, pages 378–387.

Pavel Denisov, Manuel Mager, and Ngoc Thang Vu. 2021. IMS' systems for the first IWSLT 2021 low-resource speech translation task. In *Proceedings of IWSLT*.

Mona Diab, Nizar Habash, Owen Rambow, and Ryan Roth. 2013. LDC Arabic treebanks and associated corpora: Data divisions manual. *arXiv preprint arXiv:1309.5652*.

Alia El Bolock, Injy Khairy, Yomna Abdelrahman, Ngoc Thang Vu, Cornelia Herbert, and Slim Abdennadher. 2020. Who, when and why: The 3 Ws of code-switching. In *Proceedings of Highlights in Practical Applications of Agents, Multi-Agent Systems, and Trust-worthiness*, pages 83–94.

Hassan Gadalla, Hanaa Kilany, Howaida Arram, Ashraf Yacoub, Alaa El-Habashi, Amr Shalaby, Krisjanis Karins, Everett Rowson, Robert MacIntyre, Paul Kingsbury, David Graff, and Cynthia McLemore. 1997. CALLHOME Egyptian Arabic transcripts – LDC97T19. Web Download. Philadelphia: Linguistic Data Consortium.

Marwa Gaser, Manuel Mager, Injy Hamed, Nizar Habash, Slim Abdennadher, and Ngoc Thang Vu. 2022. Exploring segmentation approaches for neural machine translation of code-switched Egyptian Arabic-English text. In *Proceedings of EACL*.

Abhirut Gupta, Aditya Vavre, and Sunita Sarawagi. 2021. Training data augmentation for code-mixed translation. In *Proceedings of NAACL-HLT*, pages 5760–5766.

Francisco Guzmán, Peng-Jen Chen, Myle Ott, Juan Pino, Guillaume Lample, Philipp Koehn, Vishrav Chaudhary, and Marc'Aurelio Ranzato. 2019. The FLORES evaluation datasets for low-resource machine translation: Nepali–English and Sinhala–English. In *Proceedings of EMNLP-IJCNLP*, pages 6098–6111.

Nizar Habash and Bonnie Dorr. 2003. CatVar: A database of categorial variations for English. In *Proceedings of Machine Translation Summit IX: System Presentations*.

Nizar Habash, Abdelhadi Soudi, and Tim Buckwalter. 2007. On Arabic Transliteration. In A. van den Bosch and A. Soudi, editors, *Arabic Computational Morphology: Knowledge-based and Empirical Methods*, pages 15–22.

Injy Hamed, Pavel Denisov, Chia-Yu Li, Mohamed Elmahdy, Slim Abdennadher, and Ngoc Thang Vu. 2022a. Investigations on speech recognition systems for low-resource dialectal Arabic–English code-switching speech. *Computer Speech & Language*, 72:101278.

Injy Hamed, Mohamed Elmahdy, and Slim Abdennadher. 2018. Collection and analysis of code-switch Egyptian Arabic-English speech corpus. In *Proceedings of LREC*.

Injy Hamed, Nizar Habash, Slim Abdennadher, and Ngoc Thang Vu. 2022b. ArzEn-ST: A three-way speech translation corpus for code-switched Egyptian Arabic-English. In *Proceedings of WANLP*.

Injy Hamed, Ngoc Thang Vu, and Slim Abdennadher. 2020. ArzEn: A speech corpus for code-switched Egyptian Arabic-English. In *Proceedings of LREC*, pages 4237–4246.

Injy Hamed, Moritz Zhu, Mohamed Elmahdy, Slim Abdennadher, and Ngoc Thang Vu. 2019. Code-switching language modeling with bilingual word embeddings: A case study for Egyptian Arabic-English. In *Proceedings of SPECOM*, pages 160–170.

Amir Hussein, Shammur Absar Chowdhury, Ahmed Abdelali, Najim Dehak, Ahmed Ali, and Sanjeev Khudanpur. 2023. Textual data augmentation for Arabic-English code-switching speech recognition. In *Proceedings of SLT*, pages 777–784.

Lars Kjeldgaard and Lukas Nielsen. 2021. NERDA. GitHub.

Philipp Koehn, Hieu Hoang, Alexandra Birch, Chris Callison-Burch, Marcello Federico, Nicola Bertoldi, Brooke Cowan, Wade Shen, Christine Moran, Richard Zens, Chris Dyer, Ondrej Bojar, Alexandra Constantin, and Evan Herbst. 2007. Moses: Open source toolkit for statistical machine translation. In *Proceedings of ACL*, pages 177–180.

Gaurav Kumar, Yuan Cao, Ryan Cotterell, Chris Callison-Burch, Daniel Povey, and Sanjeev Khudanpur. 2014. Translations of the CALLHOME Egyptian Arabic corpus for conversational speech translation. In *Proceedings of IWSLT*.

Garry Kuwanto, Afra Feyza Akyürek, Isidora Chara Tourni, Siyang Li, and Derry Wijaya. 2021a. Low-resource machine translation for low-resource languages: Leveraging comparable data, code-switching and compute resources. *CoRR*, abs/2103.13272.

Garry Kuwanto, Afra Feyza Akyürek, Isidora Chara Tourni, Siyang Li, Alexander Gregory Jones, and Derry Wijaya. 2021b. Low-resource machine translation training curriculum fit for low-resource languages. *arXiv preprint arXiv:2103.13272*.

LDC. 2002a. 1997 HUB5 Arabic transcripts – LDC2002T39. Web Download. Philadelphia: Linguistic Data Consortium.

LDC. 2002b. CALLHOME Egyptian Arabic transcripts supplement – LDC2002T38. Web Download. Philadelphia: Linguistic Data Consortium.

Grandee Lee, Xianghu Yue, and Haizhou Li. 2019. Linguistically motivated parallel data augmentation for code-switch language modeling. In *Proceedings of Interspeech*, pages 3730–3734.

Chia-Yu Li and Ngoc Thang Vu. 2020. Improving code-switching language modeling with artificially generated texts using cycle-consistent adversarial networks. In *Proceedings of Interspeech*, pages 1057–1061.

Mohamed Amine Menacer, David Langlois, Denis Jouvet, Dominique Fohr, Odile Mella, and Kamel Smaïli. 2019. Machine translation on a parallel code-switched corpus. In *Proceedings of the Canadian Conference on Artificial Intelligence*, pages 426–432.

Myle Ott, Sergey Edunov, Alexei Baevski, Angela Fan, Sam Gross, Nathan Ng, David Grangier, and Michael Auli. 2019. FAIRSEQ: A fast, extensible toolkit for sequence modeling. In *Proceedings of NAACL (Demonstrations)*, pages 48–53.

Vassil Panayotov, Guoguo Chen, Daniel Povey, and Sanjeev Khudanpur. 2015. Librispeech: an ASR corpus based on public domain audio books. In *Proceesings of ICASSP*, pages 5206–5210.

Kishore Papineni, Salim Roukos, Todd Ward, and Wei-Jing Zhu. 2002. BLEU: a method for automatic evaluation of machine translation. In *Proceedings of ACL*, pages 311–318.

Daniel S Park, William Chan, Yu Zhang, Chung-Cheng Chiu, Barret Zoph, Ekin D Cubuk, and Quoc V Le. 2019. SpecAugment: A simple data augmentation method for automatic speech recognition. In *Proceedings of Interspeech*, pages 2613–2617.

Arfath Pasha, Mohamed Al-Badrashiny, Mona Diab, Ahmed El Kholy, Ramy Eskander, Nizar Habash, Manoj Pooleery, Owen Rambow, and Ryan Roth. 2014. Madamira: A fast, comprehensive tool for morphological analysis and disambiguation of Arabic. In *Proceedings of LREC*, pages 1094–1101.

Shana Poplack. 1980. Sometimes i'll start a sentence in Spanish y termino en Español: Toward a typology of code-switching. *The bilingualism reader*, 18(2):221–256.

Maja Popović. 2017. chrF++: words helping character n-grams. In *Proceedings of the second conference on machine translation*, pages 612–618.

Matt Post. 2018. A call for clarity in reporting BLEU scores. In *Proceedings of the Third Conference on Machine Translation: Research Papers*, pages 186–191.

Adithya Pratapa, Gayatri Bhat, Monojit Choudhury, Sunayana Sitaram, Sandipan Dandapat, and Kalika Bali. 2018. Language modeling for code-mixing: The role of linguistic theory based synthetic data. In *Proceedings of ACL*, pages 1543–1553.

Adithya Pratapa and Monojit Choudhury. 2021. Comparing grammatical theories of code-mixing. In *Proceedings of the Seventh Workshop on Noisy User-generated Text (W-NUT 2021)*, pages 158–167.

Mohd Sanad Zaki Rizvi, Anirudh Srinivasan, Tanuja Ganu, Monojit Choudhury, and Sunayana Sitaram. 2021. GCM: A toolkit for generating synthetic code-mixed text. In *Proceedings of EACL (System Demonstrations)*, pages 205–211.

Caroline Sabty, Islam Omar, Fady Wasfalla, Mohamed Islam, and Slim Abdennadher. 2021. Data augmentation techniques on Arabic data for named entity recognition. *Procedia Computer Science*, 189:292–299.

Ali Shazal, Aiza Usman, and Nizar Habash. 2020. A unified model for Arabizi detection and transliteration using sequence-to-sequence models. In *Proceedings of the Arabic Natural Language Processing Workshop*, pages 167–177.

Han-Ping Shen, Chung-Hsien Wu, Yan-Ting Yang, and Chun-Shan Hsu. 2011. CECOS: A Chinese-english code-switching speech database. In *2011 International Conference on Speech Database and Assessments (Oriental COCOSDA)*, pages 120–123.

Kai Song, Yue Zhang, Heng Yu, Weihua Luo, Kun Wang, and Min Zhang. 2019. Code-switching for enhancing NMT with pre-specified translation. In *Proceedings of the Conference of the North American Chapter of the Association for Computational Linguistics: Human Language Technologies, Volume 1 (Long and Short Papers)*, pages 449–459.

Ishan Tarunesh, Syamantak Kumar, and Preethi Jyothi. 2021. From machine translation to code-switching: Generating high-quality code-switched text. In *Proceedings of ACL-IJCNLP*, pages 3154–3169.

Jennifer Tracey et al. 2021. BOLT Egyptian Arabic sms/chat parallel training data LDC2021T15. Web Download. Philadelphia: Linguistic Data Consortium.

Ashish Vaswani, Noam Shazeer, Niki Parmar, Jakob Uszkoreit, Llion Jones, Aidan N Gomez, Lukasz Kaiser, and Illia Polosukhin. 2017. Attention is all you need. *Advances in neural information processing systems*, 30.

Ngoc Thang Vu, Dau-Cheng Lyu, Jochen Weiner, Dominic Telaar, Tim Schlippe, Fabian Blaicher, Eng-Siong Chng, Tanja Schultz, and Haizhou Li. 2012. A first speech recognition system for Mandarin-English code-switch conversational speech. In *Proceedings of ICASSP*, pages 4889–4892.

Shinji Watanabe, Takaaki Hori, Shigeki Karita, Tomoki Hayashi, Jiro Nishitoba, Yuya Unno, Nelson Enrique Yalta Soplin, Jahn Heymann, Matthew Wiesner, Nanxin Chen, et al. 2018. Espnet: End-to-end speech processing toolkit. In *Proceedings of Interspeech*, pages 2207–2207.

Genta Indra Winata, Andrea Madotto, Chien-Sheng Wu, and Pascale Fung. 2018. Learn to code-switch: Data augmentation using copy mechanism on language modeling. *CoRR*, abs/1810.10254.

Genta Indra Winata, Andrea Madotto, Chien-Sheng Wu, and Pascale Fung. 2019. Code-switched language models using neural based synthetic data from parallel sentences. In *Proceedings of CoNLL*, pages 271–280.

Jitao Xu and François Yvon. 2021. Can you traducir this? machine translation for code-switched input. *arXiv preprint arXiv:2105.04846*.

Rabih Zbib, Erika Malchiodi, Jacob Devlin, David Stallard, Spyros Matsoukas, Richard Schwartz, John Makhoul, Omar F. Zaidan, and Chris CallisonBurch. 2012. Machine translation of Arabic dialects. In *Proceedings of NAACL*, pages 49–59.

Tianyi Zhang, Varsha Kishore, Felix Wu, Kilian Q Weinberger, and Yoav Artzi. 2019. BERTScore: Evaluating text generation with bert. In *Proceedings of the International Conference on Learning Representations*.

Limitations

To the best of our knowledge, this paper presents the first comparison for the mentioned lexical replacement techniques, covering human evaluation as well as three downstream tasks; automatic speech recognition, machine translation, and speech translation. However, the study is focused on the Egyptian Arabic-English language pair, and we make no assumptions on the generalizability of results to other language pairs, nor other domains. Further investigations are needed to assess how the results would differ, especially in the case of languages with less syntactic divergence. We also note another limitation in the human evaluation, which is that code-switching is a user-dependent behaviour, that differs across different users, and thus the evaluation of the naturalness of a code-switched sentence is very subjective. We have taken this into account in our human evaluation study by having each sentence evaluated by three annotators and taking the average across the three ratings.

Ethics Statement

We could not identify potential harm from using the provided models in this work. However, one concern is that code-switched ST is yet a challenging task, and the ST models trained in this work provide low performance, and thus should not be deployed as it can mislead the users.

A ArzEn-ST Corpus

In Table 7, we provide an overview on ArzEn-ST corpus. In Table 8, we show examples from the corpus.

ArzEn-ST Speech Corpus	
Duration	12h
#Speakers	40
# Sentences	6,216
% CS sentences	63.7%
% Arabic sentences	33.2%
% English sentences	3.1%

Table 7: ArzEn-ST corpus overview.

#	Example
1	←انا كتبت ال project code *AnA ktbt Al* project code I wrote the project code
2	←عملت كذا internship *Emlt k*A* internship I did several internships
3	←كنت ب overload الناس اللى معايا *knt b* overload *AlnAs Ally mEAyA* I was overloading my teammates
4	←ن detect ال traffic within period معينة *n* detect *Al* traffic within period *mEynp* to detect the traffic within a certain period

Table 8: ArzEn-ST corpus examples, showing source text, its transliteration (Habash et al., 2007), and translation. The arrows beside the sentences show the sentence starting direction, as Arabic is read right to left.

B POS Intrinsic Evaluation

As an intrinsic evaluation of the CS predictive model, we check the POS distribution of the words predicted as CS words by both the random and predictive approaches, against that of CS words in ArzEn-ST dev set. We report that the natural POS distribution is in-line with the distributions reported

POS	ArzEn	Random	Predictive
NN	48.4	33.2	67.0
VB	14.5	22.9	13.6
JJ	13.1	9.3	13.6
RB	7.6	6.5	1.7
IN	5.0	8.9	0.9
PRP	3.8	4.7	0.6
DT	2.2	3.7	0.2
CC	0.9	3.8	0.1
Total	94.7	89.3	97.6

Table 9: The POS distribution (%) of the words predicted as CS words by both the random and predictive models, against that of CS words in ArzEn-ST dev set.

for CS Egyptian Arabic-English (Hamed et al., 2018; Balabel et al., 2020), where the dominating POS tags are nouns, verbs, and adjectives, followed by adverbs, pronouns, and prepositions. We report that the predictive model gives a higher correlation (0.984) versus random approach (0.938). We present the POS distribution of the top frequent tags in Table 9. We observe that the predictive model provides a percentage of nouns that is significantly higher than that occurring in ArzEn-ST. It also provides less coverage to the tags occurring less frequently in ArzEn-ST. We believe this can be due to the predictive model being trained on limited data. The random approach on the other hand, provides higher counts for less frequent POS tags, as seen in the total, where 11% of the words identified by the random prediction to be code-switched belong to POS tags that are infrequent in natural CS data.

C Data Preprocessing

Data preprocessing involved removing corpus-specific annotations, removing URLs and emoticons through *tweet-preprocessor*,[12] tokenizing numbers, lowercasing, running Moses' (Koehn et al., 2007) tokenizer as well as MADAMIRA (Pasha et al., 2014) simple tokenization (D0), and performing Alef/Ya normalization. For LDC2017T07 (Chen et al., 2017), LDC2019T01 (Chen et al., 2019), and LDC2021T15 (Tracey et al., 2021), some words have literal and intended translations. We opt for one translation having all literal translations and another having all intended translations. For LDC2017T07, we utilize the work by Shazal et al. (2020), where the authors used a sequence-to-sequence deep learning model to transliterate SMS/chat text in LDC2017T07 from Arabizi (where Arabic words are written in Roman script) to Arabic orthography.

D MT Hyperparameters

The following is the train command:
python3 fairseq_cli/train.py $DATA_DIR –source-lang src –target-lang tgt –arch transformer –share-all-embeddings –encoder-layers 5 –decoder-layers 5 –encoder-embed-dim 512 –decoder-embed-dim 512 –encoder-ffn-embed-dim 2048 –decoder-ffn-embed-dim 2048 –encoder-attention-heads 2 –decoder-attention-heads 2 –encoder-normalize-before –decoder-normalize-before –dropout 0.4 –attention-dropout 0.2 –relu-dropout 0.2 –weight-decay 0.0001 –label-smoothing 0.2 –criterion label_smoothed_cross_entropy –optimizer adam –adam-betas '(0.9, 0.98)' –clip-norm 0 –lr-scheduler inverse_sqrt –warmup-updates 4000 –warmup-init-lr 1e-7 –lr 1e-3 –stop-min-lr 1e-9 –max-tokens 4000 –update-freq 4 –max-epoch 100 –save-interval 10 –ddp-backend=no_c10d

E MT Results

In Table 10, we present the MT and ST results of the non-constrained and constrained experiments. We report the scores on BLEU, chrF, chrF++, and BERTScore(F1). Given that each metric has its strengths and weaknesses, we also report the average of the four metrics ($AvgMT$).

F Translation Examples

In Table 11, we show examples of source-target pairs with their translations obtained from different MT models. We observe that the models trained using augmented sentences are better than the baseline MT model at retaining CS words in the source sentence in the translations.

[12] https://pypi.org/project/tweet-preprocessor/

Model	All Sentences					CS Sentences				
	BLEU	chrF	chrF++	F_{BERT}	Avg_{MT}	BLEU	chrF	chrF++	F_{BERT}	Avg_{MT}
Non-constrained Experiments										
MT										
Baseline	31.0	54.2	53.0	0.519	47.5	31.4	55.3	54.0	0.501	47.7
+DICTIONARY	30.9	53.8	52.6	0.516	47.2	31.5	54.7	53.5	0.498	47.4
+MAPRAND$_{1-1}$	$34.4^{\ddagger}$	56.6^{*}	55.2^{*}	0.545	50.2	$35.9^{\ddagger}$	$58.5^{*,\ddagger}$	57.0^{*}	0.543	51.4
+MAPPRED$_{1-1}$	$33.7^{\ddagger,\dagger}$	$56.9^{\dagger}$	$55.5^{\dagger}$	0.548	50.2	$35.2^{\ddagger,\dagger}$	$58.9^{\dagger,\ddagger}$	$57.4^{\dagger}$	0.549	51.6
+MAPRAND$_{n-n}$	34.7	57.2^{*}	$\mathbf{56.0}^{*}$	**0.552**	**50.8**	36.2	$\mathbf{59.2}^{*}$	$\mathbf{57.9}^{*}$	**0.552**	**52.1**
+MAPPRED$_{n-n}$	$\mathbf{35.0}^{\dagger}$	$\mathbf{57.3}^{\dagger}$	$\mathbf{56.0}^{\dagger}$	0.550	**50.8**	$\mathbf{36.5}^{\dagger}$	$\mathbf{59.2}^{\dagger}$	$57.8^{\dagger}$	**0.552**	**52.1**
+ExtraCS	34.8	57.2	55.7	0.547	50.6	36.2	59.1	57.6	0.546	51.9
ST										
Baseline	15.3	41.2	39.4	0.335	32.4	15.8	42.4	40.4	0.317324	32.6
+DICTIONARY	16.3	41.9	40.1	0.344	33.2	16.8	42.8	41.0	0.324	33.2
+MAPRAND$_{1-1}$	$16.5^{\ddagger,*}$	42.8^{*}	41.0^{*}	0.347	33.8	17.0^{*}	44.1^{*}	42.1^{*}	0.329	34.0
+MAPPRED$_{1-1}$	$16.1^{\ddagger,\dagger}$	$42.8^{\dagger}$	$40.9^{\dagger}$	0.348	33.6	$16.9^{\dagger}$	$44.2^{\dagger}$	$42.2^{\dagger}$	0.331	34.1
+MAPRAND$_{n-n}$	$\mathbf{17.0}^{*}$	43.3^{*}	41.4^{*}	0.349	**34.2**	$\mathbf{17.7}^{*}$	44.7^{*}	42.7^{*}	0.332	**34.6**
+MAPPRED$_{n-n}$	$16.9^{\dagger}$	$\mathbf{43.4}^{\dagger}$	$\mathbf{41.5}^{\dagger}$	**0.352**	**34.2**	$17.4^{\dagger}$	$\mathbf{44.8}^{\dagger}$	$\mathbf{42.8}^{\dagger}$	**0.335**	**34.6**
+ExtraCS	17.4	43.4	41.6	0.353	34.4	18.0	44.7	42.9	0.336	34.8
Constrained Experiments										
MT										
+c[DICTIONARY]	30.3	53.6	52.3	0.517	47.0	31.0	54.6	53.3	0.499	47.2
+c[MAPRAND$_{n-n}$]	$33.8^{\star}$	$56.9^{\star}$	$55.6^{\star}$	$\underline{0.553}$	50.4	$35.1^{\star}$	$58.7^{\star}$	$57.3^{\star}$	$\underline{0.555}$	51.7
+c[MAPPRED$_{n-n}$]	$\underline{35.0}^{\star}$	$\underline{57.4}^{\star}$	$\underline{56.0}^{\star}$	0.551	$\underline{50.9}$	$\underline{36.8}^{\star}$	$\underline{59.5}^{\star}$	$\underline{57.9}^{\star}$	0.554	$\underline{52.4}$
ST										
+c[DICTIONARY]	15.2	41.2	39.4	0.341	32.5	15.5	42.1	40.1	0.319	32.4
+c[MAPRAND$_{n-n}$]	16.4	$\underline{43.1}$	$\underline{41.2}$	0.350	33.9	17.0	$\underline{44.7}$	$\underline{42.6}$	0.335	$\underline{34.5}$
+c[MAPPRED$_{n-n}$]	$\underline{16.6}$	$\underline{43.1}$	$\underline{41.2}$	$\underline{0.353}$	$\underline{34.0}$	$\underline{17.2}$	44.6	$\underline{42.6}$	$\underline{0.337}$	$\underline{34.5}$

Table 10: MT and ST evaluation on ArzEn-ST test set for the non-constrained (using all augmentations) and constrained experiments. We report BLEU, chrF, chrF++, F1 BERTScore (F_{BERT}), and their average (Avg_{MT}), on all sentences as well as code-switched sentences only. The best performing data augmentation approach in the non-constrained setting is bolded. The best performing approach in the constrained setting is underlined. We run statistical significance tests between pairs of models to compare the effect of using MAPRAND vs. MAPPRED and 1-1 vs. n-n alignments, and mark models that are statistically significant (*p-values*$<$ 0.05) with superscript symbols ($*, \dagger, \ddagger, \star$).

Model	Example
Src	ما هو المفروض ال . . ال . . الناس اللي بت adjudicate بيبقوا poker face فهو مابنفعش يفهمني اي حاجة بس بعديها بيبقي يعني بعرف غلطي ، بس
Tgt-Ref	those one who adjudicate should have a poker face, so i can't get any signal from them, but afterwards i know my mistake, that's all
Baseline	it's supposed to be the. the. people who are a rijudi could be powder face so it can't explain anything but after that i mean i know my mistake, that's it
DICTIONARY	the.. the. the.. the people who are hurt should be thinking about face, so it can't explain anything to me, but after that, i mean, i know my mistake, that's it
MAPRAND$_{1-1}$	the.. the.. the.. the.. the people who adjudicate become a poker of face, so he can't explain anything to me, but after that i know my mistake, that's it
MAPPRED$_{1-1}$	the.. the. the.. the people that adjudicate become the poker face, so he can't understand anything but after that i mean i know my mistake, that's it
MAPRAND$_{n-n}$	the.. the.. the.. the people who are adjudicate, they become poker face, so it can't explain anything to me after that, i mean, i know my mistake, that's it
MAPPRED$_{n-n}$	the.. the. the.. the people who are adjudicate should be poker face, so he can't explain anything to me but after that, i mean, i know my mistake, that's it
Src	انا بعمل مشروع اسمه multi-robot system task allocation
Tgt-Ref	i'm working on a project called multi-robot system task allocation.
Baseline	i make a project called multi-robot system and allocation
DICTIONARY	i'm making a project called al-gamalt system for the task of allocation
MAPRAND$_{1-1}$	i make a project called multi-robot system and allocation
MAPPRED$_{1-1}$	i am making a project called multi-robot system and allocation task
MAPRAND$_{n-n}$	i am making a project called multi-robot system allocation
MAPPRED$_{n-n}$	i am doing a project called multi-robot system task allocation

Table 11: Examples of translation outputs obtained from the MT models. The words in the translations that correspond to the CS words in the input source sentence are underlined.

Measuring the Impact of Data Augmentation Methods for Extremely Low-Resource NMT

Zeyneb Kaya [1], **Annie K. Lamar**[2]
[1] Saratoga High School, Saratoga, CA
zeynebnahidekaya@gmail.com
[2] Department of Classics and Stanford Data Science
Stanford University, Stanford, CA
kalamar@stanford.edu

Abstract

Data augmentation (DA) is a popular strategy to boost performance on neural machine translation tasks. The impact of data augmentation in low-resource environments, particularly for diverse and scarce languages, is understudied. In this paper, we introduce a simple yet novel metric to measure the impact of several different data augmentation strategies. This metric, which we call Data Augmentation Advantage (DAA), quantifies how many true data pairs a synthetic data pair is worth in a particular experimental context. We demonstrate the utility of this metric by training models for several linguistically-varied datasets using the data augmentation methods of back-translation, SwitchOut, and sentence concatenation. In lower-resource tasks, DAA is an especially valuable metric for comparing DA performance as it provides a more effective way to quantify gains when BLEU scores are especially small and results across diverse languages are more divergent and difficult to assess.

1 Introduction

Neural Machine Translation (NMT) has been established as the dominant approach for developing state-of-the-art Machine Translation (MT) systems. The neural network-based architecture enables effective translation without expert linguistic knowledge while better capturing contextual information. However, many NMT systems are data-inefficient and are dependent on large amounts of parallel data pairs in order to attain reliable performance, limiting their applicability in low-resource tasks. This paper is particularly interested in applicability of DA methods in the preservation of low-resource and scarce languages. There is therefore a significant performance gap in NMT for low-resource language pairs (Zoph et al., 2016).

One way that this gap is addressed is the generation of synthetic data through unsupervised Data Augmentation (DA). DA has been largely used in other deep learning modalities like image- and tabular-based data (Yang et al., 2022; Shorten et al., 2021). Multilingual text DA, in particular, has been the frontier of DA research. Sennrich et al. (2016a) proposed the backtranslation of sentences from monolingual data to generate bitext for a pseudo-parallel corpora. Recently, many more new DA approaches have been presented in order to improve NMT systems.

As opposed to approaches for low-resource NMT exploiting auxiliary languages through transfer learning, which rely heavily on the availability of data on a rich-resourced and linguistically similar language, DA in particular has potential to expand language technologies further by addressing that many low-resource and indigenous languages tend to be the most specialized and idiosyncratic, and are often part of smaller language families that are endangered as a whole (Sennrich et al. (2016a)). DA thus is especially relevant in the preservation of low-resource and scarce languages.

However, DA methods often do not exhibit consistent improvement across translation tasks (Li et al., 2019). In the case of low-resource languages, the effectiveness of DA may be even more irregular. Synthetic pairs based on very limited amounts of data may have compromised quality,

Proceedings of the The Sixth Workshop on Technologies for Machine Translation of Low-Resource Languages (LoResMT 2023), pages 101–109
May 6, 2023

and the generalizability of these methods for scarce and orthographically diverse languages is understudied.

In this paper, we propose a method to measure the impact of DA on machine translation tasks in a low-resource environment. We then use this metric to assess the performance of three DA methods–back translation, switch-out, and sentence concatenation–on a machine translation task. We first measure the impact of DA on variously-sized subsets of high-resource language datasets, including English-Italian, English-Turkish, and German-English, to assess the generalizability and consistency of the selected DA methods. We then demonstrate how DA methods can be employed and measured in truly scarce linguistic environments by measuring the impact of DA on a machine translation task for the language pairs English-Romany, English-Māori, English-Uyghur, and English-Kabyle.

2 Background

We implement and investigate three multilingual DA approaches in our analyses. Each of these approaches have been shown to improve performance in high-resource environments, underscoring the importance of measuring the impact of such approaches in low-resource settings as well.

2.1 DA Methods for NMT

Back-translation: The augmentation procedure of back-translation (Sennrich et al., 2016a) uses monolingual data to generate more training data for a machine translation task. A backward intermediate model is trained on the available parallel corpora and then used to generate synthetic source-side translations from a target-side monolingual language corpus. Synthetic and true pairs are mixed together in the training data and not distinguished during model training.

Back-translation has shown promising results for neural machine translation tasks, particularly for large datasets. Sugiyama and Yoshinaga (2019) show that back translation has a significant positive impact on context-aware large-scale NMT tasks. Several iterations of previous work (Jin et al. 2022, Aji & Heafield 2020, Li & Specia 2019) show that back-translation can supplement other data augmentation techniques to improve performance in neural translation tasks. Such work emphasizes the need to better understand the impact of back-translation in low-resource environments so that such work can keep pace with work in high-resource settings.

SwitchOut: SwitchOut (Wang et al., 2018) independently replaces words in both the source and target sentences with words randomly sampled from their respective vocabularies to encourage smoothness and diversity. Wang et al. treat DA as an optimization problem and use hamming distance sampling to sample data pairs. Wang et al. find that these 'switches' in combination with their sampling strategy yield an improvement of 0.5 BLEU on multilingual datasets. They also find that the performance gain from SwitchOut is more significant than the gain from back translation. Notably, all the datasets used by Wang et al. are high-resource languages, including English, German, and Vietnamese.

SwitchOut has been used in combination with other DA methods in other low-resource investigations, namely that of Maimaiti et al. (2021). Maimaiti et al. compare their own, novel method of constrained sampling for machine translation to the results achieved by other DA methods, including SwitchOut, and conclude that their method is state-of-the-art. As above, such work emphasizes the need for a straightforward evaluation framework for foundational DA methods.

Sentence Concatenation: The sentence concatenation (Kondo et al., 2021) method is straightforward: sentence pairs are selected at random from the parallel corpora and concatenated with a separator token, <SEP>, in between. Notably, this method was developed with low-resource datasets in mind. Konda et al.'s method prioritizes performance on longer sentences, which are more common in low-resource datasets. Notably, Konda et al. find that their method is even more effective when combined with back-translation. For the purposes of our study, we do not combine the two methods.

2.2 Low-Resource and Scarce Languages

To evaluate the utility of the DA methods in low-resource language pairs across linguistically diverse languages from various regions, we perform our experiments on a range of low-resource languages from the Tatoeba Dataset (Tiedemann, 2020), which contains parallel data for translation systems of ranging sizes. We test DA methods for four language pairs, including English-Romany, English-Māori, English-Uyghur, and English-Kabyle.

Romany is a Balkan language classified as "definitely endangered" of the Indo-Aryan language family (New et al., 2017). It is spoken by small groups in various countries but is stateless and a minority, with a history of persecution and suppression. Availability of Romany resources is very small, with limited access to books and computers. Projects to support and Romany have arisen to help preserve the language and prevent its loss. The dataset contains English-Romany pairs, with 24K parallel sentences.

Māori, spoken in the indigenous population of New Zealand, is an endangered Eastern Polynesian language (Love, 1983). Māori is an analytical language and marks many grammatical categories. It became a minority language and English became increasingly powerful, and has since had several movements towards its revitalization. The dataset contains English-Māori pairs, with 221K parallel sentences.

Uyghur is the Turkic language spoken in the Xinjiang region of Western China (Imin et al., 2021). Primarily Muslim, the Uyghur people have been targeted by the Chinese on the basis of ethnic and religious identity. With ongoing crimes against the minority community, recognised as a genocide, teaching of the Uighur language has been banned in schools and the culture suppressed. The dataset contains English-Uyghur pairs, with 143K parallel sentences.

Kabyle in the Afro-Asiatic language of the Berbers (Rousan et al., 2018), the indigenous people of north Africa. The language has a history of brutal suppression, and today, most Berber varieties are endangered or extinct. It has limited official status, as French and Arabic are primarily used. The dataset contains English-Kabyle pairs, with 84K parallel sentences.

These languages are a selection of extremely low-resource languages from around the world with diverse linguistic features. For these languages, the development of effective NMT systems have potential to support both preservation and promotion. They are only a sample of the languages that could benefit from such technologies, and demonstrate the implications of DA towards advancing linguistic vitality and cultural preservation.

3 Datasets

In this paper, we use two groups of data. Both groups of data are from the Tatoeba Dataset (Tiedemann, 2020). The training data for the Tatoeba Dataset was obtained from OPUS' parallel corpora (Tiedemann, 2012), which is made up of translated texts from the web. First, we determine the generalizability and consistency of different DA algorithms by measuring their performance in a simulated low-resource environment, that is, using small samples of high-resource languages.

Dataset	**5%**	**10%**	**20%**	**50%**	**100%**
English-Italian	50K	100K	200K	500K	1M
English-Turkish	50K	100K	200K	500K	1M
German-English	50K	100K	200K	500K	1M
		25%	**50%**	**75%**	**100%**
English-Romany		6K	12K	18K	24K
English-Māori		55K	111K	166K	221K
English-Uyghur		36K	72K	107K	143K
English-Kabyle		21K	42K	63K	84K

Table 1: Datasets and sampling sizes for simulated and true low-resource experiments.

Second, we measure the efficacy of DA algorithms for true low-resource environments using scarce language datasets.

To simulate a low-resource setting we randomly sample 1M pairs each from the English-Italian, English-Turkish, and German-English Tatoeba Dataset training data. We train multiple models by sampling the data in increments of 5%, 10%, 20%, 50%, and 100%. We sample from the unused portions of the dataset for use in the augmentation methods requiring monolingual data. We report results on the 2021 test sets. Second, we test DA methods for four truly scarce language pairs, including English-Romany (24K pairs), English-

Māori (221K pairs), English-Uyghur (143K pairs), and English-Kabyle (84K pairs) (see section 2.2 above). We train multiple models by sampling the data in increments of 25%, 50%, 75%, and 100%.

4 Data Augmentation Advantage

Across DA methods, synthetic pairs contribute different amounts of value to the training data. In some cases, synthetic pairs have the same impact as a true pair in the training pair, while in other cases, synthetic pairs seem to have no value or even negative value within the training dataset. In this section, we offer a simple yet novel metric to quantify how many true data pairs a synthetic data pair is worth. We call this metric Data Augmentation Advantage (DAA). We calculate DAA as follows.

First, we perform linear interpolation for the baseline model, where x is the number of training pairs and y is a BLEU score. Then for a point y we calculate the interpolant as in Equation 1 below. Note that $y_a < y < y_b$ and $x_a < x < x_b$.

$$y = y_a + (y_b - y_a)\frac{x - x_a}{x_b - x_a} \quad (1)$$

For a specified target BLEU score b on the linear interpolation described above, let x_t be the number of training pairs needed to achieve b in the current experiment, and let x_b be the number of training pairs needed to achieve b in the baseline model. We can then calculate x_{adv} as in Equation 1 below.

$$x_{adv} = x_b - x_t \quad (2)$$

Using x_{adv}, we calculate Data Augmentation Advantage (DAA) as in Equation 3. This process is summarized in Figure 1.

$$DAA = \frac{x_{adv}}{x_t} \quad (3)$$

DAA represents the number of true data points that each synthetic data point is worth. For example, if DAA is 0.5, then the addition of DA is comparable to having 50% more data and a synthetic data point is worth 0.5 true data points. In the results section below, the overall DAA values of a DA method are obtained by averaging the values across the language tasks.

5 Experiments

For all the experiments, we use the OpenNMT-py toolkit (Klein et al., 2017) for the translation models. The NMT system is a 4-layer attention-

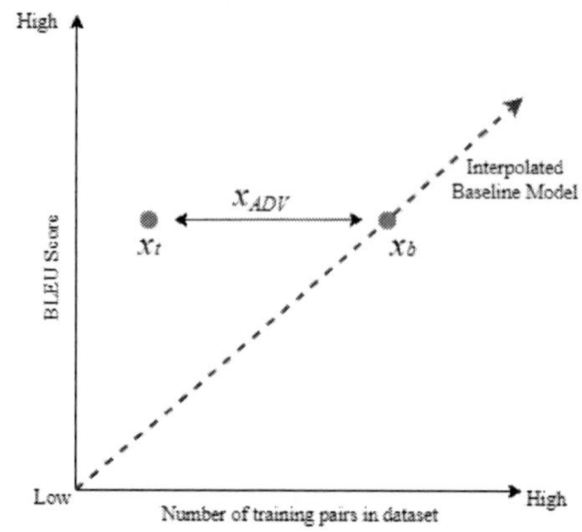

Figure 1

based encoder-decoder model (Luong et al., 2015). This system estimates the probability distribution of a sentence in the target languages given a sentence in the source language. An encoder recurrent neural network (RNN) maps each source word to a word vector; the word vectors are then mapped to a set of hidden vectors. The decoder RNN decodes the source-side hidden vectors to predict the next word in the target languages. Note that target-side decoder used is aware of the previously generated words. We train the model with hidden dimension 1024 and batch size 64. We use a dropout probability of 0.3. We employ early stopping to train until convergence in order to control for the role of training time in performance changes. The settings used in training the models are the same for each language pair.

Across the experiments we process the source and target language sentences with Byte-pair encoding (BPE) (Sennrich et al., 2016b) based on the SentencePiece subword model (Kudo & Richardson, 2018) with a vocabulary size of 8K. BPE is a method for segmenting words into subword units based on their frequency of occurrence. It enables better coverage and generalization in handling rare and out-of-vocabulary words by breaking them down, and is especially relevant in languages with complex morphology such as Turkish. SentencePiece is a powerful and flexible method for unsupervised tokenization and subword segmentation, and provides an implementation of the BPE algorithm. For models with augmentation, BPE is applied after DA, and for augmentation methods with an intermediate model, BPE is applied for each. For all DA methods, we generate synthetic data with a 1:1 ratio.

In the experiments, we compare a baseline model with no augmentation to models trained with the original training data in addition to the synthetic data obtained through each DA method. We additionally ran control experiments by simply duplicating the data to verify that any results were due to DA, and observed no improvement from the baselines. We run a model for each of the subsets of data and report our final results for each. The translation quality is measured by a single reference BLEU score (Papineni et al., 2002). Three language pairs, English-Italian, English-Turkish, and German-English, are used to assess the generalizability and consistency of the methods.

6 Results & Discussion

6.1 Simulated Low-Resource Environment

DA can obtain different benefits across different sizes of available data and examine the trends and limits as data grows smaller. In this section, we examine the trends in the performance of the three DA methods across decreasing amounts of initial language pairs on multiple translation tasks. Table 2 shows the BLEU scores achieved by the various models demonstrating the performance of the various DA methods across dataset sizes and languages. Table 3 shows the calculated DAA for each DA method and dataset size.

Training Pairs	50K	100K	200K	500K	1M
		eng → ita			
Baseline	11.1	23.9	27.8	29.6	30.4
Ba-Trans	19.9↑	20.9	28.4	28.4	29.0
Sw-Out	12.1	24.8	27.5	27.6	28.2
Sen-Con	13.6	24.8↑	28.8↑	30.7↑	31.0↑
		eng → tur			
Baseline	5.5	9.8	14.4	15.7	16.5
Ba-Trans	7.1 ↑	13.2↑	15.6↑	16.4	17.0
Sw-Out	6.1	10.4	13.0	14.1	14.2
Sen-Con	5.6	9.8	14.5	16.7↑	17.6↑
		deu → eng			
Baseline	11.1	17.7	21.0	21.5	23.1
Ba-Trans	15.1↑	19.3↑	20.7	20.9	21.1
Sw-Out	13.0	18.1	20.4	20.8	21.6
Sen-Con	11.8	18.2	21.0	23.3↑	23.0

Table 2: BLEU scores for three datasets (English-Italian, English-Turkish, and German-English) for a baseline model, back-translation (Ba-Trans), SwitchOut (Sw-Out) and sentence concatenation (Sen-Con).

Training Pairs	50K	100K	200K	500K	1M
		eng → ita			
Ba-Trans	0.69	-0.12	0.50	-0.40	-0.60
Sw-Out	0.08	0.23	-0.04	-0.61	-0.75
Sen-Con	0.20	0.23	0.83	1.38	0.38
		eng → tur			
Ba-Trans	0.37	0.74	1.38	0.87	0.31
Sw-Out	0.14	0.13	-0.15	-0.61	-0.80
Sen-Con	0.02	0.0	0.12	1.25	0.69
		deu → eng			
Ba-Trans	0.60	0.48	-0.05	-0.61	-0.74
Sw-Out	0.29	0.12	-0.09	-0.61	-0.47
Sen-Con	0.11	0.15	0.0	1.12	-0.03

Table 3: DAA scores for three datasets (English-Italian, English-Turkish, and German-English) for back-translation (Ba-Trans), SwitchOut (Sw-Out) and sentence concatenation (Sen-Con).

As expected, baseline model performance increases significantly with greater data sizes, and as the number of language pairs is less, its impact on model performance is greater. Although intuitively, DA performance might be expected to decrease with less available data with the limited quality of the generated synthetic data, it is observed that the improvement from DA increases with fewer initial pairs. DA thus shows potential and value for the development of low-resource NMT systems.

There is no single consistently best DA method across the configurations. SC shows improvement in nearly all runs. However, while BT primarily shows the best improvement, its gains are not always consistent. SO follows a similar trend, harming performance in larger data sizes, but providing near the highest gains in smaller data sizes. In multiple cases, such as in both the 200K and 500K data size models, application of SC and BT attain results that can exceed or perform competitively with the results of baseline models trained on datasets with up to over twice as many pairs. Here, synthetic data provides as much value to the models as a true pair.

The most effective methods are based on introducing lexical and syntactic diversity to the datasets, presenting potentially important characteristics of effective DA methods and opening paths for future development. Overall, the results demonstrate trends that present the limits of DA and show surprising potential for its application in low-resource conditions.

6.2 True Low-Resource Environment

Many methods presenting studies on DA and low-resource NMT have often applied methods to simulated low-resource settings, like in the previous section, to enable certain analyses (Fadaee et al., 2017; Li et al., 2020). However, with the unique linguistic characteristics of truly low-resource languages as well as the varying quality of the sentences available in such data, it is also important to understand the effectiveness of the application of DA methods in a true low-resource environment. In this section, we assess the capabilities of DA methods in developing translation systems for truly low-resource languages and demonstrate the potential of such methods in advancing language technologies for supporting these communities. We evaluate the performance of the NMT systems with and without the generated augmentations on the low-resource languages. The models used follow the architecture of those described in the simulated low-resource conditions in the Experiments section.[1]

Training Pairs	25%	50%	75%	100%
eng → rom				
Baseline	0.4	0.5	0.5	0.7
Ba-Trans	0.4	0.5	0.6	1.0↑
Sw-Out	0.7↑	0.7↑	0.9↑	0.6
Sen-Con	0.6	0.5	0.5	0.6
eng → mri				
Baseline	5.5	10.2	10.8	12.0
Ba-Trans	8.5↑	6.4	10.0	12.4
Sw-Out	7.1	10.4↑	11.4	12.6↑
Sen-Con	5.3	9.0	11.5↑	12.4
eng → uig				
Baseline	0.5	0.6	0.5	0.6
Ba-Trans	0.4	0.4	0.6	0.4
Sw-Out	0.7↑	0.5	0.7↑	0.6
Sen-Con	0.6	0.6	0.6	0.7↑
eng → kab				
Baseline	1.3	1.5	1.4	1.6
Ba-Trans	1.0	1.2	1.3	1.4
Sw-Out	1.1	1.5	1.7	1.4
Sen-Con	1.1	1.3	1.8↑	1.5

Table 4: BLEU scores for four datasets (English-Romany, English-Māori, English-Uyghur, and English-Kabyle) for a baseline model, back-translation (Ba-Trans), SwitchOut (Sw-Out) and sentence concatenation (Sen-Con).

Overall, BLEU scores (Table 4) are, as expected, lower than those in the simulated low-resource conditions, even comparing datasets of similar sizes. One reason for this may be because of the lower quality of the data. The training data for the Tatoeba Dataset was obtained from OPUS' parallel corpora (Tiedemann, 2012), which is made up of translated texts from the web. The resources on these languages are limited, and therefore not only is there less data, but also the sentences are potentially less diverse and clean. Another reason is that many of these languages that are low-resource are indigenous languages, which often have more unique linguistic characteristics. Linguistic similarity between the source and target is an influential factor in the performance of NMT systems (Subramanian & Sundararaman, 2021).

These differences also create some shifts in the performance of the DA methods. As in Section 2, the best augmentation methods are also not consistent, yet here SO seems to perform better with respect to the other augmentation methods than it did in the simulated low-resource. SC also continues to show gains in the BLEU scores as well. Across the tasks, DA was able to considerably improve results, even with extremely limited available data, establishing the value DA. In fact, comparing our models' performances to the results reported on the OPUS-MT leaderboard[2] for the 2021 Tatoeba test sets shows that in two of the tasks, eng→uig and eng→mri, the top DA methods' performances surpassed the previous best OPUS-MT scores by 0.4 BLEU points each. The previous best OPUS-MT model was trained with multilingual training, and our models' comparably better performance may demonstrate that DA is more suitable in low-resource NMT to address the differences that the condition presents. This is consistent with previous findings demonstrating the limitations of utilizing auxiliary languages in low-resource NMT (Eo et al., 2021). The results

[1] Note that for back-translation, we sample from the monolingual data presented in the Tatoeba dataset.

[2] https://opus.nlpl.eu/leaderboard/

show the potential of DA to be furthered towards multilingual NLP systems and language technologies enabling inclusivity.

The advantage provided by DA is especially significant in lower-resource settings, and generated synthetic data can provide up to as much value as a true source-target pair. Comparing the DA methods, BT provides the most considerable value, and SC is the most consistently beneficial. The DAA values for BT show a greater advantage in the eng→tur task, and SC is more effective in the eng→ita, while SO has less variation across languages. These analyses of the generalizability of the methods go beyond the information presented by the BLEU scores, where the greatest net gains are not consistent with these trends.

DAA enables further insights into the performance of DA methods that BLEU scores do not capture. The absolute gains are not comparable across languages and dataset sizes. Observing the BLEU scores of the SO method in the 11K and 221K eng→mri datasets, while there are greater net gains in the larger of the two, the DAA values show that DA has a far greater impact in the smaller dataset. DAA accounts for the non-linear variation in the worth of true data with larger corpora. DAA shows the performance of BLEU gains between language tasks; for instance, the 11K eng→mri task and the 12K eng→rom task, although shows having similar dataset sizes and BLEU gains with SO, eng→rom experiences a greater impact.

Training Pairs	**25%**	**50%**	**75%**	**100%**
		eng → rom		
Ba-Trans	0.0	0.0	0.17	0.38
Sw-Out	3.0	1.0	0.67	-0.13
Sen-Con	2.5	0.0	0.0	-0.13
		eng → mri		
Ba-Trans	0.64	-0.40	-0.35	0.08
Sw-Out	0.34	0.17	0.17	0.13
Sen-Con	-0.04	-0.13	0.19	0.08
		eng → uig		
Ba-Trans	-0.2	-0.6	0.33	-0.8
Sw-Out	1.0	-0.5	0.33	0.0
Sen-Con	1.0	0.0	0.33	1.0
		eng → kab		
Ba-Trans	-0.23	-0.54	-0.67	-0.25
Sw-Out	-0.15	0.0	1.0	-0.5
Sen-Con	-0.15	-0.5	1.66	-0.5

Table 5: DAA scores for four datasets (English-Romany, English-Māori, English-Uyghur, and English-Kabyle) for a baseline model, back-translation (Ba-Trans), SwitchOut (Sw-Out) and sentence concatenation (Sen-Con).

7 Conclusion & Future Work

Data augmentation (DA) is a popular strategy to boost performance on neural machine translation tasks. The impact of data augmentation in low-resource environments, particularly for diverse and scarce languages, is understudied. In this paper, we introduce a simple yet novel metric to measure the impact of several different data augmentation strategies. This metric, which we call Data Augmentation Advantage (DAA), quantifies how many true data pairs a synthetic data pair is worth in a particular experimental context.

Because DAA provides a consistent measure comparable across the results, we are able to determine that SwitchOut and sentence concatenation show the greatest language task generalizability, providing more consistent DAA. In general, SwitchOut is especially advantageous with less available data, most evident in the increasing DAA in eng→mri and eng→rom, while back-translation has more limitations with regards to the minimum amount of data required for best performance. In particular, in lower-resource tasks, DAA is an especially valuable metric for comparing DA performance as it provides a more effective way to quantify gains when BLEU scores are especially small and results across diverse languages are more divergent and difficult to assess.

Limitations

DA demonstrates promising gains in low-resource NMT. However, in the current exploration there are certain limitations. Our experiments use the Tatoeba Dataset, which contains varying, and sometimes quite high, levels of noise; this can impact the quality of translations, the extent of overfitting, and the effectiveness of generated synthetic data. Furthermore, such data can also affect the sensitivity of evaluations to minor changes in outputs, affecting the significance of performance changes.

Additionally, DA has limitations in its effectiveness. The quality of the data generated by augmentation is inconsistent, and can degrade model performance. DA is a tradeoff between noise vs. knowledge injection (Li et al., 2019), so it is important to understand the effects that DA can have. Although we experiment with a diverse range of languages and DA methods, the study is a limited yet promising analysis of the impact of DA for low-resource NMT.

Finally, this paper does not engage in discussion regarding the value of experiments performed with true low-resource datasets vs. simulated ones. This issue is topical and requires further investigation in an expanded work.

Ethics Statement

Global linguistic diversity is currently fragile with the rapid loss of languages. The current overlap between these fading languages and emerging technologies, natural language processing tools are especially critical towards supporting diverse languages. However, globalization has only furthered English domination across the web and available language resources as NLP advancements grow in high-data tasks, and minority languages have been unrepresented in NLP literature and technologies, leaving many behind. Language technologies are a valuable aspect of supporting minority languages, yet the low-data setting has made it difficult to fully take advantage of this critical era. The application of effective multilingual DA methods in NMT systems for these languages is valuable for greater materials in accessibility, promotion, education, and connection.

References

Alham Fikri Aji and Kenneth Heafield. 2020. Fully synthetic data improves neural machine translation with knowledge distillation. CoRR, abs/2012.15455.

Eo, S., Park, C., Moon, H., Seo, J., & Lim, H. 2021. Dealing with the Paradox of Quality Estimation. *Proceedings of the 4th Workshop on Technologies for MT of Low Resource Languages* (*LoResMT2021*), 1–10.

Fadaee, M., Bisazza, A., & Monz, C. 2017. Data Augmentation for Low-Resource Neural Machine Translation. *Proceedings of the 55th Annual Meeting of the Association for Computational Linguistics* (Volume 2: Short Papers), 567–573.

Imin, G., Ablimit, M., & Hamdulla, A. 2021. A Review of Morphological Analysis Methods on Uyghur Language. *2021 International Conference on Asian Language Processing* (*IALP*), 310–315.

Jin, C., Qiu, S., Xiao, N., & Jia, H. 2022. AdMix: A Mixed Sample Data Augmentation Method for Neural Machine Translation (arXiv:2205.04686).

Klein, G., Kim, Y., Deng, Y., Senellart, J., & Rush, A. 2017. OpenNMT: Open-Source Toolkit for Neural Machine Translation. *Proceedings of ACL 2017, System Demonstrations*, 67–72.

Kondo, S., Hotate, K., Hirasawa, T., Kaneko, M., & Komachi, M. 2021. Sentence Concatenation Approach to Data Augmentation for Neural Machine Translation. *Proceedings of the 2021 Conference of the North American Chapter of the Association for Computational Linguistics: Student Research Workshop*, 143–149.

Kudo, T., & Richardson, J. 2018. SentencePiece: A simple and language independent subword tokenizer and detokenizer for Neural Text Processing. *Proceedings of the 2018 Conference on Empirical Methods in Natural Language Processing (System Demonstrations)*, 66–71.

Li, G., Liu, L., Huang, G., Zhu, C., & Zhao, T. 2019. Understanding Data Augmentation in Neural Machine Translation: Two Perspectives towards Generalization. *Proceedings of the 2019 Conference on Empirical Methods in Natural Language Processing and the 9th International Joint Conference on Natural Language Processing* (*EMNLP-IJCNLP*), 5689–5695.

Li, J., Liu, L., Li, H., Li, G., Huang, G., & Shi, S. 2020. Evaluating Explanation Methods for Neural Machine Translation. *Proceedings of the 58th Annual Meeting of the Association for Computational Linguistics*, 365–375.

Li, Z., & Specia, L. 2019. Improving Neural Machine Translation Robustness via Data Augmentation: Beyond Back-Translation. *Proceedings of the 5th Workshop on Noisy User-Generated Text* (*W-NUT 2019*), 328–336.

Love, P. A. (1983). The Maori language in New Zealand: A case study of language shift.

Luong, M.-T., Pham, H., & Manning, C. D. 2015. Effective Approaches to Attention-based Neural Machine Translation. Stanford NLP Group.

Maimaiti, M., Liu, Y., Luan, H., & Sun, M. 2022. Data augmentation for low-resource languages: NMT guided by constrained sampling. *International Journal of Intelligent Systems*, 37(1), 30–51.

New, W., Kyuchukov, H., & Villiers, J. de. 2017. 'We don't talk Gypsy here': Minority Language Policies in Europe. *Journal of Language and Cultural Education*, 5(2), 1–24.

Papineni, K., Roukos, S., Ward, T., & Zhu, W.-J. 2002. BLEU: A method for automatic evaluation of machine translation. *Proceedings of the 40th Annual Meeting on Association for Computational Linguistics*, 311–318.

Rousan, R. A., & Ibrir, L. 2018. Language Change and Stability in Algeria: A Case Study of Mzabi and Kabyle. *Jordan Journal of Modern Languages and Literature*, 10(2), 177-198.

Sennrich, R., Haddow, B., & Birch, A. 2016a. Neural Machine Translation of Rare Words with Subword Units. *Proceedings of the 54th Annual Meeting of the Association for Computational Linguistics (Volume 1: Long Papers)*, 1715-1725.

Sennrich, R., Haddow, B., & Birch, A. 2016b. Improving Neural Machine Translation Models with Monolingual Data. *Proceedings of the 54th Annual Meeting of the Association for Computational Linguistics (Volume 1: Long Papers)*, 86–96.

Shorten, C., Khoshgoftaar, T. M., & Furht, B. 2021. Text Data Augmentation for Deep Learning. Journal of Big Data, 8(1), 101.

Subramanian, V., & Sundararaman, D. 2021. How do lexical semantics affect translation? An empirical study. arXiv preprint arXiv:2201.00075.

Sugiyama, A., & Yoshinaga, N. (2019). Data augmentation using back-translation for context-aware neural machine translation. *Proceedings of the Fourth Workshop on Discourse in Machine Translation (DiscoMT 2019)*, 35–44.

Tiedemann, J. 2012. Parallel Data, Tools and Interfaces in OPUS. *Proceedings of the Eighth International Conference on Language Resources and Evaluation (LREC'12)*, 2214–2218.

Tiedemann, J. 2020. The Tatoeba Translation Challenge – Realistic Data Sets for Low Resource and Multilingual MT. *Proceedings of the Fifth Conference on Machine Translation*, 1174–1182.

Wang, X., Pham, H., Dai, Z., & Neubig, G. 2018. SwitchOut: An Efficient Data Augmentation Algorithm for Neural Machine Translation. *Proceedings of the 2018 Conference on Empirical Methods in Natural Language Processing*, 856–861.

Whalen, D. H., & Simons, G. F. 2012. Endangered Language Families. *Language*, 88(1), 155–173.

Yang, S., Xiao, W., Zhang, M., Guo, S., Zhao, J., & Shen, F. 2022. Image Data Augmentation for Deep Learning: A Survey (arXiv:2204.08610).

Zoph, B., Yuret, D., May, J., & Knight, K. 2016. Transfer Learning for Low-Resource Neural Machine Translation (arXiv:1604.02201).

Findings from the Bambara - French Machine Translation Competition (BFMT 2023)

Ninoh Agostinho Da Silva[1], Tunde Oluwaseyi Ajayi[2], Alexander Antonov[3], Panga Azazia Kamate[4], Moussa Coulibaly[4], Mason Del Rio[5], Yacouba Diarra[4], Sebastian Diarra[4], Chris Emezue[6], Joel Hamilcaro[1], Christopher M. Homan[7], Alexander Most[8], Joseph Mwatukange[9], Peter Ohue[10], Michael Pham[11], Abdoulaye Sako[4], Sokhar Samb[12], Yaya Sy[1], Tharindu Cyril Weerasooriya[7], Yacine Zahidi[5], Sarah Luger[5*]

[1]Independent, previously Université Paris-Cité, [2]Insight Centre for Data Analytics, Masakhane, [3]Chuvash Language Laboratory, Yandex, [4]RobotsMali,[5]Orange Silicon Valley,[6]Mila Quebec AI Institute, Technical Universityof Munich, Lanfrica,[7]Rochester Institute of Technology,USA, [8]Montana State University,USA,[9]Meyabase Platforms,[10]University of Ibadan, Nigeria, [11]Swarthmore,[12]Dakar American University of Science & Technology, Senegal

[5*]sarahluger@gmail.com

Abstract

Orange Silicon Valley hosted a low-resource machine translation (MT) competition with monetary prizes. The goals of the competition were to raise awareness of the challenges in the low-resource MT domain, improve MT algorithms and data strategies, and support MT expertise development in the regions where people speak Bambara and other low-resource languages. The participants built Bambara to French and French to Bambara machine translation systems using data provided by the organizers and additional data resources shared amongst the competitors. This paper details each team's different approaches and motivation for ongoing work in Bambara and the broader low-resource machine translation domain.

1 BFMT 2023 - Competition Introduction

Orange Silicon Valley, hosted the "Bambara-French Machine Translation Competition 2023" (BFMT 2023) a low-resource machine translation (MT) competition that ended on February 15, 2023. The competition was launched on December 15, 2022. Participants had access to a Github repository with a training dataset of parallel French-Bambara aligned sentences[1]. The participants were also invited into a Slack community to share their approaches and data. An additional development dataset was provided to the teams and fewer than 48 hours before the submission deadline, a test dataset was released for generating text output to be sent to the competition organizers to evaluate translation performance using BLEU scores (Post, 2018).

The goals of the competition were to improve not only French to Bambara and Bambara to French automated translation systems, but also support a transparent and collaborative community to work on these and other language pairs, especially those (low-resource) languages spoken by West Africans. 50 people joined the online community and fourteen people competed in 6 teams. The teams contained participants from Mali, Senegal, Namibia, Nigeria, Ireland, Germany, Russia, Spain, France, the US, and the UK. Many of the participants speak or have working knowledge of a "low-resource language" or a language that does not have the digital resources that support highly accurate Natural Language Processing tool development.

Bambara is a tonal language with a rich morphology spoken by five million people as a first language and approximately 15 million people as a second language. Approximately 30–40 million people speak a language in the Mande language family, to which Bambara belongs (Lewis et al., 2014).

A predominately oral language, several competing writing systems have developed. A majority of Bambara speakers have not been taught to read or write in a standard format. Bambara's standardization is evolving and this poses challenges to automated text processing such as machine translation (Vydrin et al., 2022).

Additional contest information may be found in both French and English on the Orange Silicon Valley website[2].

[1]The dataset is available to share on request through the corresponding author.

[2]https://siliconvalley.orange.com/en/bambara-french-machine-translation-competition/

Proceedings of the The Sixth Workshop on Technologies for Machine Translation of Low-Resource Languages (LoResMT 2023), pages 110–122
May 6, 2023 ©2023 Association for Computational Linguistics

2 Background

Current state-of-the-art low-resource MT is surveyed in Haddow et al. (2022). Google Translate has integrated more low-resource languages into their language library sharing innovations as detailed in blog posts (Venugopal, 2010; Benjamin, 2019).

MT for the Bambara - French language pair has been explored in recent years in Akhbardeh et al. (2021); Tapo et al. (2020); Leventhal et al. (2020). This work is in part motivated by an increased financial and cultural focus on bringing machine learning to the Sahel region (Diarra and Leventhal, 2020).

2.1 Evaluation

MT can be evaluated by automated and manual methods. In this competition, we used automated tools to evaluate the closeness of translations to a gold standard. We use BLEU scores with sacreBLEU (Papineni et al., 2002; Post, 2018) for automated evaluation. Human evaluation would have been performed if the difference between the Team scores was less than 1 point in BLEU scale. The results were not close. Thus, we proceeded with using BLEU scores with sacreBLEU.

2.2 Datasets

The organizers provided a training dataset of aligned parallel Bambara - French sentences from the medical and dictionary domains as described in the original data collection (Akhbardeh et al., 2021). Each line in the dataset corresponds to a single sentence. The characteristics of the dataset provided by the organizers is shown in Table 1. In addition to the competition data, all participants were encouraged to gather, utilize, and share additional resources with other members of the competition community. The additional datasets used in the competition are shown in Table 2, with the Bayelemabaga (Vydrin et al., 2022) dataset being notable for the amount of additional data it gave to participants.

2.3 Baseline

The competition guidelines did not provide any baseline models nor baseline scores for the competition participants. The closest baseline to compare for this competition was from the findings of WMT21 (Akhbardeh et al., 2021), with BLEU scores of 1.32 for French to Bambara, and 3.62 for Bambara to French, using the Marian NMT (Junczys-Dowmunt et al., 2018) pre-trained model.

Data Split	Number of Sentences
Train	3,150
Dev	460
Test	460

Table 1: The characteristics of the dataset provided by the competition organizers.

Dataset	Teams
MAFAND (Adelani et al., 2022)	All Teams
NLLB-SEED (Team et al., 2022)	All Teams
FLORES (Goyal et al., 2022)	All Teams
BAYELEMABAGA (Vydrin et al., 2022)	All Teams
XP3 (Muennighoff et al., 2022a)	Yacine Zahidi
Wikipedia	Team Alpha

Table 2: Additional Bambara datasets used by the teams. Team Alpha use the Wikipedia dataset that is available through Wikimedia.org [3].

Technique	Reference
BART	(Lewis et al., 2019)
BLOOM-z 560M, mt0-small	(Muennighoff et al., 2022b)
byt5	(Xue et al., 2021a)
DeltaLM	(Ma et al., 2021)
HuggingFace	(Wolf et al., 2020)
LION optimizer	(Chen et al., 2023)
LoRA	(Hu et al., 2021)
M2M100 model	(Fan et al., 2020)
MarianNMT/Opus-MT	(Junczys-Dowmunt et al., 2018)
mt5	(Xue et al., 2021b)
NLLB model	Team et al., 2022
PEFT library	(Mangrulkar et al., 2022)
Sockeye	(Hieber et al., 2020)

Table 3: Techniques and models used by the teams.

2.4 Machine Translation Systems

Table 3 shows the different techniques and models used by the teams with transformer (Vaswani et al., 2017) and BERT models (Mishra et al., 2022; Sheshadri et al., 2023) inspiring much of the development.

3 Team-by-Team Machine Translation Findings from BFMT 2023

Six teams submitted system output that could be evaluated using sacreBLEU. Team Peter-Sokhar (Section 3.7) built an MT system but did not submit an output for scoring. Nonetheless, their findings from training and error analysis are included in this paper. In the following sections, each team first describes their methodology, then they describe their error analysis. See Table 2 for the datasets used by each team.

3.1 Team Alpha

We used an additional dataset from Wikipedia[4] which provided us with an extra 892 lines of data. Next, we made a list of MT models that contained Bambara and French in their dataset during pre-training. As a result, we started with the NLLB-200 (Team et al., 2022) pre-trained model. We fine-tuned both the 600M and the 1.3B (in order to test the impact of scaling on model capacity) parameter versions, from the Huggingface Hub. We found the NLLB model to be under-performing. Next, we switched to an M2M-100 (Fan et al., 2020) model after we discovered it had fine-tuned multilingual MT models separately for each language direction, which outperformed NLLB-200 (Adelani et al., 2022)

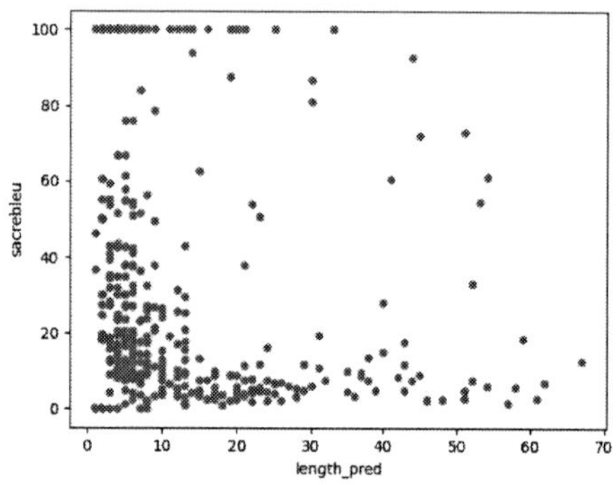

Figure 1: Scatterplot showing length of predicted sentences against sentence BLEU scores for FR → BAM.

To gain further insight into the challenges posed by certain sentence characteristics in our MT model, we conducted an analysis of the per-sentence BLEU scores plotted against the length of the predicted sentences. Initially, we postulated that our MT model would perform better with shorter sentences and perform worse with longer sentences. However, as illustrated in Figure 1, which presents a scatterplot of the lengths of the predicted sentence against their sentence BLEU scores, our model struggled even with shorter sentences. This led us to reconsider our hypothesis and explore the possibility that our model was underfitting. Next, we decided to investigate the potential benefits of implementing backtranslation.

[4]https://dumps.wikimedia.org

Algorithm 1 Team Alpha's Backtranslation Approach

$n\_epochs \leftarrow$ number of fine-tuning epochs
$D_{train} \leftarrow$ training dataset of French- Bambara parallel sentences
$D_{bam}^{wiki} \leftarrow$ 892 monolingual cleaned sentences from Wikipedia.
$D_{fr} \leftarrow$ dataset of French sentences only. For our case it was gathered by taking the French instances of D_{train}
$D_{bam} \leftarrow$ dataset of Bambara sentences only. For our case it was gathered by taking the Bambara instances of D_{train} and additional monolingual sentences from D_{bam}^{wiki}

$M_{fr \longrightarrow bam}^{0} \leftarrow$ fine-tuned MT model of (Adelani et al., 2022) for French $\longrightarrow$ Bambara

$M_{bam \longrightarrow fr}^{0} \leftarrow$ fine-tuned MT model of (Adelani et al., 2022) for Bambara $\longrightarrow$ French.

$D_{train}^{0} \leftarrow D_{train}$.
for $k \leftarrow [0, 1, 2...n]$ **do**
  $M_{fr \longrightarrow bam}^{k+1} \leftarrow$ fine-tune $M_{fr \longrightarrow bam}^{k}$ on D_{train}^{k} for n_epochs epochs.

  $M_{bam \longrightarrow fr}^{k+1} \leftarrow$ fine-tune $M_{bam \longrightarrow fr}^{k}$ on D_{train}^{k} for n_epochs epochs.

  $D_{bam}^{k} \leftarrow$ generated synthetic translations to Bambara from D_{fr} using $M_{fr \longrightarrow bam}^{k+1}$.

  $D_{fr}^{k} \leftarrow$ generated synthetic translations to French from D_{bam} using $M_{bam \longrightarrow fr}^{k+1}$.

  $D_{train}^{k+1} \leftarrow$ concatenated training dataset gotten from $D_{train}^{0} \cup \{D_{bam}^{k} \leftrightarrow D_{fr}\} \cup \{D_{fr}^{k} \leftrightarrow D_{bam}\}$
end for

3.1.1 Team Alpha's Backtranslation Approach

Several papers have highlighted the positive effect of backtranslation (Sennrich et al., 2016a; Poncelas et al., 2018; Zhang et al., 2020; Dossou and Emezue, 2020; Fan et al., 2020; Emezue and Dossou, 2021; Adelani et al., 2022; Team et al., 2022). Inspired by random online backtranslation (Zhang et al., 2020), we created our version, explained in Algorithm 1, to help our model better utilize the training dataset, and the 892 monolingual Bambara sentences from Wikipedia. Our approach, dubbed *Cyclic backtranslation* (Lam et al., 2021), would theoretically enable the model to leverage the available training and monolingual dataset by compelling the MT model for each direction, at each step k, to learn from a concatenation of the original training dataset, its synthetically generated sentences, and those generated by the MT model of the opposite direction in the previous step.

Despite its potential benefits, implementing backtranslation presented several challenges. First, it was a difficult process to set up, particularly in achieving a high degree of automation and reducing the need for human intervention. Secondly, it was computationally expensive and time-consuming, as each iteration of the backtranslation process involved working with three times more data than the previous iteration. Consequently, we were only able to complete one backtranslation successfully.

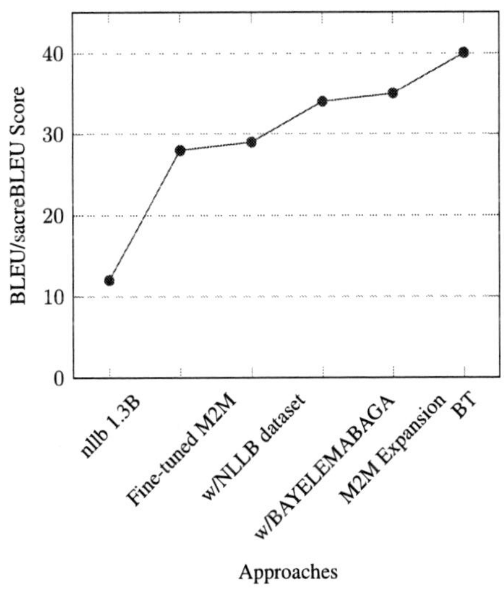

Figure 2: Timeline of Team Alpha efforts and BLEU score on dev set. The chart begins with our use of NLLB, switches to fine-tuned M2M, incorporates NLLB Seed dataset, then includes the BAYELEMABAGA dataset, and ends in our hypothetical performance using our cyclic backtranslation approach. The scores reported are for doing French → Bambara translation.

We included a potential impact in Figure 2 which shows the timeline of our activities and their corresponding evaluation results on the French → Bambara direction.

One of the major challenges facing machine translation for African languages is the limited availability of high-quality datasets (Nekoto et al., 2020; Caswell et al., 2021; Adelani et al., 2022). This became apparent in our study, where the use of the BAYELEMABAGA dataset resulted in a significant increase in the performance of our MT model. The scarcity of such resources highlights the need for continued efforts to develop and curate datasets for African languages, which could significantly improve the performance of machine translation models for African languages.

3.2 Team Most-Pham

We used a pre-trained MarianMT transformer model (Junczys-Dowmunt et al., 2018) which was pre-trained for Romance languages to English due to the non-existence of Bambara-French pre-trained weights for the MarianMT model. The model was then trained using a set of hyperparameters which were inspired by findings from Araabi and Monz (2020); Van Biljon et al. (2020) where the authors found the hyperparameters that would achieve the highest BLEU scores when dealing with low-resource languages. Our implementation was limited due to insufficient computing power (we were not able to increase attention heads without the GPU crashing during training).

We use the following set of hyperparameters; optimizer: adam, learning rate: $2e^{-5}$, beta 1:0.9, beta 2: 0.999, epsilon: $1e^{7}$, batch size: 64, and attention heads: 8.

3.2.1 Error analysis

Due to limited computing power, we were not able to fully train our MT model until convergence. It is plausible our model could have achieved higher accuracy or lower bias with more iterations of gradient descent. We also were not able to fine-tune our hyper-parameters as much as we would have liked.

In the seq2seq translation output, one word would get repeated multiple times back-to-back. This hallucination could be reduced by using a model that was pre-trained in French, so it would know from experience that French sentences do not normally include back-to-back repeated words.

There were words that appeared infrequently in the training set and were frequently mistranslated. With more time in this competition, this could have been alleviated with Byte Pair Encoding (BPE).

3.2.2 Discussion

While the existing literature suggests that Transformer models typically need a large training corpus to do well, our model suggests otherwise. With minor (out-of-the-box) modifications made to the architecture, the Transformer seq2seq model was still able to achieve a BLEU of 14.81 despite a limited training corpus, lack of a pre-trained Bambara model, computing power, and hyper-parameter tuning. In hindsight, we should have used a model that was pre-trained for Bambara to any Romance language, because it would be easier to learn Bambara to French if it had been pre-trained in Bambara to English, for example. We hypothesize that the difference between Bambara and the pre-trained data is very large, thereby making the model struggle to learn a different language with such a small dataset.

3.3 Team JYN

Our team had previously worked on MT tasks on languages such as French, Reunionese Creole, Portuguese, Umbundu, and Kimbundu, where we observed sub-optimal outcomes when training an autoregressive generative transformer model, either encoder-only or decoder-only, starting from scratch. Hence, for the given task, we wanted to use a Sequence to Sequence (seq2seq) model with prior training on the Bambara language. We evaluated different models of different sizes and with different number of training steps. We evaluated the following models on the development datasets: mt0-small, BLOOM-z 560M (Muennighoff et al., 2022b), NLLB 600M distilled, NLLB 1.3B, NLLB 1.3B distilled, and NLLB 3.3B (Team et al., 2022).

Upon evaluating the dev dataset, NLLB 600M distilled and NLLB 1.3B distilled exhibited superior performance. However, due to computational limitations even with our optimizations, training the NLLB 3B version would have been impossible. For an auto-regressive/instruction model, BLOOM-z exhibited more potential than mt0-small, and after two epochs, it produced acceptable scores. Nevertheless, it appears that general-purpose models of such small sizes do not rival specialized seq2seq models of similar dimensions, especially in a low-resource scenario.

We focused our scarce GPU hours to the two most promising models (NLLB 600M and NLLB 1.3B, which are both distilled models) and fine-tune them until the competition deadline. This provided an avenue to utilize and fine-tune distilled models. 1.3B distilled was better than not distilled models. Without fine-tuning, by using the default HuggingFace *generate* method, the 600M distilled model

Model size/Training steps	BAM → FR	FR → BAM
600M/3000 steps	21.7641	18.8674
600M/6000 steps	21.5270	**21.3773**
600M/9000 steps	21.3773	17.8374
1.3B/1500 steps	20.3349	17.8032
1.3B/3000 steps	18.6542	17.6243
1.3B/4500 steps	24.2556	19.3324
1.3B/6000 steps	25.3816	18.7743
1.3B/7500 steps	**26.0991**	18.1205

Table 4: BLEU Scores on development set (Team JYN), with increasing training steps showing a constant increase in translation for Bambara to French.

had a BLEU score of 19.8157 and 17.9217 for BAM to FR and FR to BAM, respectively. And the non-fine-tuned distilled 1.3B model had 24.5496 and 25.5610 for BAM to FR and FR to BAM, respectively. Both were tested on the dev corpus provided by the competition organizers. Table 4 shows the BLEU scores using different models and training steps, the latter indicating the amount of training a model should undergo.

The hyperparameters used for fine-tuning the NLLB models are: Optimizer: Adafactor; Learning rate: $1e^{-04}$; Batch size (1.3B model): 4; Batch size (600M model): 10; Gradient acc. (1.3B model): 16; and Gradient acc. (600M model): 10.

3.3.1 Error Analysis

We made a challenging discovery during this competition. In the NLLB paper, the source and target sequences are fed to the model with this scheme: (src_sequence, src_lang) for the source sequence and (tgt_lang, tgt_sequence) for the target sequence. On the other hand, the NLLB tokenizer in the HuggingFace transformer tokenizes the pair of sequences as (src_squence, src_lang) and (tgt_sequence, tgt_lang). Once we fixed this issue, the sacreBLEU scores of our finetuned NLLB models started to improve, consistently with the decrease of the loss, and with the quality differences that we could observe. However, we discovered and fixed this issue less than 24 hours before the deadline, and we had lost quite a bit of time by trying other fixes. Considering French is our native language, and a member of our group has some understanding of Bambara, we were able to compare the outputs of the model to the targets of the development set. Prior this discovery, the BLEU scores of our fine-tuned models were not impressive and inconsistent with the steadily decreasing loss on the dev set, and our observations of the outputs. After this fix, the BLEU scores showed improvements, even when we did not resolve the difference in behaviour between the two translation directions. The Bambara to French translations got marginally better in terms of BLEU scores compared to the French to Bambara, which was dramatically worse than the base performance.

3.3.2 Discussion

For our next MT project, we would explore large language models (LLM). We believe it would be a good idea to investigate the performance of few-shot prompting on these LLMs, because we have seen that the most promising model is still very limited for languages like Bambara.

Since Bambara, like many languages, is primarily spoken, we will try speech-based approaches in future work. These approaches will potentially have more impact and be more useful to these communities, especially to those who cannot write in their languages.

3.4 Yacine Zahidi

For pre-trained models, we explored several models available on the HuggingFace Hub, including M2M-100 (Fan et al., 2020), NLLB (Team et al., 2022), mT5 (Xue et al., 2021b) and byt5 (Xue et al., 2021a) models each pre-trained by the Masakhane Organization (Nekoto et al., 2020). Each model was evaluated on the dev set provided by the organizers with respect to the BLEU score. The M2M-100 (Fan et al., 2020) was chosen as a starting point since it scored the highest. It is a 483 million parameters distilled version of the original 1.2 billion parameters encoder-decoder transformer model.

Fine-tuning on the challenge dataset was promising, but the model validation loss curves showed overfitting despite fine-tuning for weight decay, small learning rate with decreasing linear schedule, warmup, and dropout. In addition, the BLEU score would not exceed 15 on the dev dataset, but upon manual investigation, the produced translations were shallow and sometimes semantically unrelated to the ground truth.

3.4.1 Error analysis

We examined the generated translations for common issues such as mistranslations, omissions, and word order errors. The resulting training process consisted of two steps: fine-tuning on the additional dataset in Table 2 and a step involving the challenge data. Yielding a BLEU score of **27** on the dev set, this approach produced a better result than fine-tuning on a mix of both extended and challenge data. The challenge data would then be under-represented, which would allow for a low BLEU score since the model is evaluated on a dev set from the challenge data distribution and not the additional data in Table 2.

The score was further improved by changing the generation algorithm and number of beams, resulting in the final dev BLEU score of **28.93** seen in Figure 3. This improved the score by 2 points.

Error analysis showed the gap in BLEU score between the dev set medical data and dictionary data. An average of 10 points difference was reported from one distribution to the other, which could be explained by two main differences: that in sequence length (the dictionary data was notably shorter) and in vocabulary distribution (the medical data was more domain-specific).

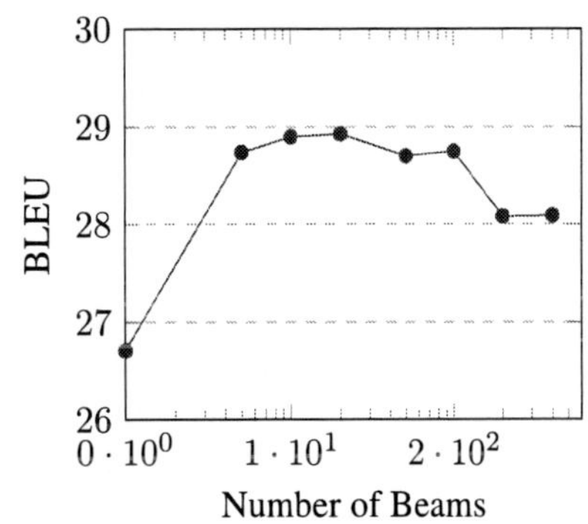

Figure 3: BLEU as a function of the number of beams. A value of one implies greedy decoding while bigger values correspond to the beam-search algorithm. Not surprisingly, the score dramatically improves before plateauing around 10 and reaching diminishing returns. Notably, the optimum is reached at 15 and increasing the number of beams further has a negative impact on the score.

3.4.2 Discussion

In addition to the data in Table 2, we extended our training data by processing a many-to-Bambara dataset from BigScience: the Bambara split of XP3-all (Muennighoff et al., 2022a). XP3-all contains 265,180 many-to-Bambara lines, but we only included the French-to-Bambara subset, and enriched it with the English-to-Bambara subset that was translated with the opus-mt-en-fr model from Helsinki-NLP (Tiedemann and Thottingal, 2020) resulting in 8,377 additional lines of training data.

In the future, we would spend more time automating tasks, including hyper-parameter tuning, to improve the efficiency of the system. Notably, the cross-entropy loss function is only a differentiable proxy for the metric we are trying to optimize i.e. the BLEU score (which is not differentiable). With the recent success of Reinforcement Learning techniques in natural language generation tasks (Stiennon et al., 2020), we plan to further fine-tune the model using the BLEU metric as a task reward, similar to Pinto et al. (2023).

In the future we will explore techniques, such as the recently introduced PEFT (Mangrulkar et al., 2022), which allows for fine-tuning of LLM on very small datasets using parameter efficient fine-tuning methods. IA3 (Liu et al., 2022), Prompt-Tuning (Lester et al., 2021), Prefix-Tuning (Liu et al., 2021), and Low Rank Adaptation (LoRA) (Hu et al., 2021) methods are currently leveraged to train large models efficiently on as few as 10 examples. In comparison to classic fine-tuning that involves training all the weigths of the model, these methods have the added advantage of achieving similar (sometimes even better) results by training only a small subset of the weights (by freezing the pre-trained weights and adding trainable adapter weights as seen in the case of LoRA and IA3). We therefore expect these methods to be increasingly used for any low-resource task in the near future.

Moreover, it seems that the Adam optimizer has finally found a worthy, artificially evolved rival (Chen et al., 2023). We look forward to testing it using the parameters of this task.

Finally, we would suggest the use of learned metrics for the evaluation of the translations instead of the BLEU metric (that ignores synonyms and idioms) building on the works of (Zhang* et al., 2020). Although such models are not yet trained on Bambara, Eddine et al. (2021) seems to offer part of the solution, and an alternative would simply be computing the cosine-distance between the embedding representation of the produced translation and that of the reference (Reimers and Gurevych, 2020).

3.5 Alexander Antonov

All of our models were trained using Sockeye (Hieber et al., 2020). In this task, we focused on building models *from scratch* and utilized 4 checkpoints averaging model parameters in our system. We averaged the parameters of the best 4 checkpoints, which helped to improve results. In addition we used BPE for word segmentation (Sennrich et al., 2016b).

3.5.1 Error analysis

We performed error analysis based on the BLEU metric, and used it as an optimized metric while training. We also used the sacreBLEU (Post, 2018).

3.5.2 Discussion

There are other extended techniques, such as back translation and pre-trained models that we intend to explore in future research. In addition, we also plan to add additional training datasets that were provided and used by the other teams.

3.6 Team Mali

The team attempted multiple approaches concurrently, first pre-training a bilingual Bambara-French denoising Seq2Seq-based foundational model with a lower quality dataset, inspired by Lewis et al. (2019), then fine-tuning it with a higher-quality dataset. This approach yielded non-optimal translations and performance, with all the scores being sub-8 BLEU (it was also resource-heavy and time-consuming). We fine-tuned with DeltaLM (Ma et al., 2021), the training failed to converge with both the base checkpoint and large checkpoint. The problem could be attributed primarily to limited compute resources.

We were able to double our performance from the previous approaches when we re-trained with the NLLB-200 (Team et al., 2022) 600M parameters pre-trained model, with a learning rate of 2, batch size of 512, and training steps of 20k with the lower-quality dataset. Using both DABA-assisted and non-Daba-assited pre-processing[5].

Furthermore, we obtained another peak in performance when we unfreeze the model and then tuned it with the competition dataset with the same configuration, for an understanding of the type of text used for the competition (although we suspected over-fitting). We have seen similar results from both directions, Bambara to French and French to Bambara.

3.6.1 Error analysis

We knew that Bambara is a complex and morphologically sophisticated language. Bambara and French have a one sentence to many translation

[5]https://github.com/maslinych/daba

scheme, where one sentence can have multiple interpretations in the other language, in a polysemous phrasal relationship. Additionally, with Bambara being predominantly a spoken language, there are many fluidities that only native speakers can pick up from translations, compared to a more structured language. We chose to weigh human evaluation higher than automated metrics. Both evaluation techniques gave an insight into the overall performance of our models.

Human Evaluation We came up with our own defined method for manual evaluation, described as follows: For every model trained, we sampled 50 lines from our test set and classified each line into three classes manually *BAD*, *ACCEPTABLE*, and *GOOD*. Where *BAD* was given a value of 0; it is chosen when the hypothesis does not relay any information from the source or is a bad translation. *ACCEPTABLE* was given a value of 1; it is chosen when the hypothesis is a literal translation of the source without context. *GOOD* was given a value of 2; it is chosen when the hypothesis is an accurate translation of the source with context.

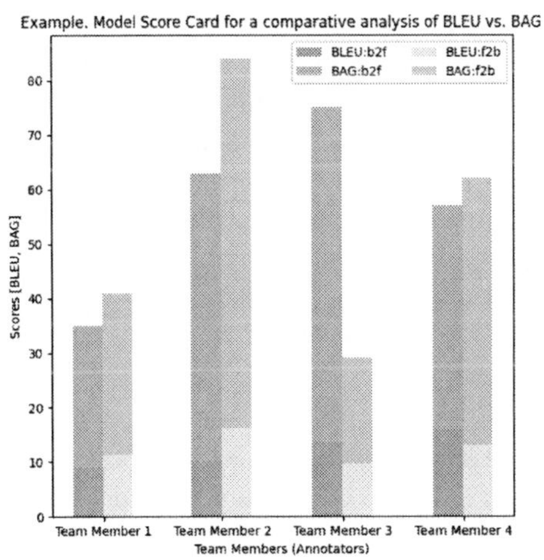

Figure 4: Example model score card analysis comparing human-evaluation vs BLEU. where **b2f**: Bambara-French, **f2b**: French to Bambara. **BAG**: Bad, Acceptable, Good

Each member of the team evaluated a batch of 50 lines per model trained, given the source text, a reference translation, and the hypothesis generated by the model. They were tasked to evaluate the manual score and to compute the BLEU score of the batch, for a comparative analysis of the two results, an example evaluation is shown in Figure 4.

Acknowledging the subjective nature of human evaluation, we should state that while the human evaluations was used to guide our analysis of the performance of our models for the competition, further investigations are needed to validate its viability.

3.6.2 Discussion

Bambara's complexity made it challenging to find the best possible approach, as each aspect of the training required analysis. From pre-processing to evaluation, we found that fine-tuning with the NLLB200 600M model to be more performant. The most significant aspect in our method was the human-in-the loop approach, where coupling human annotation and automated metrics was the primary indicator that informed our decisions during the competition.

3.7 Team Peter-Sokhar

We experimented with transformer-based models and utilized the attention mechanism, which enables one component of the model to concentrate on another part of the model. Due to the issue of vanishing gradient and the weakness of limited levels of parallelization, respectively, both recurrent neural networks (RNNs) and Long Short Term Memory (LSTM) were not considered (Vaswani et al., 2017). The selected transformer model was Facebook/nllb-200-distilled-600M (Team et al., 2022), which was fine-tuned on the training dataset, which allowed for the design of the encoder, latent representation, and decoder. By using semi-supervised learning, the decoder fed features to the model. The team explored training the model for 100 epochs.

3.7.1 Error Analysis

By using Google Translate, the team was able to avoid having a native speaker as a teammate. In the future, a native speaker will be a part of the team.

3.7.2 Discussion

Beyond needing additional compute and a powerful internet connection, we would like to consider other alternative models for cross-validation.

Team Name	BLEU Score (BAM to FR)	BLEU Score (FR to BAM)
Team Alpha	16.31	17.45
Team JYN	13.12	11.1
Yacine Zahidi	19.05	N/A
Alexander Antonov	7.54	8.06
Team Most-Pham	14.81	N/A
Team Mali	5.82	N/A

Table 5: BLEU score results by team for Bambara - French and French - Bambara, with placement ordering.

4 BFMT 2023 Results and Discussion

Table 5 shows the BLEU scores for both Bambara to French and French to Bambara translations. Not all of the teams attempted both translation directions and the scores were averaged across both language pairs to determine the winners.

The BFMT 2023 competition aimed to increase research in low-resource language machine translation by providing training and evaluation data and supporting community-building around scientific transparency. Community-building included teams being constructed from individuals with complementary skills and all relevant training data discovered by one team being shared amongst the teams.

Nonetheless, there were key themes to the submissions. All of the teams used the same core datasets, with two teams bootstrapping alternatives as shown in Table 2. Additional data provided a significant advantage in this low-resource situation. From a machine learning perspective, many of the teams shared similar approaches with effectively utilizing the M2M-100 model (Fan et al., 2020) as the differentiator between the top performing teams. Notably, the NLLB-200 (Adelani et al., 2022) model comparatively under-performed. We believe this is because the M2M-100 model had fine-tuned MT models separately for each language direction.

Subsequent insights were that the winning team used a backtranslation approach, *cyclic backtranslation*, and another successful team used a beam search optimization. Also, we learned that smaller distilled models could beat larger models with limited amounts of data (i.e., fine-tuning distilled models yields more accurate results).

Only one team had members that spoke Bambara but many participants are speakers of other low-resource languages and hope to extend their experience with MT system development to languages that their families and friends speak.

5 Conclusion and Future Work

Because of BFMT 2023, researchers have successfully implemented innovative low-resource machine translation systems. These implementations are extensible to other language pairs, which is helpful since low-resource languages continue to face numerous challenges in terms of research focus and funding. We believe BFMT 2023 has not only supported increased visibility of the Bambara language, but it has also showcased the talent that is working on using creative techniques to address these technical challenges globally.

The BFMT 2023 competition community would like to extend this work by holding other competitions. Ideally, the next competition will utilize automatic speech recognition data. Including spoken data in MT might circumvent a challenge in low-resource language, where only a few online datasets support predominately oral language text processing.

The output of BFMT 2023 is a viable baseline for French - Bambara and Bambara - French machine translation. In addition, the competition dataset is now available to researchers seeking to exceed this baseline or evaluate their translation systems. Similar to the practice in some Kaggle competitions, we can also provide a baseline model in the next competition iteration that is based on the top scoring competition submission [6].

Finally, we would like to provide greater financial support to the participating teams by sponsoring equal and standard access to computational resources. This could better illuminate which machine learning models are the highest performers.

Limitations

There are several limitations we observed during the BFMT 2023 competition. We hope these limitations and findings help researchers to understand the challenges of organizing an MT shared task and use them to improve their competitions.

1. Bambara is a low-resource language and the amount of data needed to significantly improve MT is very large. Inconsistent Bambara orthographies might mitigate translation quality improvement even with additional data collection. There are very high rates of illiteracy for Malians (35%, the 5th highest in the world (Diarra and Leventhal, 2020)) and

[6] https://www.kaggle.com/competitions

Bambara speakers. We would like to gather and translate spoken Bambara audio data to counter these challenges.

2. The test set used for BLEU score evaluation was data previously used in WMT21 (Akhbardeh et al., 2021). It contained transcripts of conversations between translators and Bambara speakers, and translations of medical information[7]. Nonetheless, this dataset was extensively re-aligned and post-processed to remove encoding errors. Due to this additional data cleaning, the processed, competition dataset is of higher quality and thus has no exact baseline for comparison. Further, many competitors trained models with additional data, potentially leading to over-fitting of models to a different format of Bambara-French translations, rather than the original dataset.

3. BLEU has known limitations for meaningful evaluation including how well it corresponds to human evaluation of language correctness and naturalness. In the future we would like to conduct human evaluation of the MT competition output. Many of the diverse competition participants speak other low-resource languages, but only Team Mali had Bambara speakers. Team Mali performed human evaluation and gave human results more weight than automated ones. Human evaluation was used to guide the analysis of the performance of their models. They would like to extend this work but were limited due to the time constraints required for a competition. Finally, the participants' BLEU scores did not meet the closeness threshold (within 1 point) the judges deemed necessary for supplementary human evaluation.

4. We understand human evaluation of the translation predictions can be a strategic piece for judging translation quality and naturalness. Human evaluation can give insight on how systems actually perform and direct focus for improvement based on linguistic analysis. As a low-resource language, it is difficult to find human evaluators with translator-level written French and Bambara skills on the data annotation platforms used in conducting and collecting supplemental human evaluation. We hope these observations will help future MT competition organizers to plan and allocate resources for human evaluation for judging.

5. The importance of compute power was also evident in this competition but the MT systems were not compared in regards to computational resources. In future work we will support equal computational resources for all teams.

[7]The dataset is available to share on request through the corresponding author.

Ethics Statement

Any evaluation system that incorporates human workers motivates reflection on the ethical implications of their contribution. Two of the teams competing in the competition had members that were able to annotate their system's output for translation quality due to their Bambara knowledge. This was part of their team's evaluation efforts and all the team members had already consented to participate in the competition.

In addition to considering how participating in the competition affected the team members, this work also affects the many millions of Bambara speakers who have not historically had access to technology. A recent focus on Machine Learning by the Malian government aims to change that (Diarra and Leventhal, 2020). As a consequence, increasing awareness and access to MT data, tasks, and their applications has wide global impact.

Finally, due to the BLEU scores the competing teams produced, these current translation systems should not be used in critical situations where inaccurate translations could lead to harm.

Acknowledgements

The data used in this work was supported by funding from the Artificial Intelligence Journal promoting AI research and previously utilized for *WMT* (Akhbardeh et al., 2021). We would like to thank Marcos Zampieri, David Talbot, and Francois Lefevre, Alexandra Mephon, and Douglas Cramer for their extremely helpful insight and time they contributed to the competition. We would like to thank Orange Silicon Valley for their support of the machine translation competition including the monetary awards for the winners.

References

David Adelani, Jesujoba Alabi, Angela Fan, Julia Kreutzer, Xiaoyu Shen, Machel Reid, Dana Ruiter, Dietrich Klakow, Peter Nabende, Ernie Chang, Tajuddeen Gwadabe, Freshia Sackey, Bonaventure F. P. Dossou, Chris Emezue, Colin Leong, Michael Beukman, Shamsuddeen Muhammad, Guyo Jarso, Oreen Yousuf, Andre Niyongabo Rubungo, Gilles Hacheme, Eric Peter Wairagala, Muhammad Umair Nasir, Benjamin Ajibade, Tunde Ajayi, Yvonne Gitau, Jade Abbott, Mohamed Ahmed, Millicent Ochieng, Anuoluwapo Aremu, Perez Ogayo, Jonathan Mukiibi, Fatoumata Ouoba Kabore, Godson Kalipe, Derguene Mbaye, Allahsera Auguste Tapo, Victoire Memdjokam Koagne, Edwin Munkoh-Buabeng, Valencia Wagner, Idris Abdulmumin, Ayodele Awokoya, Happy Buzaaba, Blessing Sibanda, Andiswa Bukula, and Sam Manthalu. 2022. A few thousand translations go a long way! leveraging pre-trained models for African news translation. In *Proceedings of the 2022 Conference of the North American Chapter of the Association for Computational Linguistics: Human Language Technologies*, pages 3053–3070, Seattle, United States. Association for Computational Linguistics.

Farhad Akhbardeh, Arkady Arkhangorodsky, Magdalena Biesialska, Ondrej Bojar, Rajen Chatterjee, Vishrav Chaudhary, Marta R. Costa-jussà, Cristina España-Bonet, Angela Fan, Christian Federman, Markus Freitag, Yvette Graham, Roman Grundkiewicz, Barry Haddow, Leonie Harter, Kenneth Heafield, Christopher M. Homan, Matthias Huck, Kwabena Amponsah-Kaakyire, Jungo Kasai, Daniel Khashabi, Kevin Knight, Tom Kocmi, Philipp Koehn, Nicholas Lourie, Christof Monz, Makoto Morishita, Masaaki Nagata, Ajay Nagesh, Toshiaki Nakazawa, Matteo Negri, Santanu Pal, Allahsera Tapo, Marco Turchi, Valentin Vydrin, and Marcos Zampieri. 2021. Findings of the 2021 conference on machine translation (wmt21). In *Proceedings of the Sixth Conference on Machine Translation*, pages 1–88, Online.

Ali Araabi and Christof Monz. 2020. Optimizing transformer for low-resource neural machine translation. In *Proceedings of the 28th International Conference on Computational Linguistics*, pages 3429–3435.

Martin Benjamin. 2019. Teach You Backwards: An In-Depth Study of Google Translate for 108 Languages — teachyoubackwards.com. `https://www.teachyoubackwards.com/`. [Accessed 04-Apr-2023].

Isaac Caswell, Julia Kreutzer, Lisa Wang, Ahsan Wahab, Daan van Esch, Nasanbayar Ulzii-Orshikh, Allahsera Auguste Tapo, Nishant Subramani, Artem Sokolov, Claytone Sikasote, Monang Setyawan, Supheakmungkol Sarin, Sokhar Samb, Benoît Sagot, Clara Rivera, Annette Rios Gonzales, Isabel Papadimitriou, Salomey Osei, Pedro Ortiz Suarez, Iroro Orife, Kelechi Ogueji, Andre Niyongabo Rubungo, Toan Q. Nguyen, Mathias Muller, Andre Matthias Muller, Shamsuddeen Hassan Muhammad, Nanda Firdausi Muhammad, Ayanda Mnyakeni, Jamshidbek Mirzakhalov, Tapiwanashe Matangira, Colin Leong, Nze Lawson, Sneha Kudugunta, Yacine Jernite, M. Jenny, Orhan Firat, Bonaventure F. P. Dossou, Sakhile Dlamini, Nisansa de Silva, Sakine cCabuk Balli, Stella Rose Biderman, Alessia Battisti, Ahmed Baruwa, Ankur Bapna, Pallavi N. Baljekar, Israel Abebe Azime, Ayodele Awokoya, Duygu Ataman, Orevaoghene Ahia, Oghenefego Ahia, Sweta Agrawal, and Mofetoluwa Adeyemi. 2021. Quality at a glance: An audit of web-crawled multilingual datasets. *Transactions of the Association for Computational Linguistics*, 10:50–72.

Xiangning Chen, Chen Liang, Da Huang, Esteban Real, Kaiyuan Wang, Yao Liu, Hieu Pham, Xuanyi Dong, Thang Luong, Cho-Jui Hsieh, Yifeng Lu, and Quoc V. Le. 2023. Symbolic discovery of optimization algorithms.

Haby Sanou Diarra and Michael Leventhal. 2020. Developing machine learning competence in africa in the francophone sahel region.

Bonaventure F. P. Dossou and Chris C. Emezue. 2020. Ffr v1.0: Fon-french neural machine translation. *arXiv preprint arXiv: Arxiv-2003.12111*.

Moussa Kamal Eddine, Guokan Shang, Antoine J. P. Tixier, and Michalis Vazirgiannis. 2021. Frugalscore: Learning cheaper, lighter and faster evaluation metricsfor automatic text generation.

Chris Chinenye Emezue and Bonaventure F. P. Dossou. 2021. MMTAfrica: Multilingual machine translation for African languages. In *Proceedings of the Sixth Conference on Machine Translation*, pages 398–411, Online. Association for Computational Linguistics.

Angela Fan, Shruti Bhosale, Holger Schwenk, Zhiyi Ma, Ahmed El-Kishky, Siddharth Goyal, Mandeep Baines, Onur Celebi, Guillaume Wenzek, Vishrav Chaudhary, Naman Goyal, Tom Birch, Vitaliy Liptchinsky, Sergey Edunov, Edouard Grave, Michael Auli, and Armand Joulin. 2020. Beyond english-centric multilingual machine translation. *arXiv preprint*.

Naman Goyal, Cynthia Gao, Vishrav Chaudhary, Peng-Jen Chen, Guillaume Wenzek, Da Ju, Sanjana Krishnan, Marc'Aurelio Ranzato, Francisco Guzmán, and Angela Fan. 2022. The FLORES-101 evaluation benchmark for low-resource and multilingual machine translation. *Transactions of the Association for Computational Linguistics*, 10:522–538.

Barry Haddow, Rachel Bawden, Antonio Valerio Miceli Barone, Jindřich Helcl, and Alexandra Birch. 2022. Survey of low-resource machine translation. *Computational Linguistics*, 48(3):673–732.

Felix Hieber, Tobias Domhan, Michael Denkowski, and David Vilar. 2020. Sockeye 2: A toolkit for neural machine translation. In *Proceedings of the 22nd Annual Conference of the European Association for*

Machine Translation, pages 457–458, Lisboa, Portugal. European Association for Machine Translation.

Edward Hu, Yelong Shen, Phil Wallis, Zeyuan Allen-Zhu, Yuanzhi Li, Lu Wang, and Weizhu Chen. 2021. Lora: Low-rank adaptation of large language models.

Marcin Junczys-Dowmunt, Roman Grundkiewicz, Tomasz Dwojak, Hieu Hoang, Kenneth Heafield, Tom Neckermann, Frank Seide, Ulrich Germann, Alham Fikri Aji, Nikolay Bogoychev, André F. T. Martins, and Alexandra Birch. 2018. Marian: Fast neural machine translation in C++. In *Proceedings of ACL 2018, System Demonstrations*, pages 116–121, Melbourne, Australia.

Tsz Kin Lam, Shigehiko Schamoni, and Stefan Riezler. 2021. Cascaded models with cyclic feedback for direct speech translation. In *ICASSP 2021-2021 IEEE International Conference on Acoustics, Speech and Signal Processing (ICASSP)*, pages 7508–7512. IEEE.

Brian Lester, Rami Al-Rfou, and Noah Constant. 2021. The power of scale for parameter-efficient prompt tuning. *CoRR*, abs/2104.08691.

Michael Leventhal, Allahsera Tapo, Sarah Luger, Marcos Zampieri, and Christopher M Homan. 2020. Assessing human translations from french to bambara for machine learning: a pilot study. *arXiv preprint arXiv:2004.00068*.

Mike Lewis, Yinhan Liu, Naman Goyal, Marjan Ghazvininejad, Abdelrahman Mohamed, Omer Levy, Ves Stoyanov, and Luke Zettlemoyer. 2019. Bart: Denoising sequence-to-sequence pre-training for natural language generation, translation, and comprehension. *arXiv preprint arXiv:1910.13461*.

M.P. Lewis, G.F. Simons, and C.D. Fennig. 2014. *Ethnologue: Languages of Africa and Europe*. SIL International.

Haokun Liu, Derek Tam, Mohammed Muqeeth, Jay Mohta, Tenghao Huang, Mohit Bansal, and Colin Raffel. 2022. Few-shot parameter-efficient fine-tuning is better and cheaper than in-context learning.

Xiao Liu, Kaixuan Ji, Yicheng Fu, Zhengxiao Du, Zhilin Yang, and Jie Tang. 2021. P-tuning v2: Prompt tuning can be comparable to fine-tuning universally across scales and tasks. *CoRR*, abs/2110.07602.

Shuming Ma, Li Dong, Shaohan Huang, Dongdong Zhang, Alexandre Muzio, Saksham Singhal, Hany Hassan Awadalla, Xia Song, and Furu Wei. 2021. Deltalm: Encoder-decoder pre-training for language generation and translation by augmenting pretrained multilingual encoders. *arXiv preprint arXiv:2106.13736*.

Sourab Mangrulkar, Sylvain Gugger, Lysandre Debut, Younes Belkada, and Sayak Paul. 2022. Peft: State-of-the-art parameter-efficient fine-tuning methods. urlhttps://github.com/huggingface/peft.

Swaroop Mishra, Matthew Finlayson, Pan Lu, Leonard Tang, Sean Welleck, Chitta Baral, Tanmay Rajpurohit, Oyvind Tafjord, Ashish Sabharwal, Peter Clark, and Ashwin Kalyan. 2022. Lila: A unified benchmark for mathematical reasoning.

Niklas Muennighoff, Thomas Wang, Lintang Sutawika, Adam Roberts, Stella Biderman, Teven Le Scao, M Saiful Bari, Sheng Shen, Zheng-Xin Yong, Hailey Schoelkopf, Xiangru Tang, Dragomir Radev, Alham Fikri Aji, Khalid Almubarak, Samuel Albanie, Zaid Alyafeai, Albert Webson, Edward Raff, and Colin Raffel. 2022a. Crosslingual generalization through multitask finetuning.

Niklas Muennighoff, Thomas Wang, Lintang Sutawika, Adam Roberts, Stella Biderman, Teven Le Scao, M Saiful Bari, Sheng Shen, Zheng-Xin Yong, Hailey Schoelkopf, Xiangru Tang, Dragomir Radev, Alham Fikri Aji, Khalid Almubarak, Samuel Albanie, Zaid Alyafeai, Albert Webson, Edward Raff, and Colin Raffel. 2022b. Crosslingual generalization through multitask finetuning.

Wilhelmina Nekoto, Vukosi Marivate, Tshinondiwa Matsila, Timi Fasubaa, Taiwo Fagbohungbe, Solomon Oluwole Akinola, Shamsuddeen Muhammad, Salomon Kabongo Kabenamualu, Salomey Osei, Freshia Sackey, Rubungo Andre Niyongabo, Ricky Macharm, Perez Ogayo, Orevaoghene Ahia, Musie Meressa Berhe, Mofetoluwa Adeyemi, Masabata Mokgesi-Selinga, Lawrence Okegbemi, Laura Martinus, Kolawole Tajudeen, Kevin Degila, Kelechi Ogueji, Kathleen Siminyu, Julia Kreutzer, Jason Webster, Jamiil Toure Ali, Jade Abbott, Iroro Orife, Ignatius Ezeani, Idris Abdulkadir Dangana, Herman Kamper, Hady Elsahar, Goodness Duru, Ghollah Kioko, Murhabazi Espoir, Elan van Biljon, Daniel Whitenack, Christopher Onyefuluchi, Chris Chinenye Emezue, Bonaventure F. P. Dossou, Blessing Sibanda, Blessing Bassey, Ayodele Olabiyi, Arshath Ramkilowan, Alp Öktem, Adewale Akinfaderin, and Abdallah Bashir. 2020. Participatory research for low-resourced machine translation: A case study in African languages. In *Findings of the Association for Computational Linguistics: EMNLP 2020*, pages 2144–2160, Online. Association for Computational Linguistics.

Kishore Papineni, Salim Roukos, Todd Ward, and Wei-Jing Zhu. 2002. Bleu: a method for automatic evaluation of machine translation. In *Proceedings of the 40th annual meeting of the Association for Computational Linguistics*, pages 311–318.

André Susano Pinto, Alexander Kolesnikov, Yuge Shi, Lucas Beyer, and Xiaohua Zhai. 2023. Tuning computer vision models with task rewards.

Alberto Poncelas, Dimitar Shterionov, Andy Way, Gideon Maillette de Buy Wenniger, and Peyman Passban. 2018. Investigating backtranslation in neural machine translation. *arXiv preprint arXiv: Arxiv-1804.06189*.

Matt Post. 2018. A call for clarity in reporting BLEU scores. In *Proceedings of the Third Conference on Machine Translation: Research Papers*, pages 186–191, Brussels, Belgium. Association for Computational Linguistics.

Nils Reimers and Iryna Gurevych. 2020. Making monolingual sentence embeddings multilingual using knowledge distillation. In *Proceedings of the 2020 Conference on Empirical Methods in Natural Language Processing*. Association for Computational Linguistics.

Rico Sennrich, Barry Haddow, and Alexandra Birch. 2016a. Improving neural machine translation models with monolingual data. *ACL*.

Rico Sennrich, Barry Haddow, and Alexandra Birch. 2016b. Neural machine translation of rare words with subword units. In *Proceedings of the 54th Annual Meeting of the Association for Computational Linguistics (Volume 1: Long Papers)*, pages 1715–1725, Berlin, Germany. Association for Computational Linguistics.

Shailashree K Sheshadri, Deepa Gupta, and Marta R Costa-Jussà. 2023. A voyage on neural machine translation for indic languages. *Procedia Computer Science*, 218:2694–2712.

Nisan Stiennon, Long Ouyang, Jeffrey Wu, Daniel Ziegler, Ryan Lowe, Chelsea Voss, Alec Radford, Dario Amodei, and Paul F Christiano. 2020. Learning to summarize with human feedback. In *Advances in Neural Information Processing Systems*, volume 33, pages 3008–3021. Curran Associates, Inc.

Allahsera Auguste Tapo, Bakary Coulibaly, Sébastien Diarra, Christopher Homan, Julia Kreutzer, Sarah Luger, Arthur Nagashima, Marcos Zampieri, and Michael Leventhal. 2020. Neural machine translation for extremely low-resource african languages: A case study on bambara. *arXiv preprint arXiv:2011.05284*.

NLLB Team, Marta R. Costa-jussà, James Cross, Onur Çelebi, Maha Elbayad, Kenneth Heafield, Kevin Heffernan, Elahe Kalbassi, Janice Lam, Daniel Licht, Anna Sun Jean Maillard, Skyler Wang, Guillaume Wenzek, Al Youngblood, Bapi Akula, Loic Barrault, Gabriel Mejia Gonzalez, Prangthip Hansanti, John Hoffman, Semarley Jarrett, Kaushik Ram Sadagopan, Dirk Rowe, Shannon Spruit, Chau Tran, Pierre Andrews, Necip Fazil Ayan, Shruti Bhosale, Sergey Edunov, Angela Fan, Cynthia Gao, Vedanuj Goswami, Francisco Guzmán, Philipp Koehn, Alexandre Mourachko, Christophe Ropers, Safiyyah Saleem, Holger Schwenk, and Jeff Wang. 2022. No language left behind: Scaling human-centered machine translation.

Jörg Tiedemann and Santhosh Thottingal. 2020. OPUS-MT – building open translation services for the world. In *Proceedings of the 22nd Annual Conference of the European Association for Machine Translation*, pages 479–480, Lisboa, Portugal. European Association for Machine Translation.

Elan Van Biljon, Arnu Pretorius, and Julia Kreutzer. 2020. On optimal transformer depth for low-resource language translation. *arXiv preprint arXiv:2004.04418*.

Ashish Vaswani, Noam Shazeer, Niki Parmar, Jakob Uszkoreit, Llion Jones, Aidan N Gomez, Łukasz Kaiser, and Illia Polosukhin. 2017. Attention is all you need. *Advances in neural information processing systems*, 30.

Ashish Venugopal. 2010. Five more languages on translate.google.com — translate.googleblog.com. `https://translate.googleblog.com/2010/05/five-more-languages-on.html`. [Accessed 04-Apr-2023].

Valentin Vydrin, Jean-Jacques Meric, Kirill Maslinsky, Andrij Rovenchak, Allahsera Auguste Tapo, Sebastien Diarra, Christopher Homan, Marco Zampieri, and Michael Leventhal. 2022. Machine learning dataset development for manding languages. urlhttps://github.com/robotsmali-ai/datasets.

Thomas Wolf, Lysandre Debut, Victor Sanh, Julien Chaumond, Clement Delangue, Anthony Moi, Pierric Cistac, Tim Rault, Rémi Louf, Morgan Funtowicz, Joe Davison, Sam Shleifer, Patrick von Platen, Clara Ma, Yacine Jernite, Julien Plu, Canwen Xu, Teven Le Scao, Sylvain Gugger, Mariama Drame, Quentin Lhoest, and Alexander M. Rush. 2020. Transformers: State-of-the-art natural language processing. In *Proceedings of the 2020 Conference on Empirical Methods in Natural Language Processing: System Demonstrations*, pages 38–45, Online. Association for Computational Linguistics.

Linting Xue, Aditya Barua, Noah Constant, Rami Al-Rfou, Sharan Narang, Mihir Kale, Adam Roberts, and Colin Raffel. 2021a. Byt5: Towards a token-free future with pre-trained byte-to-byte models.

Linting Xue, Noah Constant, Adam Roberts, Mihir Kale, Rami Al-Rfou, Aditya Siddhant, Aditya Barua, and Colin Raffel. 2021b. mT5: A massively multilingual pre-trained text-to-text transformer. In *Proceedings of the 2021 Conference of the North American Chapter of the Association for Computational Linguistics: Human Language Technologies*, pages 483–498, Online. Association for Computational Linguistics.

Biao Zhang, Philip Williams, Ivan Titov, and Rico Sennrich. 2020. Improving massively multilingual neural machine translation and zero-shot translation. In *Proceedings of the 58th Annual Meeting of the Association for Computational Linguistics*, pages 1628–1639, Online. Association for Computational Linguistics.

Tianyi Zhang*, Varsha Kishore*, Felix Wu*, Kilian Q. Weinberger, and Yoav Artzi. 2020. Bertscore: Evaluating text generation with bert.

Evaluating Sentence Alignment Methods in a Low-Resource Setting: an English-Yorùbá study case

Edoardo Signoroni and **Pavel Rychlý**
NLP Centre
Faculty of Informatics
Masaryk University
e.signoroni@mail.muni.cz, pary@fi.muni.cz

Abstract

Parallel corpora are still crucial to train effective Machine Translation systems. This is even more true for low-resource language pairs, for which Neural Machine Translation has been shown to be less robust to domain mismatch and noise. Due to time and resource constraints, parallel corpora are mostly created with sentence alignment methods which automatically infer alignments. Recent work focused on state-of-the-art pre-trained sentence embeddings-based methods which are available only for a tiny fraction of the world's languages. In this paper, we evaluate the performance of four widely used algorithms on the low-resource English-Yorùbá language pair against a multidomain benchmark parallel corpus on two experiments involving 1-to-1 alignments with and without reordering. We find that, at least for this language pair, earlier and simpler methods are more suited to the task, all the while not requiring additional data or resources. We also report that the methods we evaluated perform differently across distinct domains, thus indicating that some approach may be better for a specific domain or textual structure.

1 Introduction

Parallel corpora are vital training data for Machine Translation (MT) systems, especially for low-resource languages where data is scarce (Steingrímsson et al., 2020). While unsupervised methods trained only on monolingual data have been proposed for Neural MT, they are still sensitive to noise and domain mismatch (Khayrallah and Koehn, 2018), and are outperformed by supervised and semi-supervised systems trained on relatively small parallel corpora (Kim et al., 2020). Collecting and curating data for the creation of a parallel corpus manually is a costly and time consuming task that requires expertise in the languages involved. It is even more difficult for low to no-resource languages, for which the number of speakers and research may be lower.

Thus, today parallel corpora are mostly created by employing automatic methods for sentence alignment. Sentence alignment is the task of taking parallel documents split into sentences and finding a bipartite graph which matches minimal groups of sentences that are translation of each other (Thompson and Koehn, 2019). In other words, to find target sentences with the same meaning to that of the source segments in multilingual texts (Steingrímsson et al., 2020). Several approaches have been proposed, from simple length-based algorithms (Gale and Church, 1993), to more complex methods employing multilingual sentence embeddings (Thompson and Koehn, 2019).

Our work evaluates four commonly used sentence alignment methods using Menyo20k (Adelani et al., 2021), a high-quality benchmark English-Yorùbá[1] parallel corpus, as reference. We experiment with 1-to-1 alignments with and without reordering. Our results show that, at least for this language pair, earlier, simpler systems may be more suited, as they perform better and do not require other data than the documents to be aligned, allowing them to be employed even when no other text or knowledge of the languages is available. Moreover, we leverage the domain annotation of the Menyo20k corpus to observe that the alignment methods in our evaluation perform differently across various domains. This indicates that some approach may be better suited to a specific domain or textual structure.

After this Introduction, we report on some recent work aimed at evaluating and improving sentence alignment for low-resource language pairs in Section 2. Then, in Section 3 we describe briefly

[1]Yorùbá is the third most spoken language in Africa, with 40 million native speakers. It is native to south-western Nigeria and the Republic of Benin and belongs to the Niger-Congo family.

Proceedings of the The Sixth Workshop on Technologies for Machine Translation of Low-Resource Languages (LoResMT 2023), pages 123–129
May 6, 2023

the alignment methods in our evaluation, which methodology is outlined in Section 4. Section 5 reports the results of our experiments and Section 6 draws some conclusions.

2 Related Work

Some recent work deals with sentence alignment in a low-resource setting, focusing on evaluating and improving modern sentence embedding-based methods.

Tien et al. (2021) finds that Vecaling has several limitations: it performs poorly in aligning sentences which are located far apart in source and target documents, or it may align sentences which are not translations of one another, but have a high similarity score. Moreover, the error can be propagated to from one pair to another, since the sentence that should be in one alignment is moved to a further one. They propose a new method that overcomes these limitations by firstly aligning paragraphs and generating candidate sentence pairs only among the aligned paragraph's sentences. They work with the Vietnamese-Lao low-resource language pair by translating the Lao documents to Vietnamese, on which LASER has been trained. Then they find the sentence pairs with cosine similarity weighted for the ratio of text length and then retrieve the target sentence in the original language. They report significant improvements in precision and recall over Vecaling on their test set.

Chimoto and Bassett (2022) experiment with LASER and LaBSE (Feng et al., 2021) to extract bitext for two unseen low-resource African languages, Luhya and Swahili. They find that both pre-trained models perform poorly at zero-shot alignment on Luhya. They thus fine-tune the embeddings on a small set of parallel Luhya sentences and report significant gains, with the accuracy of LaBSE increasing from 22% to 53.3%. This is further improved to over 85% by restricting the datastet to sentence embedding pairs with cosine similarity above 0.7.

Fernando et al. (2022) evaluates the effectiveness of pre-trained language models such as LASER, XLM-R (Conneau et al., 2020), and LaBSE on document and sentence alignment in the context of the low-resource languages of Sinhala, Tamil, and English. They introduce a weighting mechanism based on small-scale bilingual lexicons to improve the semantic similarity measure used by the methods they evaluate, thus improving the resulting alignments. Contrarily to our work, they find that the multilingual sentence embeddings-based methods significantly outperform the Hunalign baseline on their test language pairs. This discrepancy should be investigated in future work.

3 Baselines

The works introduced in Section 2 deal mostly with sentence embeddings-based methods.[2] While these methods were shown to be effective and able to generalize to unseen languages in some instances (Thompson and Koehn, 2019; Conneau et al., 2020), this did not hold in other low-resource test cases, for which further work on both the system and the model was needed to reach a satisfactory performance (Chimoto and Bassett, 2022). Moreover, they are still not free from issues in handling sentences which are found far apart in the documents and employ non-optimal scoring functions, such as raw sentence embedding cosine similarity (Tien et al., 2021). Lastly, they still require resource-heavy pre-trained models which are available only for a tiny fraction of the world's languages. Thus, we also include earlier methods in our evaluation. Table 1 summarizes the methods we have taken into account.

The earliest widely documented statistical-based methods were explored by Gale and Church (1993) on the assumption that the length of a sentence is highly correlated with the length of its translation. Moreover, they concluded that there is a stable ratio between the sentence lengths in any two language. Their method assigns a probabilistic score to each correspondence of sentences, based on the scaled difference of lengths, in number of characters, of the two sentences and the variance of this difference. The score is used in a dynamic programming framework to find the maximum likelihood alignment of sentences. They worked on a trilingual corpus of economic reports issued by the Union Bank of Switzerland (UBS) in English, French, and German, and a bilingual sample of 90 million words from proceedings of the Parliament of Canada in English and French.

Varga et al. (2007) describe *Hunalign*, a hybrid method, combining a dictionary with a length-based approach. Hunalign starts by producing a crude word to word translation for each word token in the dictionary according to the token with the

[2]Fernando et al. (2022) cites Hunaling as one of their baselines, however.

Baselines	**Scoring Function**	**Reference**
Gale-Church	Sentence length	Gale and Church (1993)
Hunaling	Sentence length + dictionary	Varga et al. (2007)
Bleualign	Machine translation metric (BLEU)	Sennrich and Volk (2010, 2011)
Vecalign	Sentence embedding cosine similarity	Thompson and Koehn (2019)

Table 1: Summary of the sentence alignment methods in our evaluation.

highest frequency in the target corpus. The pseudo target language is then compared to the actual target text on a sentence to sentence basis with a similarity score based on the number of shared words, which is the heaviest component of the scoring, and the sentence length in characters based on the ratio of longer to shorter. Once the similarity matrix is obtained for the relevant pairs, dynamic programming is used to find the optimal alignment with penalties for skipping and coalescing sentences. The algorithm works even in the absence of a dictionary in which case the texts are first aligned with the source text as the crude translation of itself and then a simple dictionary can be bootstrapped by collecting source-target token pairs with an association score higher than 0.5. They mainly experiment on Hungarian, but cite also Romanian and Slovenian, motivated by the need to build parallel corpora for "medium density languages".

Sennrich and Volk (2010) presents *Bleualign*, an automatic alignment method based on MT. They propose to use automatically translated text and a measure of the quality of this translation, in this case BLEU (Papineni et al., 2002), as a similarity score to find reliable alignments to be used as anchor points. Sennrich and Volk (2011) details an iterative approach for Bleualign. They build a rough alignment using the Gale-Church algorithm and then train a first MT system on these aligned data. They then use the generated translations to compute the sentence level BLEU score and employ it as a measure of alignment. They work on a corpus of French and German text obtained by OCR from the yearbooks of the Swiss Alpine Club between 1864-1982. They claim the system to be more resilient to noise and fairly language independent, despite depending heavily on the provided translation, and thus on a MT system with reasonable performance for their language pair. This is problematic in resource-poor conditions due to the need for enough data to train the MT system and it is computationally more demanding due to the need of an automatic translation.

Thompson and Koehn (2019) presents *Vecalign*. They propose a sentence alignment scoring function based on the similarity of bilingual sentence embeddings, which has been shown to be effective in related tasks such as filtering non-parallel sentences and locating parallel sentences in comparable corpora. Moreover, blocks of sentences can be represented as the average of their embeddings, which does not depend on the number of sentences being compared, thus reducing the computational complexity. They use the LASER multilingual sentence embeddings (Artetxe and Schwenk, 2019) and compute similarity as cosine similarity, normalized with randomly selected embeddings to avoid hubness (Radovanovic et al., 2010; Lazaridou et al., 2015), i.e. the tendency of some vectors ("hubs") to appear in the top neighbour lists of many items. To align the text, they start by creating an approximate sentence alignment using the average embeddings of adjacent sentences. Then they refine this alignment with the original sentence vectors, limiting the search in a small window around the approximate alignment. They claim state-of-the-art results on the Bleualign dataset and on Bible test sets (Christodouloupoulos and Steedman, 2015). In this low-resource setting, they work on Arabic, Turkish, Somali, Afrikaans, Tagalog, and Norwegian. All these languages but Norwegian appear in the training data for LASER, albeit in different sizes. They consider *verse-alignments* as their gold-standard, for which they report an average improvement of 28 verse-level F_1 score on Hunalign in bootstrap mode. As we will show in Section 5, this improvement in performance does not hold in our experiments on English-Yorùbá.

4 Methodology

The objective of our work is to evaluate the widespread sentence alignment methods briefly described in Section 3 in a low-resource setting. To achieve this, we carry out two experiments on Menyo20k (Adelani et al., 2021), a high quality English-Yorùbá multidomain parallel corpus. Over-

Shorthand	N of sentences	Data source
book	2014	"Out of His Mind" Book
cc	193	Creative Commons license
digital	941	ICT/digital & Kolibri Tech sentences
jw	3508	JW news
misc	687	Short text from various domains
movie	774	Movie transcript
news	5980	News articles
proverbs	2700	Yoruba proverbs
radio	258	Radio transcripts
tedTalks	2945	Ted Talks transcripts
udhr	100	Universal Declaration of Human Rights
menyo	**20100**	**TOTAL**

Table 2: Domains of the Menyo20k corpus and their sizes in number of sentences.

all the dataset contains 20.100 sentences gathered from various domains such as news articles, TED talks, movie and radio transcripts, science and technology text, Yorùbá proverbs, books, and short articles curated from the web. Monolingual text crawled from the web were professionally translated and verified by native speakers. We thus assume the corpus as a a gold-standard for our experiments.

For our purposes we concatenate the train, dev, and test splits in which the corpus is divided into one text file containing 1-to-1 alignments. Table 2 gives the sizes of the corpus and its different domain splits.[3]

The first experiment, dubbed *NATURAL-ORDER*, is straightforward: we apply the alignment methods mentioned in Section 3 to each section of the corpus and on the corpus as a whole. We then evaluate the resulting alignments against the reference with an algorithm that iterates over both the proposed alignments and the reference to return a pair as correct only when the candidate alignment is identical to the one in the reference.

The second experiment, *SHUFFLED-ORDER*, is similar to *NATURAL-ORDER*, with the addition of reordering: we artificially shuffle the target side by randomly scrambling the sentences in a window of 3. More precisely, we start from sentences at lines 1 to 3 and we randomly shuffle them in this group; we then move on to sentences at lines 4 to 6, and scramble them as well. We continue in this manner until the end of the document is reached. This is done to avoid creating unrealistic data, since it is not usual for sentences that should be aligned to be very far apart in the translation of same text. We then proceed as in *NATURAL-ORDER*, by applying the alignment methods and evaluating their outputs against the gold standard.

Whenever possible, we used the implementations available online[4] with the configuration that required the least amount of pre-existing resources or further work, such as fine-tuning. For the Gale-Church method we employed the implementation provided with Bleualign. We use LASER (Artetxe and Schwenk, 2019) to compute the sentence embeddings for Vecalign. While the encoder for Yorùbá was provided in the library as part of the LASER3 extension (NLLB Team, 2022), we had to train our own `sentencepiece` (Kudo, 2018) model.[5] Hunalign was run without a precompiled dictionary. Since no end-to-end iterative implementation of Bleualign was found, we applied the method without a reference translation. We also attempted to train a NMT model only on the Menyo20k corpus aligned with the Gale-Church algorithm, as the Bleualign authors suggest in their second paper. For this, we trained a standard transformer (Vaswani et al., 2017) using `fairseq` (Ott et al., 2019) with the following parameters: vocabulary size 2000, *adam* optimizer, dropout 0.1, label smoothing 0.1, max tokens 4096, and optimizing for BLEU. After 60 epochs, however, the model failed to reach more than 5 BLEU in both translation directions, with its output hallucinated and noisy, and was thus deemed not useful to further alignment steps with Bleualign.

5 Results

Table 3 summarize the results of our evaluation.

The upper rows of the table report the results for *NATURAL-ORDER*, the simple 1-to-1 alignment without reordering. The Gale-Church baseline perform best in 8 out of 12 domains, with the percentage of correct alignments between 82.95% for the *radio* domain, and the 100% of *udhr*. It scores 99.96% on *menyo-all*.

Bleualign is the least performing method in 9 out of 12 domains, sharing its only 100% on *udhr* with all the other methods. It fares particularly badly for the literary domain, getting just 37.87% of alignments correctly for *book* and 56.07% on *proverbs*. On *menyo-all*, it returns 79.16% of correct align-

[3]For a full breakdown on the sources and data collection of the Menyo20k corpus, we defer to their paper.

[4]Hunalign: https://github.com/danielvarga/hunalign; Bleualign: https://github.com/rsennrich/Bleualign; Vecalign: https://github.com/thompsonb/vecalign

[5]We used the Yorùbá Wikipedia as training data and the same parameters for the other models in LASER3. Limiting the training data to the Menyo20k corpus failed to achieve the necessary vocabulary size needed by LASER3.

Split			*book*	*cc*	*digital*	*jw*	*misc*	*movie*	*news*	*proverbs*	*radio*	*tedTalks*	*udhr*	*menyo-all*	*avg*
Score	NAT	***bleu***	37.87%	85.49%	91.73%	86.55%	84.86%	66.54%	90.72%	56.07%	80.23%	92.87%	100.0%	79.16%	79.34%
		ga	99.6%	100.0%	100.0%	99.43%	99.71%	100.0%	99.92%	99.93%	82.95%	99.29%	100.0%	99.96%	98.40%
		hun	99.85%	100.0%	99.36%	97.86%	90.6%	97.67%	99.31%	35.83%	100.0%	99.56%	100.0%	90.6%	92.55%
		vec	97.72%	95.85%	94.17%	96.29%	97.82%	99.1%	97.98%	89.12%	78.68%	98.64%	100.0%	94.4%	94.99%
	SHF	***bleu***	11.07%	35.75%	28.21%	38.0%	27.07%	22.09%	41.94%	18.84%	35.27%	31.23%	21.0%	31.36%	28.48%
		ga	24.22%	33.68%	25.77%	24.2%	30.28%	32.04%	24.52%	25.24%	21.71%	25.7%	21.0%	25.26%	26.15%
		hun	34.99%	47.15%	36.9%	42.76%	38.86%	35.01%	45.95%	9.88%	39.92%	39.88%	48.0%	38.53%	38.15%
		vec	26.1%	32.12%	25.66%	28.56%	29.69%	32.04%	29.07%	24.02%	21.71%	31.4%	41.0%	28.63%	29.17%

Table 3: Percentage of correct 1-to-1 alignments for each method and domain in *NORMAL-ORDER* (NAT) and *SHUFFLED-ORDER* (SHF). The abbreviations for the alignment methods are the following: *bleu* : Bleualign, *ga* : Gale-Church, *hun* : Hunalign, *vec* : Vecalign. The last column reports the average score for each method.

ments.

Hunalign and Vecalign perform similarly, with scores over 90% for most domains, and 90.6% for *menyo-all*. Hunalign fails for *proverbs*, correctly aligning only 35.83% of the sentences. The lowest score for Vecalign is on *radio*, with 78.68%.

It is apparent that the structured nature of the Universal Human Rights Declaration generally favours alignment. Conversely, the more fluid nature of *proverbs* may hamper methods such as Hunalign, which rely on lexical information for alignment. This domain, however, seems to be better handled using just length information.

The lower half of Table 3 reports the results for *SHUFFLED-ORDER*, 1-to-1 alignments with reordering. All methods fail to reach 50% of found correct alignments. Hunalign scores highest in 11 domains out of 12, achieving its best score of 48.0% on *udhr*. It also detains the lowest score of the experiment, 9.88% on *proverbs*. Hunalign correctly aligns 38.53% of *menyo-all*. The other methods all perform inadequately, with values close to random for the window of 3 chosen for reordering. Apart from the aforementioned Hunalign on *proverbs* other low outliers are the Bleualign scores on *book* and *proverbs*. Again, these domains seem to be more problematic, significantly hampering the systems. Moreover, reordering appears to invalidate the accuracy even on the highly structured text in *udhr*.

6 Conclusions

In this paper we presented an evaluation of four commonly used sentence alignment methods when applied to a low-resource language pair, such as English-Yorùbá.

While working well for high resource languages and domains, more recent sentence embedding-based alignment methods do not perform similarly for a low-resource pair such as the one in our study. Earlier methods, based on sentence length statistics and bootstrapped dictionaries, returned better alignments on the Menyo20k corpus. All of these methods, however, do not seem suitable when sentence reordering is involved. Some methods appear to perform better for specific domains, as shown by the difference in scores for the literary domain, such as with the *book* and *proverbs* splits where text is less structured and translations may not be literal. Conversely, all methods return perfect alignments on the highly structured text of the *udhr*.

Even without these results, one may argue that simpler methods, which do not require a huge amount of resources, both in term of computation and data, and are mostly language-independent, are better suited to the low-resource setting. Bleualign assumes the use of machine translated data, and thus a MT system, which has to be trained to satisfactory quality. This is usually not possible in a low- and no resource settings. Vecalign requires multilingual sentence embeddings, in our case LASER, which in turn need language specific encoders and a sentencepiece model. In turn, these components need further data than simply the documents to be aligned.

Limitations and Future Work

One obvious limitation of the present work is given by its testing dataset, which includes just one corpus and one low-resource language pair. Future work may expand the study to further language pairs, leveraging other benchmark parallel corpora such as FLORES (Goyal et al., 2022), which would allow to explore other variables, e.g. the effect of typological differences.

Another limitation is that the experiments and their evaluation is currently confined to 1-to-1 alignments. Moving to more complex combinations would require costly manual intervention. However, a qualitative analysis of peculiar cases could be undertaken.

Acknowledgements

We thank the reviewer for their useful inputs. The work of the author is supported by the Internal Grant Agency of Masaryk University, Lexical Computing, and the Ministry of Education of the Czech Republic within the LINDAT-CLARIAH-CZ project LM2018101.

References

David Adelani, Dana Ruiter, Jesujoba Alabi, Damilola Adebonojo, Adesina Ayeni, Mofe Adeyemi, Ayodele Esther Awokoya, and Cristina España-Bonet. 2021. The effect of domain and diacritics in Yoruba–English neural machine translation. In *Proceedings of Machine Translation Summit XVIII: Research Track*, pages 61–75, Virtual. Association for Machine Translation in the Americas.

Mikel Artetxe and Holger Schwenk. 2019. Massively multilingual sentence embeddings for zero-shot cross-lingual transfer and beyond. *Transactions of the Association for Computational Linguistics*, 7:597–610.

Everlyn Chimoto and Bruce Bassett. 2022. Very low resource sentence alignment: Luhya and Swahili. In *Proceedings of the Fifth Workshop on Technologies for Machine Translation of Low-Resource Languages (LoResMT 2022)*, pages 1–8, Gyeongju, Republic of Korea. Association for Computational Linguistics.

Christos Christodouloupoulos and Mark Steedman. 2015. A massively parallel corpus: The bible in 100 languages. *Lang. Resour. Eval.*, 49(2):375–395.

Alexis Conneau, Kartikay Khandelwal, Naman Goyal, Vishrav Chaudhary, Guillaume Wenzek, Francisco Guzmán, Edouard Grave, Myle Ott, Luke Zettlemoyer, and Veselin Stoyanov. 2020. Unsupervised cross-lingual representation learning at scale. In *Proceedings of the 58th Annual Meeting of the Association for Computational Linguistics*, pages 8440–8451, Online. Association for Computational Linguistics.

Xiachong Feng, Xiaocheng Feng, Libo Qin, Bing Qin, and Ting Liu. 2021. Language model as an annotator: Exploring DialoGPT for dialogue summarization. In *Proceedings of the 59th Annual Meeting of the Association for Computational Linguistics and the 11th International Joint Conference on Natural Language Processing (Volume 1: Long Papers)*, pages 1479–1491, Online. Association for Computational Linguistics.

Aloka Fernando, Surangika Ranathunga, Dilan Sachintha, Lakmali Piyarathna, and Charith Rajitha. 2022. Exploiting bilingual lexicons to improve multilingual embedding-based document and sentence alignment for low-resource languages. *Knowledge and Information Systems*, 65:1–42.

William A. Gale and Kenneth W. Church. 1993. A program for aligning sentences in bilingual corpora. *Computational Linguistics*, 19(1):75–102.

Naman Goyal, Cynthia Gao, Vishrav Chaudhary, Peng-Jen Chen, Guillaume Wenzek, Da Ju, Sanjana Krishnan, Marc'Aurelio Ranzato, Francisco Guzmán, and Angela Fan. 2022. The Flores-101 evaluation benchmark for low-resource and multilingual machine translation. *Transactions of the Association for Computational Linguistics*, 10:522–538.

Huda Khayrallah and Philipp Koehn. 2018. On the impact of various types of noise on neural machine translation. In *Proceedings of the 2nd Workshop on Neural Machine Translation and Generation*, pages 74–83, Melbourne, Australia. Association for Computational Linguistics.

Yunsu Kim, Miguel Graça, and Hermann Ney. 2020. When and why is unsupervised neural machine translation useless? In *Proceedings of the 22nd Annual Conference of the European Association for Machine Translation*, pages 35–44, Lisboa, Portugal. European Association for Machine Translation.

Taku Kudo. 2018. Subword regularization: Improving neural network translation models with multiple subword candidates. In *Proceedings of the 56th Annual Meeting of the Association for Computational Linguistics (Volume 1: Long Papers)*, pages 66–75, Melbourne, Australia. Association for Computational Linguistics.

Angeliki Lazaridou, Georgiana Dinu, and Marco Baroni. 2015. Hubness and pollution: Delving into cross-space mapping for zero-shot learning. In *Proceedings of the 53rd Annual Meeting of the Association for Computational Linguistics and the 7th International Joint Conference on Natural Language Processing (Volume 1: Long Papers)*, pages 270–280, Beijing, China. Association for Computational Linguistics.

James Cross Onur Çelebi Maha Elbayad Kenneth Heafield Kevin Heffernan Elahe Kalbassi Janice Lam Daniel Licht Jean Maillard Anna Sun Skyler Wang Guillaume Wenzek Al Youngblood Bapi Akula Loic Barrault Gabriel Mejia Gonzalez Prangthip Hansanti John Hoffman Semarley Jarrett Kaushik Ram Sadagopan Dirk Rowe Shannon Spruit Chau Tran Pierre Andrews Necip Fazil Ayan Shruti Bhosale Sergey Edunov Angela Fan Cynthia Gao Vedanuj Goswami Francisco Guzmán Philipp Koehn Alexandre Mourachko Christophe Ropers Safiyyah Saleem Holger Schwenk Jeff Wang NLLB Team, Marta R. Costa-jussà. 2022. No language left behind: Scaling human-centered machine translation.

Myle Ott, Sergey Edunov, Alexei Baevski, Angela Fan, Sam Gross, Nathan Ng, David Grangier, and Michael Auli. 2019. fairseq: A fast, extensible toolkit for sequence modeling. In *Proceedings of the 2019 Conference of the North American Chapter of the Association for Computational Linguistics (Demonstrations)*, pages 48–53, Minneapolis, Minnesota. Association for Computational Linguistics.

Kishore Papineni, Salim Roukos, Todd Ward, and Wei-Jing Zhu. 2002. Bleu: a method for automatic evaluation of machine translation. In *Proceedings of the 40th Annual Meeting of the Association for Computational Linguistics*, pages 311–318, Philadelphia, Pennsylvania, USA. Association for Computational Linguistics.

Milos Radovanovic, Alexandros Nanopoulos, and Mirjana Ivanovic. 2010. Hubs in space: Popular nearest neighbors in high-dimensional data. *Journal of Machine Learning Research*, 11:2487–2531.

Rico Sennrich and Martin Volk. 2010. MT-based sentence alignment for OCR-generated parallel texts. In *Proceedings of the 9th Conference of the Association for Machine Translation in the Americas: Research Papers*, Denver, Colorado, USA. Association for Machine Translation in the Americas.

Rico Sennrich and Martin Volk. 2011. Iterative, MT-based sentence alignment of parallel texts. In *Proceedings of the 18th Nordic Conference of Computational Linguistics (NODALIDA 2011)*, pages 175–182, Riga, Latvia. Northern European Association for Language Technology (NEALT).

Steinþór Steingrímsson, Hrafn Loftsson, and Andy Way. 2020. Effectively aligning and filtering parallel corpora under sparse data conditions. In *Proceedings of the 58th Annual Meeting of the Association for Computational Linguistics: Student Research Workshop*, pages 182–190, Online. Association for Computational Linguistics.

Brian Thompson and Philipp Koehn. 2019. Vecalign: Improved sentence alignment in linear time and space. In *Proceedings of the 2019 Conference on Empirical Methods in Natural Language Processing and the 9th International Joint Conference on Natural Language Processing (EMNLP-IJCNLP)*, pages 1342–1348, Hong Kong, China. Association for Computational Linguistics.

Ha Nguyen Tien, Dat Nguyen Huu, Huong Le Thanh, Vinh Nguyen Van, and Minh Nguyen Quang. 2021. KC4Align: Improving sentence alignment method for low-resource language pairs. In *Proceedings of the 35th Pacific Asia Conference on Language, Information and Computation*, pages 354–363, Shanghai, China. Association for Computational Lingustics.

Daniel Varga, Péter Halácsy, Andras Kornai, Viktor Nagy, László Németh, and Viktor Trón. 2007. *Parallel corpora for medium density languages*, pages 247–258.

Ashish Vaswani, Noam Shazeer, Niki Parmar, Jakob Uszkoreit, Llion Jones, Aidan N Gomez, Ł ukasz Kaiser, and Illia Polosukhin. 2017. Attention is all you need. In *Advances in Neural Information Processing Systems*, volume 30. Curran Associates, Inc.

Author Index

Association for Computational Linguistics
209 N. Eighth Street
Stroudsburg, Pennsylvania 18360

ISBN 978-1-7138-7385-3